THE LUDDITE
REBELLION

THE LUDDITE REBELLION

Brian Bailey

SUTTON PUBLISHING

First published in the United Kingdom in 1998 by
Sutton Publishing Limited · Phoenix Mill
Thrupp · Stroud · Gloucestershire · GL5 2BU

British Library Cataloguing in Publication Data
A catalogue record for this book is available from the British Library.

ISBN 0-7509-1353-3

 ALAN SUTTON™ and SUTTON™ are the
trade marks of Sutton Publishing Limited

Typeset in 11/13 pt Bembo Mono.
Typesetting and origination by
Sutton Publishing Limited.
Printed in Great Britain by
Butler & Tanner, Frome, Somerset.

Contents

List of Illustrations

Maps

The author and publisher are grateful to the following sources of prints and copyright photographs:

British Museum: pages 10, 72, 77, 152
Huddersfield Library & Art Gallery: page 107
Leicester Mercury: page 131
Nottingham Castle Museum: page 23
Nottinghamshire County Library: pages 6, 17, 21, 92
Ruddington Framework-Knitters' Museum: pages 4, 124, 143
Tolson Memorial Museum, Huddersfield: pages 27, 51, 54, 60.

The photographs and drawings on pages 26, 44, 61, 75, 82, 89, 98, 115 and 136 are by the author. The maps are by Mike Komarnyckyj.

Preface

This book deals with the period in the early nineteenth century when workers in the textile industries of the Midlands and north of England took to destroying machinery. Many of my relatives in my native county, Leicestershire, including my father and his father before him, spent their whole working lives in the hosiery industry, where the riots had their origins, and I have always had more than a passing interest in the social and political history of the business which provided for my well-being in my childhood. In the 1930s, Leicester itself was identified by the League of Nations as Europe's most prosperous city. The hosiery industry was the foundation of that prosperity, but only after many vicissitudes during the course of three centuries. The so-called Luddite Rebellion is the best known of them, though still widely misunderstood.

Seen at its simplest level, the movement was a prolonged outbreak of machine-breaking by desperate textile workers intent on self-preservation. But the Luddite period has become something of an historical enigma. Nothing is ever that simple, after all, and recent historians have been posing fresh questions and re-examining the documents in their efforts to establish the 'Truth' – that elusive ideal. Who were the Luddites? What were their ultimate aims, if indeed they had any? How were they organised? Who were their leaders? Can the word rebellion, which suggests armed insurrection against the State, be properly used in relation to these nocturnal saboteurs? Did they, in fact, have a hidden agenda? Was there a long-term political aim, as well as the obvious short-term economic purpose, in their actions? The known facts need very careful consideration before any answers are attempted.

My chief object in this volume, however, is to tell as clearly and accurately as possible what actually happened. The sequence of events, and the people involved in them, have latterly become rather obscured by preoccupation with detailed analysis and interpretation, while some accounts have dealt only with particular areas involved in the Luddite movement, so that it is not easy today to find a chronological and comprehensive account of the whole episode from beginning to end. There are, for instance, many more publications dealing exclusively with Luddism in Yorkshire's woollen industry than there are about the Midland hosiery workers or the riots in north-west England. In attempting to remedy this situation, I have thought it fitting to use the title by which the episode is commonly known, though I am well aware that it is contentious, with some authorities objecting to the word 'rebellion', others to the word 'Luddite'.

Whether there was any notion among the Luddites of a revolt against the State is a question we shall have to face up to in due course. But a rebellion is properly defined as 'open resistance to any authority' (*Concise Oxford Dictionary*, 1978 edn); and a rebel as 'one who resents and resists authority or grievous conditions' (*Chambers English Dictionary*, 1988). Nothing could be plainer.

The machine-breakers themselves, according to the popular tale, adopted the name of a backward youth, Ned Ludd, or Ludlam, of Anstey in Leicestershire. This lad, legend has it, smashed the needles of a stocking-frame he was working at, in or around 1779, in bad-tempered retaliation for a punishment he had received; and thus unwittingly wrote his name in the pages of history. This myth, discovered, apparently, by the *Nottingham Review*,[1] has been repeated endlessly by generations of social and industrial historians. If there were strong evidence that machine-breaking spread from Anstey, or Leicester itself, we should perhaps be on firmer ground with this tale. But the facts entirely refute that scenario. Leicester, which possessed more stocking-frames than Nottingham, remained remarkably free of machine-breaking, for reasons that we shall discover. It *may* be that the story has a basis of truth – Ludlam is still a relatively common surname in Leicestershire (and Derbyshire). The implication, of course, is that Ludd's spontaneous resentful reaction was imprinted in the minds of fellow-workers, perhaps as a powerful symbol of injustice and workers' solidarity, and that the story spread throughout the hosiery industry by word of mouth until the moment came when a growing movement, needing an identity, remembered Ned Ludd, and took his name as its figurehead – a sort of industrial Robin Hood, operating ostensibly from Sherwood Forest, on behalf of men who had learned by experience that machine-breaking was an effective weapon in fighting against wage reductions and other iniquities, when there were no legal means of collective bargaining.

On the other hand, if Ned Ludd did not exist, it would not have been necessary to invent him. It is possible that the name Luddism has a much more venerable, and indeed more appropriate, origin, I would like to suggest. There was an ancient British king named Lud who was, Geoffrey of Monmouth tells us, the elder brother of Cassivellaunus. He it was who, according to tradition, built the original Lud Gate in London in 66 BC. He was buried 'nigh unto that gate, which even yet is called Porthlud in British, but in Saxon Ludgate'.[2] A posthumous statue of King Lud from the rebuilt medieval gateway survives in the church of St Dunstan-in-the-West in Fleet Street. The hall of the Framework Knitters' Company, long demolished, once stood only half a mile away in Redcross Street.

Admittedly, Geoffrey of Monmouth, a twelfth-century Benedictine monk, is as unreliable an authority as we could hope to find. He claimed that he had based his *Histories of the Kings of Britain* on ancient British texts which have never come to light. Nevertheless, there is ample circumstantial evidence to support him, and in Leicestershire, too. There are villages here called Loddington and Lyddington, as well as others such as Luddenden in West Yorkshire, Luddenham in Kent and Ludham in Norfolk, which place-name experts vaguely define as land occupied by 'Luda's people'. There is a River Lud in the Lindsey division of Lincolnshire, rising in the Wolds west of Louth. There is also a village in Lincolnshire named Ludborough, which seems plain enough, with the earthworks of a larger medieval settlement remaining round its fringes. In the east of Leicestershire, moreover, near the Lincolnshire border on Saltby Heath, are mysterious linear earthworks long known as 'King Lud's Entrenchments', where a ruler named Lud was supposedly buried. Perhaps this was really Ludeca, a Mercian king killed in battle in AD 827.[3] At any rate, it surely seems much more likely that folk memory adopted the name of an ancient British king for a serious engagement with the 'enemy', than that working men took a village idiot as the eponymous hero of a desperate campaign.

Acknowledgements

My grateful thanks are due to the unfailingly helpful staffs of the York University Library, the Public Record Office and the Leeds City Archives, as well as those of the North Yorkshire County Library at York and Thirsk, and the West Yorkshire County Library at Leeds.

I am also indebted for assistance from the Local Studies departments at Nottingham County Library and Manchester Central Library, and from the Leicestershire Record Office at Wigston.

My wife's contribution, as always, has been invaluable in so many ways.

Introduction

The later years of the reign of George III encompassed a period of stark contrasts in British society. The prosperous and imaginative surface appearance of the country obscured a host of social evils, like a made-up face and upholstered body disguising the true features of an ageing prostitute. The nation was poised on the threshold of new standards of triumph and civilisation. The third quarter of the eighteenth century saw the inventions of Hargreaves' spinning jenny, Arkwright's spinning frame and Crompton's mule. James Watt built his first steam engine, and the pioneering Bridgewater Canal was constructed between Worsley and Manchester to carry coal to industry. Cartwright's power-loom was on the horizon. Mass-production machinery, powered by water or steam, was soon inducing capitalist manufacturers to build huge mills of brick in Lancashire and of stone across the Pennines. Alongside the rise of the cotton industry in Lancashire, the West Riding of Yorkshire was becoming dominant in the woollen industry, succeeding the smaller early mills in rural parts of England such as the Cotswolds and East Anglia. Silk manufacturing was becoming important to Cheshire and Derbyshire, and the latter county has the distinction of hosting the first factory in the modern sense, with many employees going out to work in one building at machinery operated, in this case, by water power. This was the Lombe brothers' silk spinning mill on the River Derwent at Derby.

The rise of manufacturing industries and the beginning of the railway revolution were accompanied by the abolition of slavery and reforms of prison and factory conditions. John Nash and the Adam brothers brought new architectural elegance to London and Edinburgh. It was the age of Byron and Wordsworth, Jane Austen and Sir Walter Scott, Gainsborough and Turner, Richard Sheridan and Sarah Siddons. But there was a reverse side to this fashionable Georgian facade, and the object of this introduction is to describe briefly the development of an economic and social climate in the textile industries of the Midlands and north of England that made them ripe for unrest and the advent of Luddism.

The revolution in industry was about to cause the biggest destabilisation of British civilisation since the Black Death in the fourteenth century. Since that time, once the Peasants' Revolt had been suppressed and some social stability restored, economic development had progressed at a pace which the working population of the country could cope with. But the rapid changes in technology which began three centuries later were responsible for huge upheavals throughout working-class society. A mass movement of workers from rural to urban centres was accompanied by vast population increases: in the course of the eighteenth century the population of England almost doubled. The new manufacturing towns soon became overcrowded, with the inevitable consequences of slums, widespread disease and rising crime rates. The notorious Black Act of 1723, popularly known as the 'Bloody Code', was extended until, towards the end of the century, there were well over two hundred capital crimes on the statute book. The majority of them were crimes against property – the obsession of Georgian criminal law.

Dealing with the large increase in crime was one of the chief preoccupations of local authorities. But these authorities were made up largely of land-owning country squires, while law and order lay in the hands of parish constables. The latter were becoming as unequal to their hugely mounting task as the squires were to bringing about urgently needed social reforms. The wealthy and powerful believed there was a 'criminal class' which must be eliminated for the sake of society as a whole, and acted upon this delusion with a barbarity almost unparalleled in the peacetime history of Europe. In 1801 a boy of thirteen was hanged for stealing a spoon, and only a year before the advent of Luddite machine-breaking, Lord Ellenborough, the Lord Chief Justice, made his notorious speech against abolition of the death penalty for stealing goods up to the value of five shillings from shops. If the Bill went through, he said, no man would be able to 'trust himself for an hour out of doors without the most alarming apprehensions, that on his return, every vestige of his property will be swept off by the hardened robber'.

Such hysterical fear and suspicion of the 'lower orders' found expression in political terms, too, in the measures taken by Pitt's government against what it perceived as a Jacobin tendency among the working populace during the heightened tension of the war years. In 1799 the Corresponding Societies Act suppressed the circulation of radical literature by bodies such as the London Corresponding Society, which had been founded after the publication of Thomas Paine's *The Rights of Man*, with a membership composed chiefly of artisans and tradesmen, and called by Edmund Burke 'the mother of all mischief'. And in 1799 and 1800 repressive Combination Acts reinforced existing laws against trade unions, making it a criminal offence for workers to join forces in pressing their employers for higher wages or the reduction of working hours; or indeed, to gather together for any industrial or political purpose whatever. One of the chief proponents of the new laws was none other than William Wilberforce, that saintly philanthropist and MP for Hull, who fought so long for the abolition of the slave trade. All combinations, he thought, were 'a general disease in our society'. In the matter of suppressing the Luddites, Wilberforce was to become one of the most reactionary members of the House of Commons.

The Combination laws were passed by Pitt's government in an atmosphere of near panic. The rise of working-class radicalism in England at the same time as revolution in France and the apparent inability of the primitive policing system to maintain law and order in rapidly expanding industrial towns had already led to several repressive measures. The Combination Acts served a dual purpose. Not only did they render workmen who combined to protect their wages and conditions liable to prosecution for conspiracy – a capital felony – they also eliminated one of the cradles of subversive intercourse. But there could be no moral justification for leaving workers at the mercy of unscrupulous employers, without, in the first place, any right to protect themselves by joining trade unions which could represent their interests fairly and legally, and, in the second place, without any regulation of their wages and working conditions. The government's policy of non-intervention in industrial disputes was called *laissez-faire*. It had become, since Adam Smith, the political dogma of the English bourgeoisie. In fact, it represented freedom for the employers and intolerable repression of the workers. Individual freedom after the Combination Acts meant the freedom of capitalist employers to exploit their workers in any way they chose. But drive men into a corner, and their only defence is attack.

The effectiveness of the legislation varied from trade to trade. Unions were often merely driven underground, or survived in the guise of friendly societies. Many illegal unions continued to exist, in one way or another, in the textile industries. In theory, the law prevented manufacturers, as well as workers, from combining in a common interest, but this reminds one rather of Joad's comment on the 'impartiality of the law which forbids rich and poor alike to sleep in doorways'. Besides, a workman breaking the law could be sentenced to two months of hard labour, whereas a convicted master was liable only to a fine of £20. Benjamin Hobhouse objected that the 'journeymen alone were to be imprisoned for breaking the law', and Sheridan condemned the Bill as 'replete with the grossest aggressions against the principles of the law of the land and against the rights of the subject'.[1]

On to this precariously balanced ship of state was loaded the economic burden of the war with France. Although Nelson's naval victories had established Britain's supremacy at sea, Napoleon was boycotting British trade with France's allies, as well as with other countries, through the so-called Continental System of blockade. The Milan Decree of December 1807 issued a threat to neutral countries that any ship trading with Britain would be regarded as a British vessel and dealt with accordingly. This was the first attempt in the history of Europe to conduct major economic warfare. Spencer Perceval, Chancellor of the Exchequer, retaliated with Orders in Council which closed off European ports to neutral shipping, including American vessels. The response of the United States government was a Non-Intercourse Act, which came into effect in February 1811. In 1810 British exports to the United States had amounted to more than eleven million pounds worth of goods. In the following year, they fell to less than two million.[2] The woollen and cotton industries in the north of England were particularly hard hit. Manufacturers laid off workers as stocks of cloth mounted in the warehouses. In the West Riding of Yorkshire alone more than a thousand manufacturers went out of business.

Other factors in the early years of the nineteenth century combined to make the living standards of the working population even more hazardous. The summers of 1809–12 saw disastrous harvests in Britain, but the political situation (not to mention poor harvests on the continent as well) precluded the importation of wheat, thus producing a huge increase in the price of bread and other foods. The government's series of twenty-four Orders in Council was soon doing as much harm to the home economy as Napoleon's blockades were. A healthy balance of trade was vital to Britain in order to finance the war against the French emperor. The Continental System and the Orders in Council between them might have resulted in total defeat for Britain if Napoleon had not gradually lost his grip on Europe.

The government was preoccupied with the apparent madness of the king and the consequent matter of the Regency, as well as with the war against Bonaparte and the economic crisis. In January 1812, for instance, when stocking and lace frames were being smashed almost daily in the Midlands, a Parliamentary Committee was in session to hear the opinion of the royal doctors, who believed that the recovery of the king was 'highly improbable'. It was necessary to make the temporary Regency permanent and give the Prince of Wales full powers.[3] And the Home Office had another crime wave on its hands which was causing widespread anxiety and distress among the poorer classes throughout the country. The body-snatching trade was at its height, and offences against common decency were occurring regularly in burial grounds from southern England to Aberdeen. During the winter of 1811–12, for example, when the Luddite riots were at their height, a London gang of body-snatchers sold 360 recently buried corpses, including fifty-six babies and children, at an average price of four guineas for adults and 'so much an inch' for 'small ones'.[4] Eminent surgeons and physicians were earnestly exhorting the Home Secretary to turn a blind eye to these nocturnal offences, despite public outrage and the distress they were causing to friends and relations of the deceased, because there were no legal means of obtaining the corpses necessary for training the new surgeons needed urgently for the British army on the continent and the rapidly rising urban population at home. This parallel crime wave, arising from government procrastination, is not entirely irrelevant to the Luddite story, as we shall see. Both were symptomatic of the disordered times.

This book is concerned only with the textile machinery saboteurs who became known as Luddites, between 1811 and 1816, but the upheavals in working-class life and economy during the Industrial Revolution and the Napoleonic Wars were felt throughout the country and in other trades at the same time. The Luddites, who often had the sympathy and sometimes the bodily reinforcement of other, non-textile workers and tradesmen, were simply organised exponents of physical resistance to worsening conditions. The introduction of the spinning jenny and the gig-mill to the Cotswold wool towns had already caused much hardship to spinners and shearmen in an area threatened by the growing monopoly of Yorkshire in the woollen industry. Arthur Young noted that there were 'many begging children' in Chippenham in 1796. Stroud and other places had fallen into decay and 'almost wholly into beggary', while at Seend, 'the poor, from the great reduction in the price of spinning, scarcely have the heart to earn the little that is obtained by it'.[5]

The net result of so much inequality and repression in an ill-prepared new industrial society was the development of a class war. The decade preceding the Luddite outbreaks was characterised by rising food prices while trade depression was causing falling wages. In the north the growth of factory industry was having a huge impact on the lives of working people. Domestic textile occupations were being slowly destroyed, and as large manufacturing towns grew rapidly at the expense of the rural economy, capitalist manufacturers were discovering that women and children could be employed to operate factory machinery, and they cost a good deal less in annual wage bills than men.

The inevitable reaction of hard-pressed working men, unable to feed their families and denied the recourse of peaceful collective bargaining to settle their grievances, was to riot and resort to violence. As M.I. Thomis has written: 'If social tension can be expected in years following bad harvests and in times of high food prices, then 1812 was, by universal agreement of historians, a year of inevitable social tension.'[6] Direct action in the textile industries was led by the Midland framework-knitters, and we must begin by considering who these people were, and why they became the unlikely vanguard of violent revolt.

CHAPTER ONE

The Midland Framework-knitters

In the first quarter of the eighteenth century, Daniel Defoe, riding through the Midland shires, noted that the town of Leicester had 'considerable manufacture carried on here, and in several of the market towns round for weaving of stockings by frames; and one would scarce think it possible so small an article of trade could employ such multitudes of people as it does; for the whole county seems to be employed in it'.[1]

There were about eight thousand stocking frames in operation in England around that time, and roughly half of them were in Leicestershire and Nottinghamshire.[2] The centre of the hosiery trade was shifting to the Midland counties from London, where the Framework Knitters' Company had been granted its charter as a City Livery Company by Charles II in 1657. But within little more than half a century some machine-breaking had occurred in the capital, in reaction to the excessive number of boys apprenticed to each journeyman. When the Framework Knitters' Company restricted the number of apprentices allowed into the local trade, however, the Midlands, aided by low wages and changes in fashion which brought plain Midland hosiery into favour against the fancy patterns and colours of the London manufacturers, were able to take a large proportion of the industry away from the capital. A degree of county specialisation began to take place, with Leicestershire predominant in woollen knitting, Nottinghamshire in cotton and Derbyshire in silk.

The 'small article of trade' that Defoe referred to had provided employment for vast numbers of people in various parts of Britain for a long period. Stockings were worn by both men and women, and besides supplying the market at home, there was a healthy demand abroad for stockings made in England. The knitting of stockings and other woollen garments by hand had been carried on mainly, but not exclusively, by women and girls. Women would sit outside their cottages in fair weather so as to consort happily with their neighbours while knitting. At Bala, in north Wales, 'knitters, of both sexes, and all ages' would gather in summer-time on a mound called Tomen-y-Bala, at the town's south-eastern outskirts, to do their knitting together. Bala had what

Thomas Pennant described as 'a vast trade in woollen stockings', and at its markets every Saturday morning,

> from two to five hundred pounds worth are sold each day, according to the demand. Round the place, women and children are in full employ, knitting along the roads; and mixed with them *Herculean* figures appear, assisting their *omphales* in this effeminate employ. During winter the females, through love of society, often assemble at one another's houses to knit; sit round a fire, and listen to some old tale, or to some ancient song, or the sound of a harp; and this is called *Cymmorth Gwau*, or, the knitting assembly.[3]

At Dent, then in the West Riding of Yorkshire, the pace at which women produced knitted garments became almost legendary, earning them an unwonted reputation as 'the terrible knitters of Dent'. At the beginning of the nineteenth century hosiery masters at Kendal, Westmorland, were collecting over eight hundred pairs of hand-knitted woollen stockings a week from Dent and the nearby village of Sedbergh, as well as a thousand pairs from Ravenstonedale and more than five hundred from Orton. The finest of the woollen stockings knitted here were sent by packhorse to London, while knitted woollen caps were exported to the Netherlands for use by seamen.[4] Joseph Budworth described local men and women in the last years of the eighteenth century 'knitting stockings as they drove their peat carts into the town'.[5] Defoe, writing of the North Riding regions of Richmondshire and North Allertonshire, says: '. . . here you see all the people, great and small, a-knitting; and at Richmond you have a market for woollen or yarn stockings, which they make very coarse and ordinary, and they are sold accordingly.'[6] Defoe also mentions the making of stockings along the Dorset/Somerset border, where the 'finest, best and highest-prized knit stockings in England' came from;[7] while at Wells, Glastonbury and other towns in Somerset they knitted stockings mainly for export to Spain. F.A. Wells quotes an eighteenth-century *Dictionary of Trade and Commerce* as saying that the town of Bridgnorth in Shropshire was 'as famous as any other for the making of stockings'.[8] There was a strong tradition of stocking knitting in Scotland, too.

Leicestershire folklore has it that the first pair of knitted silk stockings worn by Queen Elizabeth I, given to her by her silkwoman, Mistress Montague,[9] was made in the county thirty years before the stocking-frame was invented by a Nottinghamshire clergyman, Revd William Lee. Mr Lee, curate of Calverton, is thought to have been a native of either that village or neighbouring Woodborough, and in 1589 his imagination was set in motion, according to the romantic legend, by watching a young lady he was courting, or possibly his wife, knitting stockings by hand. He invented the knitting-frame, on which there was a separate needle for each loop, making a whole row of stitches at one operation, instead of casting all the loops on to one needle. The thread still had to be placed over the needles by hand, and it was to be more than two hundred years before this operation was successfully mechanised, but even so, Lee's ingenious device eventually created a major local industry.[10]

Nothing was ever invented, however, which did not bring some immediate – if temporary – misery to some, though it might eventually be a blessing to all. There was strong opposition to Lee's machine from the hand-knitters at first, and the queen herself understood and sympathised with their anxieties. When Lee's patron, Lord Hunsdon, asked her to grant the inventor a patent, she refused. 'My Lord,' she said, 'I have too much love for my poor people who obtain their bread by the employment of knitting, to give my money to forward an invention that will tend to their ruin by depriving them of employment, and thus make them beggars.'[11]

The queen had a notable precedent for her cautious attitude to new machinery. A statute of Edward VI in 1552 had banned the rotary gig-mill, a device invented to raise the nap on woollen cloth. The gig-mill, or teazeling machine, reduced the time required for this finishing operation from a week's to little more than a day's work, but it had also been used dishonestly by some clothiers to overstretch their cloth.

The Revd Mr Lee received no better encouragement from the government of Stuart England. Professor Wells quotes a letter in the State Papers of 1611 which suggests that the use of knitting-frames was actually prohibited; a correspondent having referred to the 'silk loom stocking weaving which is not permitted in England for fear of ruining the knitters'.[12] So Lee took his knitting-frame to France, where his invention found favour with Henri IV until the king's assassination in 1610, after which Mr Lee fell foul of the persecution of Protestants and died in poverty in Paris. His brother James and his friends eventually returned to Nottinghamshire with their frames, and gradually the machines came into common use.

Lee's frame could make six hundred stitches a minute, as against the average one hundred of a good hand-knitter. It was a man-powered mechanical device for producing various garments, including shirts and gloves as well as socks and stockings. As it was not dependent on a central source of power such as steam or water, which would later enable wool and cotton textile manufacturing to become major factory industries in Yorkshire and Lancashire, framework-knitting remained a domestic occupation.

The first frame set up in Leicestershire belonged to William Iliffe, brother-in-law of the Royalist poet John Cleveland. Iliffe bought it in 1640 and set it up in his native town, Hinckley, which was eventually to be nicknamed 'Stockingopolis'. Leicester itself did not acquire its first frame until about 1670, when one Nicholas Alsop set up in business as a framework-knitter (although he is reputed to have worked in his cellar by night, to keep it secret), but within a

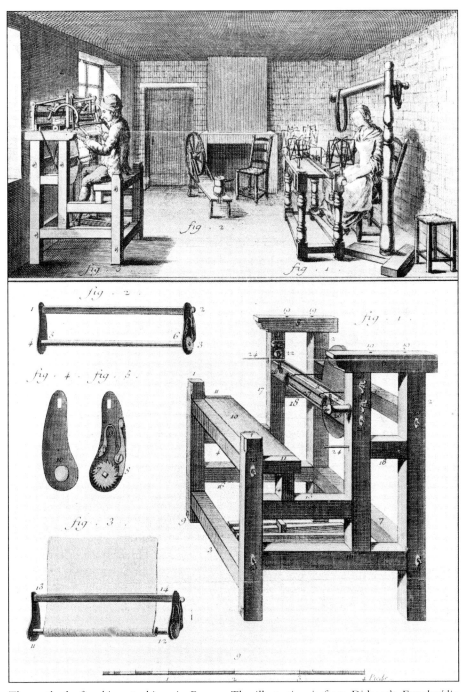

The method of making stockings in France. The illustration is from Diderot's *Encyclopédie*, published in the mid-eighteenth century, and shows a framework-knitter and his wife at work.

hundred years Leicestershire possessed more frames than Nottinghamshire, and knitting-frames were providing the earliest answer on any significant scale in this region to the economic problem of the age: 'setting the poor to work'.

Although their wages were always low, the framework-knitters appear to have been, on the whole, a generally contented body of workers, labouring in their own homes and enjoying their self-determined hours of leisure. There was little education among them, and most were illiterate. But the Leicester hosier and amateur musician William Gardiner (who sent a gift of six pairs of cotton stockings to his hero Joseph Haydn, with themes from the maestro's works woven into them), recalled that,

> the lower orders were comparatively in a state of ease and plenty . . . what contributed to their solid comforts was the common and open field, upon which they kept their pig and poultry, and sometimes a cow . . . the stocking-maker had peas and beans in his snug garden, and a good barrel of humming ale. To these comforts were added two suits of clothes, a working suit and a Sunday suit; but, more than all, he had leisure, which in the summer-time was a blessing and delight. The year was chequered with holidays, wakes, and fairs; it was not one dull round of labour. Those who had their frames at home seldom worked more than three days in a week.[13]

Although this is undoubtedly a rosy and idealised picture of the daily lives of the average stockingers, it does not appear to have been a wild exaggeration for the time. A large number of the frames in Leicestershire then were the property of the master framework-knitters themselves, not of the hosiers. The agriculturalist Arthur Young, during one of his tours through the country, found trading conditions so good in Leicester in 1791 that a stockinger who owned his own frame could earn up to thirty shillings a week. The typical knitter's home was a three-storey cottage with living room on the ground floor, bedroom above that, and on top a workroom with a long mullioned window under the eaves to provide maximum light. Those who did not own knitting-frames hired them from the hosiers, operating them in their own homes. The clatter of the wooden stocking-frames was an ever-present sound in well over a hundred towns and villages in Leicestershire alone, and the importance of stocking knitting to the local economy was indicated for all to see in a procession in 1763, when a stage, built on a waggon, was drawn through the streets of Leicester with 'two combers at work, two doublers, two spinners [and] a framework-knitter at his calling . . .'.[14]

During the course of the eighteenth century many improvements were made to Lee's original invention. Jedediah Strutt, originally a Derbyshire farmer, developed rib-knitted hosiery by adding another set of needles to Lee's frame, so as to reverse the loops and produce a ribbed effect. Around 1760 the stocking-frame was also

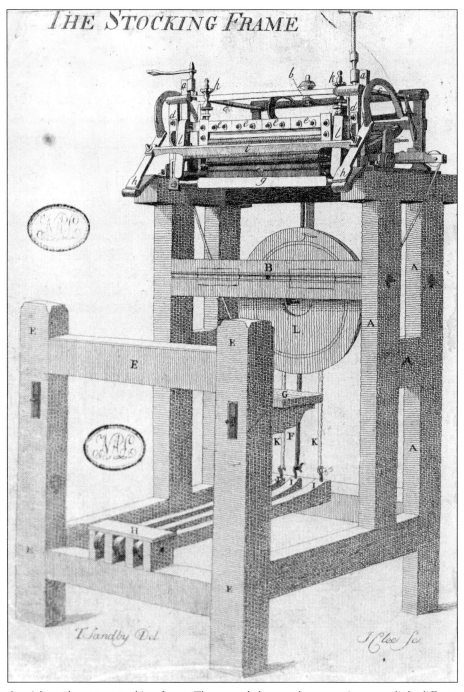

An eighteenth-century stocking frame. The general shape and construction were little different from Lee's original invention.

adapted to make lace. This development again belonged to Nottinghamshire. The lace thus produced, however, was never entirely satisfactory, and in 1808 John Heathcoat, a framesmith in business at Loughborough, Leicestershire, invented a bobbin net machine which was a complete departure from the stocking-frame.[15]

It has been estimated that by the first decade of the nineteenth century there were around thirty thousand knitting frames at work in England, twenty-five thousand of them in the three Midland shires of Leicester, Derby and Nottingham. Leicestershire had more than 11,000 frames, Nottinghamshire over 9,000 and Derbyshire nearly 5,000.[16] About 75,000 people were making their livings in the Midland hosiery trade, and up to 50 per cent of the population of Leicester had been dependent on it for a hundred years or more. By 1812 the number of Midland knitting frames comprised 85 per cent of all the frames in the United Kingdom, and nearly 60 per cent of all those believed to be in use throughout the world.[17]

But economic conditions were to alter the circumstances of framework-knitters beyond recognition within the space of a quarter-century. Capitalism and exploitation were ever-present ingredients of the Midland social scene, and inevitably led to conflict in due course. By the beginning of the nineteenth century it had become a rarity for a stockinger to own his own frame, which at that time cost between £50 and £60. There were no agreed minimum rates, and each knitter, as well as paying a weekly rent for the frame, also had to pay a wage to a woman seamer and buy oil for the machine. He might also have to spend many hours a week travelling to collect his raw materials and then deliver his goods. The yarn was usually distributed at warehouses on Monday mornings, and finished stockings had to be delivered there on Saturdays. Settling up and the weighing of work (to ensure that the stockinger had converted all his week's yarn) could take the whole day, so there was not time to distribute new yarn on Saturdays as well. And it was not unknown for hosiers to give out raw material which was slightly damp, thus increasing its weight, so that when the knitter returned it he had wages deducted for short measure. F.A. Wells gives a typical week's deductions from a stockinger's wage of 13s 3¼d in 1811:

	s	d
Seaming	1	1
Needles		3
Oil		½
Candles		3
Coals		1½
Frame standing		3
Expenses taking in work	1	
Frame rent	1	
Total:	4s	0d [18]

It was not long before 'middlemen' and 'bag hosiers' intervened in the hosiery trade. The manufacturers who owned stocking-frames hired them out to agents or 'undertakers' instead of directly to the knitters. The knitters earned their wages at piece-work rates according to the number of stockings they made, and they were completely at the mercy of these middlemen, who also made profits from frame-rents, charging the knitters more than they paid the owners of the frames. Furthermore, if a machine broke down, the knitter was expected to be his own mechanic, so that every hour spent on repairs was an hour's less production towards his scanty wages. And all this out of the mere pittance he earned for sitting at his frame for perhaps fourteen hours a day. The bag hosiers were generally rural owners of frames set up in small workshops, who took low profits to undercut the larger manufacturers, and so paid the workers lower wages. They sometimes employed knitters to work with stolen raw materials.

The iniquitous practices of 'truck' and 'stinting' put further intolerable pressures on the knitters. 'Truck' was the system whereby middlemen and bag hosiers, who frequently had other business interests, often in the form of retail trade, used their profits to acquire stocking-frames of their own, and then paid the knitters they employed with goods instead of money. As the knitters relied on these frame-owners for their work, they were in no position to refuse. 'Stinting' meant that when there was a shortage of work, the middlemen distributed it out thinly over a large number of workers. But the knitters still had to pay the full week's frame rent, though the frame might be idle for several days. The knitters were thus contributing to the masters' and middlemen's profits from both retail trade and frame-rents. Moreover, a young and inexpert knitter had to pay the same frame-rent as an older and much more experienced workman. Growing desperation led the knitters to adopt the only apparent solution to their problems of earning a living – they rented extra frames and taught their children to operate them. Child labour existed long before the factory system made it a public scandal, and when it helped to earn the family's bread, the obvious advantage of child labour led to a further increase in the birth-rate. 'Even the child,' a Leicester hosier wrote in 1778 with apparent approval, 'as soon almost as it has dropped its leading strings, can earn something towards its maintenance.' [19] Government committees in 1778 and the following year heard of 'pauper children enslaved to long hours at work which destroyed the nerves and the bodily strength of grown men and women, toiling from 5 a.m. to 10 p.m., day after day, for a pittance of 4s 6d a week'.[20]

In addition to Bonaparte's boycott of British trade with France's allies, the damaging effect of Orders in Council and the high price of food, there were several events in the first decade of the nineteenth century which combined to make the living standards of Midland hosiery workers even more precarious. Trousers were beginning to replace the elegant leg in male fashion, drastically reducing the demand for stockings. Manufacturers, responding to a demand for cheaper stockings, introduced 'cut-ups'. These were unfashioned stockings cut to shape from knitted fabric made on wide frames, and sewn together with a seam at the back. Other cheap products were shaped by heating and steaming, and lost their shape as soon as they were washed. The 'three-at-once' or 'four-at-once' wide frame could make several stockings in the time it had hitherto taken to make one. Wide knitting-frames had been employed previously to make pantaloons, but Europe was the major market for these garments and Napoleon's embargo had put an end to the trade. The worthless cut-ups, or 'shoddy', which saved the wide frames from redundancy, caused great resentment among the knitters of traditional hosiery because they glutted a market that was already overstocked and undercut the prices of fully fashioned stockings.

As all these factors came into play in causing distress, another problem developed, which London had experienced a hundred years earlier. There were too many workers trying to earn a living from the depressed trade. Stockingers were training too many apprentices. One framework-knitter in Nottingham had twenty-four apprentices in 1810, and two men at Hinckley had a hundred between them.[21] In a test case brought by the framework-knitters in 1809 a hosier named Payne at Burbage, near Hinckley, was charged with 'colting' – taking on youngsters who were not formally apprenticed – in defiance of the by-laws of the Framework Knitters' Company. Payne defended the action before the King's Bench at the cost of all his capital, but the jury found for the plaintiff, awarding damages of one shilling.[22] Although this derisory award was merely a grudging recognition of the law as it stood, Mr Payne was ruined and went to prison for debt.

By the last years of the eighteenth century many stocking-knitters were living at subsistence level, and many were dependent on poor relief. Wages did not keep pace with the rising price of food, and bread riots were the inevitable result. As the war against France drained the economy, the most desperate among the framework-knitters resorted to rioting and the sabotage of machinery. Food rioting was a widespread feature of the social scene in Britain throughout the eighteenth century, but occurring with increasing frequency towards the end of the century, when poor harvests and the wars with France raised the price of wheat to alarmingly high levels. Bread and potatoes were the most important staple foods of the working population, and the price of bread, in particular, was a major item in the family expenditure. It was a matter of obvious concern to the poorest when the high price of bread put it beyond their means, and riots usually ensued. In 1795, for instance, the price of a bushel of wheat shot up from 7s to 11s 6d, and the cost of a quartern loaf in London rose from 7½d to 12¼d. There were riots throughout England and Wales, from Carlisle to Chichester, and from Conway to Ipswich.[23] When a mob in Leicester tried to seize a wagon of wheat,

The British Butcher. Gillray's cartoon of 1795 shows Pitt offering an impoverished worker meat, which the Prime Minister had recommended as a substitute for bread; both are beyond the poor man's means.

the Duke of Rutland, Lord Lieutenant of the county, called out the Leicester Troop of Cavalry. Some rioters were killed or seriously injured in the resulting affray, which became known locally as the 'Barrow Butchery'. Nottingham also experienced several food riots in the second half of the century.

It is not surprising to find that there was a close link between food riots and machine-breaking. One thing led to the other. When a man was unable to earn enough to feed his family, his wife's anxieties about their children would cause him to demand higher wages, by peaceful means if possible, but by violent ones if not. All public disturbances, according to the *Leicester Journal* in 1800, 'generally commence with the clamour of women . . .'.[24]

★   ★   ★

There was no lack of precedent for machine-breaking as a means of winning bargaining power against capitalist owners when more legitimate methods of negotiation had been tried and failed. Machine-breaking was not an invention of the Luddites, nor was it exclusive to textile workers. The only difference between the Luddites and other machine-breakers in other industries at other times is that the Midland Luddites, in particular, organised and maintained a sustained campaign of industrial sabotage. Weavers in London had rioted against engine-looms for four days in 1675, protesting that one machine could do the work of twenty men. The wooden machines were wrecked and burnt in the streets.[25] John Kay's home at Bury, Lancashire, had been attacked in 1753 by workers who saw his 'flying shuttle' as a threat to their livelihoods. Spinners at Blackburn rioted against Hargreaves' 'jenny' in 1768, attacking the inventor's home and breaking up the frames of twenty prototype machines on his premises. Richard Arkwright was driven to move from his home town, Preston, to Nottinghamshire, because of widespread animosity towards his new machinery. In September 1776 crowds said to number eight thousand attacked machinery in cotton towns and villages around Blackburn and Manchester; and on 4 October 'a most riotous and outrageous Mob' assembled at Birkacre, near Chorley, where Arkwright had just built a factory, and destroyed most of the carding machines and set fire to the building.[26]

In June 1779 framework-knitters raided various premises in Nottingham, smashing up machines and throwing them into the streets until the Riot Act was read and troops were called out to restore order. This disturbance was in reaction to the failure of two petitions, in 1778 and 1779, for establishing a minimum wage and regulation of 'the Art and Mystery of Frame-Work Knitting'. The mob destroyed three hundred machines belonging to Richard Arkwright and Samuel Need, and burnt down a house.[27] These workers were demanding higher wages, and got them. The point was not lost on anyone that rioting and machine-breaking had worked, whereas repeated appeals to parliament had not.

In 1787 there was a riot in Leicester when an angry mob broke up a new worsted spinning machine invented by Joseph Brookhouse, and attacked the homes of its owners, John Coltman and Joseph Whetstone. The town's mayor read the Riot Act and tried to pacify the mob. 'Come, my lads,' he shouted, 'give over – you've done enough – quite enough. Come, give over, there's good lads, and go away.'[28] But someone in the crowd threw a stone which struck the mayor on the head. He died later from his injuries. Nevertheless, this outbreak of violence had the desired effect. The masters agreed to standard price lists which kept the knitters contented for a few years. But it also lost Leicester the lead in worsted spinning, for it was driven out of the town for more than two decades.

A man, a woman and a boy were killed at Bradford-on-Avon in 1791 when armed civilians opened fire while helping a clothier named Phelps to defend his mill against a crowd of five hundred opposing the use of new machinery. And in March of the same year, two years after the opening of Grimshaw's mill in Manchester (the first to install Cartwright's power loom), the factory was burnt down by hand-loom weavers who objected to the use of such machinery. In 1802 Yorkshire woollen workers attempted to bring Benjamin Gott's mill at Leeds to a standstill because he had taken on as apprentices two men who were over the age limit, and were naturally regarded by the other workers as cheap labour. There were also strikes in the region against the use of gig-mills. Arson was suspected, but not proven, when fire broke out in Ottiwells Mill at Marsden and Bradley Mill near Huddersfield in 1803. The owners of these buildings, William Horsfall and the Atkinson family respectively, were using both gig-mills and shearing machines. The operations performed by both these devices had formerly been done by hand, by skilled workmen, for centuries.

A serious spate of machine-breaking had already occurred in the West Country in the previous year. A shearing machine invented by Joseph Lewis, a Stroudwater clothier, had caused a great deal of resentment throughout the Cotswold wool towns. A letter dated 7 April 1799, purporting to be written on behalf of the cloth workers of Trowbridge, Bradford-on-Avon, Chippenham and Melksham, asserted that they were 'the greatest part of Us Oute of work and Wee are fully Convinst that the gretests of the Cause is your dressing work by Machinery . . .'. The letter threatened that, so far from destroying the mills, the united workers would put 'you Damd Villions' to death.[29]

In 1802 a manufacturer at Woodchester, near Stroud, received an unnerving letter:

Wee Hear in Formed that you got Shear in mee sheens and if you Dont Pull them Down in a Forght Nights Time Wee will pull them Down for you Wee will you Damd infernold Dog. And Bee four Almighty God we will pull down all the Mills that heave Heany Shearing me Shens in We will cut out Hall your Damd Hearts as Do keep them and We will meaock the rest Heat them or else We will Searve them the Seam.[30]

A more peaceful local attempt at finding a solution to the shearmen's problems, when a deputation of seven men went to see a master clothier at Bradford-on-Avon in July to protest at the use of the machinery, came to nothing. Although the manufacturer himself was conciliatory, the Attorney General, Spencer Perceval, considered that the seven should be charged with conspiracy under the Combination Act. The employer, Mr Jones, refused to act on this advice, having given the men his word that he would take no action against them.[31] Manufacturers became generally reluctant, in fact, to prosecute workers under the Combination Acts because, as John Beckett, Under-Secretary at the Home Office, pointed out later, an employer would thereby lose his trade for three months prior to the trial, by virtue of being under an interdict.[32] Subsequent destructive raids on local mills resulted in the arrest and execution of a nineteen-year-old rioter recognised by a nightwatchman. Thomas Helliker, refusing to name his accomplices, was convicted on the evidence of the mill manager, Ralph Heath, of leading the rioters, and was hanged at Salisbury in 1803. Five men charged at the same time with administering illegal oaths were acquitted. The execution, it was hoped, would 'answer all the Ends of Public Justice'.[33] Helliker's corpse was carried by his fellow-workers to Trowbridge, and buried in the churchyard there, where a headstone was duly erected 'by the cloth making factories of the Counties of York, Wilts and Somerset'. The 'more than common respect' shown at his funeral caused some alarm to the local master clothiers. The shearmen's trade union, the so-called 'Brief Institution', provided a small allowance to the dead man's mother. The Brief Institution had been founded in Yorkshire in 1796 to bar unapprenticed and unskilled workers from the trade, and a Select Committee of 1806 was told that there were scarcely twenty workers in Yorkshire who were not members.

Helliker was arguably the first Luddite martyr, even though the term 'Luddite' did not come into use until eight years later. If the large-scale wave of machine-breaking in 1811 had commenced with the shearmen in the woollen industry, instead of the hosiery framework-knitters, the episode might well be known today as the Hellikite Rebellion! A witness told the 1806 Select Committee that if shearing frames had not been introduced into the Cotswolds, 'there would not be so many boys running about the streets without shoes or stockings on, and nearly half-starved'.[34] This Select Committee was set up by the House of Commons to enquire into the state of the woollen industry. Among its members were William Wilberforce and Sir Robert Peel (father of the future Prime Minister), a wealthy cotton manufacturer and a factory owner on the grand scale, with twenty-three mills in the north and Midlands.

Lancashire hand-loom weavers obtained 130,000 signatures on a petition for a Minimum Wage Bill in 1807, and when it was thrown out in May of the following year, there were strikes and riots in Manchester and Rochdale,

Burnley and Blackburn, Preston and Wigan. Some machinery was wrecked, the Rochdale House of Correction was burnt down and a Manchester mill owner was forced to sign a minimum wage agreement while on his knees in the street.

By the beginning of 1811 the poorest among the Midland stocking-knitters were reduced to penury. Nearly half the population of Nottingham was in need of relief out of the poor rates, and skilled workers in Leicester, Nottingham and Derby were sweeping the streets for the pittance it offered them. Threatened with starvation, framework-knitters turned to the well-tried and often successful means of protest – violence against the machinery whose misuse was increasing their suffering. It is important to emphasise that the Midland framework-knitters were *not* protesting against the introduction of new machines. The domestic stocking-frame had been in use for two hundred years, with relatively little technical improvement. Opposition to machinery *per se* by the framework-knitters would have been cutting the ground from under their own feet. It was only the use of wide frames for making cheap merchandise and the undermining of skilled workmen's livelihoods that was the object of their violent protests. It must be borne in mind that the majority of stockingers lived and worked in relative isolation in small villages scattered throughout the western half of Leicestershire, south-western Nottinghamshire and eastern Derbyshire. They were unsophisticated and often illiterate men who had little or no knowledge of trade union activity on their behalf in the larger towns, and were economically worse off than urban workers. Resorting to violence must have seemed the only way for them to draw attention to their plight.

There are strong grounds for suggesting, in fact, that Luddism in the Midlands was chiefly a rural movement: that the incentive to violence came from those workers who were ignorant of, or out of touch with, negotiations on behalf of everyone in the trade. It was not in the big towns like Leicester, Derby, Hinckley or Loughborough that machine-breaking was rife, nor even in Nottingham at first. It began in the scattered villages and smaller towns, and continued most strongly there. Nottingham became a curious exception. As the textile industries grew, and the town's population increased as people moved from the country to find employment, every conceivable piece of land had to be used to accommodate them. But Nottingham's outward expansion was restricted by the surrounding open fields, which had remained unenclosed. So pressure on space increased, and Nottingham's workers soon found themselves living in appalling conditions in overcrowded slums. The enclosure of Nottingham's common fields was not achieved until 1845, by which time it was much too late. These social factors cannot be ignored when considering why Nottingham suffered more industrial unrest than other large hosiery towns. The population of Nottingham in 1811/12 was about 34,000; of Leicester about 23,000; and Derby about 13,000.

Midland workers have a long tradition of law-abiding moderation in industrial relations. Social history and anthropology help to attest to the sheer desperation which drove men in the Midlands to such unlawful reaction to their conditions. Geology, too, has an incalculable and little-explored role in determining the character of any region's indigenous population. The small, dark people of Celtic origin who settled in the English Midlands were bound to become a race of miners, engineers and mechanics. The hard rock beneath their feet dictated the rigorous pattern of their lives. They established a permanent preoccupation with winning a living in the face of a hostile environment. They formed a close-knit society insulated, to some extent, from outside influences. They had no coastline to make them wonder about distant horizons, no mountains to induce a spirit of adventure, no natural spectacle to challenge their imagination. They were materialistic, with little romance or sophistication in their make-up. Their modern descendants inherited a philosophy of hard work and independence, and were non-conformist in both religious and secular matters, tending to keep their own counsel and indifferent to both southern affectation and northern bluster. Their Protestant work ethic made them discipline their children to prepare for hard-working lives, taught them to despise illness and find their own remedies rather than take time off; and made them practical and independent. The Midland framework-knitters were, in short, a relatively dull, unimaginative and stoical people, of poor physique owing to their sedentary occupation. Only the real horror of starvation could have made them resort to violence as a means of coercing their employers into paying adequate wages and abandoning the wide frames which were threatening the workers' ability to earn their daily bread.

It became clear, as machine-breaking increased, especially in Nottinghamshire, that ordinary stocking-frames were being left intact, and only wide frames destroyed. When Luddite gangs broke into workshops where hosiers owned frames of both types, they were usually scrupulous in sabotaging only the wide frames, leaving the standard frames alone. They did not smash frames owned by masters who had not reduced wages, nor those of men whose frames were making fully fashioned stockings at the proper price. This restraint implies a good deal of discipline and single-minded purposefulness among them.

CHAPTER TWO

The Advent and Escalation of Luddism

The début of Luddism seems to have taken place in the small town of Arnold, Nottinghamshire, where, in the early weeks of 1811, knitters broke into workshops and removed the jack-wires from wide frames which were being used to make cut-ups. This example of direct action was copied by knitters in other Nottinghamshire villages during February and March. The removal of these machine parts constituted disablement rather than destruction. Jack-wires could soon be replaced and the frames put in working order again.

On 11 March a large demonstration took place in the market-place at Nottingham; stockingers from all over that part of the county that was chiefly engaged in framework knitting gathered and made threats against hosiery masters who were reducing wages. The crowd was dispersed by the local militia and no damage was done. But that night, between dusk and dawn, a mob at Arnold swarmed through the town, forcibly entered the homes of frame owners and smashed up sixty-three wide frames. Dragoons were called out to restore order, but during the next three weeks another two hundred frames were broken in the area, at Sutton-in-Ashfield, Mansfield, Bulwell and other places.[1]

Rewards were promptly offered by the frame owners to anyone giving information which would lead to conviction of the criminals. But no arrests were made: the sympathies of the public were with the rioters, and a high level of secrecy was maintained regarding their identities and activities. No individual, in fact, would be denounced for frame-breaking during the entire course of the troubles in the Midlands, although, as E.J. Hobsbawm has remarked, the owners 'must have known perfectly well who broke their frames'.[2]

No stocking-frames had been smashed in Nottingham itself up to this point, but F.O. Darvall was mistaken in his belief that the disturbances had not 'extended over the county borders to Derbyshire or Leicestershire'.[3] Frames had been wrecked at Ilkeston, for instance, and on 11 April stockingers at Hinckley went on a rampage through the town, breaking windows and plundering and burning houses.

Ironically, however, the county which reputedly gave the machine-breaking movement its popular title suffered relatively little from frame destruction.

WHEREAS,

Several EVIL-MINDED PERSONS have assembled together in a riotous Manner, and DESTROYED a NUMBER of

FRAMES,

In different Parts of the Country:

THIS IS

TO GIVE NOTICE,

That any Person who will give Information of any Person or Persons thus wickedly

BREAKING THE FRAMES,

Shall, upon CONVICTION, receive

50 GUINEAS

REWARD.

And any Person who was actively engaged in RIOTING, who will impeach his Accomplices, shall, upon CONVICTION, receive the same Reward, and every Effort made to procure his Pardon.

☞ Information to be given to Messrs. COLDHAM and ENFIELD.

Nottingham, March 26, 1811.

A poster printed at Nottingham in March 1811, offering a reward for information leading to the conviction of machine-breakers.

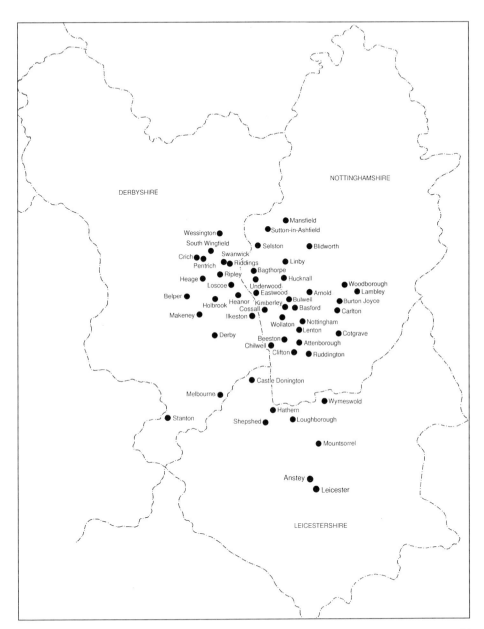

The geography of Luddite riots and machine-breaking in the Midland counties, 1811–16. (Old county boundaries)

Although in some parts of Leicestershire knitters were hardly less distressed than their counterparts to the north, the county generally did not experience the worst of the depression, owing to its manufacture of expensive worsted garments of fine quality. It owed this relative economic success to 'Dawson's Wheels' – an invention by a Leicester framework knitter, William Dawson – which successfully mechanised former hand operations. Thus, so far from attacking new inventions, many local workers were actually *saved* from the worst effects of the time by a new machine! In Leicester itself, the stockingers were noted for their 'very peacable and orderly disposition'. The protests of those workers in Leicestershire who did suffer took different forms from the physical violence of the Nottinghamshire men. They disabled machinery by removing jack-wires, wrote a few threatening letters, and collected money for the support of those in direst need, but did not generally resort to violent extremes, except along the county's northern fringes, where the workers had something of a reputation for turbulence, in places such as Loughborough, Shepshed, Castle Donington and Wymeswold.[4] In Derbyshire, where there were fewer frames, and they were more widely scattered, there was comparatively little destruction of machinery in this early phase, especially as the hosiers in that county were more inclined to give in to the knitters' demands.[5] At Pentrich, for instance, a gang of Luddites 'after passing through the village, and examining the frames, and their holders, as to the work they made and the prices they received, they retired without doing any mischief . . .'.[6]

It is fairly obvious from the known sequence of events that there was never a decisive meeting among the Midland knitters, at which they formulated any concerted plan of campaign. No knowledge of any inaugural message or plot has come down to us. One or two malcontents at Arnold mischievously removed jack-wires from their frames, and then others went a step farther, and so a growing mobilization took place under its own impetus. Such a spontaneous movement does not always require a common justification, or the incentive of an ultimate target. It just gathers momentum like a runaway train. Rationalisation comes later.

In Nottinghamshire the summer and early autumn were fairly quiet, although some frames were wrecked at Sutton-in-Ashfield in July, but organised violence resumed as winter approached. On the night of Monday, 4 November, six wide frames used for making cut-ups were smashed at Bulwell.[7] Six days later a mob of about seventy armed men from Arnold and the surrounding villages gathered in Bulwell Forest and, led by a commander calling himself 'Ned Lud', marched to the Bulwell premises of Edward Hollingsworth, an unpopular hosier with many frames. Mr Hollingsworth and his men tried to defend the property by shooting at the rioters, and one of them, John Westley of Arnold, was shot dead. His companions carried his body from the scene, then returned, more inflamed than ever, and broke into Hollingsworth's house, where they destroyed his furniture and a number of stocking-frames.[8]

After this incident, sabotage escalated rapidly. Frames were wrecked at Basford, Old Radford and Sutton-in-Ashfield during the next few days. The large number of frames smashed at Sutton-in-Ashfield (about seventy) all belonged to one hosier, named Betts, who – according to Felkin – 'died deranged' shortly afterwards.[9] On this occasion, however, four men were arrested and committed for trial.

The Lord Lieutenant of Nottinghamshire, the 4th Duke of Newcastle, wrote to the Home Secretary from Clumber House on 16 November, pointing out that the disturbances were of a 'local and partial nature, totally unmixed as yet with any political notions', although 'the high price of corn very much tends to aggravate their grievances'.[10] This more or less confirmed the Secretary of State's own view. He had spoken in February about the Midland disturbances as a purely local industrial matter. The Home Secretary in Spencer Perceval's administration was Richard Ryder, long-standing Member of Parliament for Tiverton, Devon. His Under-Secretary, John Beckett, was a member of a prominent Leeds family of merchants and bankers. These two ministers were as determined to subdue the Luddites as the Foreign Secretary, Lord Wellesley, was to prosecute the war against Napoleon.

The Prince Regent issued a proclamation offering a reward of £50 for information leading to the conviction of anyone involved in machine-breaking, and a free pardon to any informant who was himself a participant in such actions. But this temptation to tell tales, like the previous one, fell on stony ground. A manifesto from 'Ned Ludd's Office, Sherwood Forest', claimed somewhat extravagantly that the seventeenth-century Framework Knitters' Charter had empowered them to destroy frames that were used dishonestly.[11] On the night of 23/24 November the first frame-breaking was recorded in Nottingham itself, as well as other instances at Basford, Chilwell and Ilkeston, and during the following day and night, more frames were smashed in Nottingham, Basford, Heanor, Cossall and Eastwood.

Nevertheless, on the 26th, the Duke of Newcastle informed the Home Secretary that it was with 'great satisfaction' that he could now report that 'the late disagreeable disturbances in the County are entirely got under'. The Lord Lieutenant went on to express his sympathy with the plight of the framework knitters, especially as

> the high price of every thing necessary for their subsistence presses now still heavier upon these poor people . . . They certainly are very much to be pitied and when every thing is perfectly tranquil and that they find themselves sub-dued by being obliged to submit to the Laws I hope we may be able by some means to relieve them.[12]

The Duke of Newcastle, Lord Lieutenant of Nottinghamshire during the Luddite period.

The Duke's compassionate sentiments contrast with his startling optimism. What can have led him to believe that the disturbances had been largely subdued, so soon after two nights of machine-breaking in several places? Was he misinformed by those he relied on for advice? There seems to have been a general air of complacency for a time among members of the government and aristocracy. The

subject of frame-breaking was not raised in parliament until February 1812, and
when it was, few Members attended the debates. Only four days after his sanguine
letter to the Home Secretary, the Duke had to write again to report that he had
found it necessary to call out the Volunteer Yeomanry Cavalry, as the riots had
'become more serious'.[13] In the few days between his two letters, frames had been
wrecked at Beeston, Basford and other places. Altogether, during November,
around two hundred stocking- and lace-frames had been destroyed in the Midland
counties, the vast majority of them in Nottinghamshire. Many hosiers had been
sufficiently alarmed and intimidated to give in to the rioters' demands, and agreed
to abandon the manufacture of cut-ups and to increase knitters' wages, provided
that the attacks on machinery were stopped.[14] This attempt at conciliation broke
down, however, because only about half the manufacturers were prepared to make
such concessions, and in the first days of December more frames were smashed up
in Nottingham; the spate of attacks spread into Leicestershire and Derbyshire
when around fifty frames were wrecked at Shepshed and Ilkeston.

Those responsible in practical day-to-day terms for law and order were far
from being as complacent as the aristocratic Lord Lieutenant. The Nottingham
town clerk, George Coldham, was in constant and anxious communication with
the Home Office about the worsening situation, while a county magistrate,
William Sherbrooke, insisted that no half measures would be sufficient to
suppress the 'Lawless mob'.[15] Sabotage continued throughout the first half of
December, often accompanied by threatening letters in the name of 'General
Ludd', in Nottingham and the surrounding villages, and in Derbyshire. 'The
great body of the present Mischief', George Coldham advised the Home Office,

> arises from the endeavours of the labouring Classes by terror to compel their
> Employers to increase the price of their labour and otherwise conduct the
> Manufactory in a manner more agreeable to the Interests or prejudice of the
> Artizan and this System must be kept down by Force before we can expect
> the restoration of Public Tranquillity . . . Since the first origin of these distur-
> bances which have now existed more or less Six or Seven Months the great
> Engine of Terror with the people has been to destroy the Stocking Frames of
> those Manufacturers who have been most odious to their Eyes and it is sup-
> posed that in the whole about Eight hundred Frames have been destroyed of
> the value of Eight thousand Pounds, depreciated as this species of Property is
> by the dreadful state of the Manufactory . . . If the People are once taught
> that they can accomplish the objects of their wishes by a system of Terror
> I feel assured that they will proceed further than breaking Frames and it is
> Difficult to say who may be the next Objects of their Vengeance.[16]

Mr Coldham, it is worth remarking, was also Secretary of the Hosiers' Association.

George Coldham, Town Clerk of Nottingham, and spokesman for local manufacturers who demanded government action to protect their property.

Baron Middleton of Wollaton Hall was alarmed by a threat to seize two hundred stand of arms kept there, and had thirty armed men stationed at the house day and night. He believed that a small force of mixed cavalry and infantry in each of the hosiery towns and villages would be sufficient to suppress 'popular tumult in any direction'.[17]

By 16 December the Lord Lieutenant was reporting that the authorities in Nottinghamshire were 'working entirely in the dark' in their efforts to trace the 'real designs' of the Luddites and apprehend the ringleaders, and that 'Foreign agency is strongly suspected to be the support and mover of the whole . . .'.[18] The *Leeds Intelligencer* declared that the causes of the machine-breaking conspiracies could not be ascribed merely to the economic distresses of the time.[19] The clear implication of these suspicions was that the French were behind the rioting, just as the French had been rumoured to be behind the Gordon riots in London in 1780. The object this time was obviously to disrupt Britain's war effort. A rumour was soon in circulation that Napoleon was prepared to supply both men and arms to support a general uprising. Ten thousand men and thirty thousand guns were supposed to be available in Ireland, ready to reinforce a revolution in Britain.[20] 'The Insurrectional state to which this country has been reduced for the last month', a *Leeds Mercury* correspondent wrote, 'has no parallel in history, since the troubled days of Charles the First.'[21]

By this time, after several abortive appeals to the Secretary of State to draft in the military, nine troops of cavalry and two regiments of infantry had finally been sent to the Midland counties from various parts of the kingdom. Their commander, General Dyott, had a force of nearly two thousand men at his disposal. It was, Mr Ryder told the House of Commons, 'a larger force than had ever been found necessary in any period of our history to be employed in the quelling of any local disturbance'.[22]

'My friend,' the indignant young poet Shelley wrote to Elizabeth Hitchener, 'the military are gone to Nottingham – Curses light on them for their motives if they destroy *one* of its famine wasted inhabitants . . . Southey thinks that a revolution is inevitable; this is one of his reasons for supporting things as they are.'[23] In fact, Southey, the future Poet Laureate, despite being tucked away beyond the Cumbrian Mountains at Keswick, had felt the necessity to 'take down a rusty gun and manfully load it for the satisfaction of the family', in case the 'ugly fellows' should turn up there.[24]

Sir Joseph Banks, President of the Royal Society, received information from Ashover in December that

the stocking frame-breaking system which has caused so much alarm and disturbance in the neighbourhood of Nottingham has extended its baneful

effects into this neighbourhood. At Pentridge, about six miles from hence, a person of the name of Topham has had frames destroyed to the amount of £500.[25]

The Lord Lieutenant of Nottinghamshire told the Home Secretary on 21 December that special constables had taken to entering suspects' homes in the middle of the night and taking them from their beds. This was causing alarm to the culprits, he thought, because they feared their friends were informing against them. He hoped that the public peace would be restored within a fortnight.[26] But the first weeks of the new year saw stocking-frames smashed in Bulwell and Basford, Arnold and Hucknall, Heanor and Old Radford, and lace-frames were attacked in Nottingham.

At length Mr Ryder responded to repeated requests for Bow Street officers to be sent to assist the local authorities. N. Conant and R. Baker arrived in Nottingham to investigate the rioting and discover those responsible for organising it. Conant's first report to his chiefs in London said that the 'frames are here and there for ten miles round which are all open to the depredators – who take their own time and in five minutes destroy the Frame and disappear . . . But the result in my own mind is, that much mischief is not to be apprehended.'[27] Conant and Baker also investigated reports that Napoleon was already pouring money into the country to aid those engaged in industrial sabotage, but they found no evidence to support such rumours.

Then there was a more ominous development. On Sunday, 19 January, while stocking- and lace-frames were being wrecked at various places in Nottinghamshire and Derbyshire, fire was discovered at a woollen mill in Leeds. The Oatlands Mill of Messrs Oates, Wood & Smithson, near Woodhouse Carr, went up in flames; arson was suspected, with good reason. The factory contained gig-mills, and threats had already been made, when a crowd of men with blackened faces had assembled in the town a few nights earlier, that machinery would be destroyed in certain unspecified premises.[28] Luddism had made its Yorkshire début. If any doubts were entertained on this score, they were dispelled three days later when shearing frames were destroyed by gangs at Joseph Hirst's dressing shop at Marsh, near Huddersfield, and at James Balderstone's premises at Crosland Moor.

It is vital at this point to establish clearly that there was, right from the first act of violence in the north, an essential difference between the attacks on machinery in the Midland hosiery industry and those in the Yorkshire woollen industry. Any question of political motives apart, the economic aims of the two groups of workers were quite different. We have already seen that the framework-knitters were not antagonistic to new machinery as such. The Yorkshiremen, on the other hand, were violently opposed to machinery itself.

They were protesting against the introduction of new labour-saving machinery which was threatening to make them redundant. The body of workers chiefly involved there were the shearmen, or 'croppers', as they were more commonly called in Yorkshire. They were a tiny group compared with the Midland knitters, who numbered fifty thousand. There were only around four thousand croppers, and only half of them were in the northern Luddite epicentre, Huddersfield and its district, which became known as the 'metropolis of discontent'. The croppers were highly skilled finishers who raised the uneven nap on woollen cloth with the spiky bracts of the teazel plant, *Dipsacus fullonem*, and then cropped it with large and heavy iron hand-shears to produce a smooth surface. The shears weighed about 40 lb (18 kg), and the croppers had to be strong men. (They had to be strong to smash the machines, too: the stocking-frame in the Midlands was built of wood, with only the working parts of metal, whereas the shearing machines and gig-mills in the north were made entirely of iron.) The croppers worked in small workshops which had been established in the valleys of the River Calder and its tributary, the Spen, between Leeds and Huddersfield. They were the most highly paid of all the workers in the woollen industry, because it was on the quality of their work that the value of the finished cloth finally depended. One newspaper reported that the croppers could spend 'twice or three times as much money at the ale house than the weaver or dyer'.[29] George Walker, the contemporary author of *The Costume of Yorkshire*, wrote:

The head of the teazel plant, *Dipsacus fullonem*. Its spiky bracts, fixed in wooden frames, were used by the hand-finishers to raise the nap on woollen cloth.

Hand cropping shears. These heavy implements, weighing about 50lb (18kg), and nearly 4ft long (1.2m), required both strength and skill in the user.

The Cloth-dressers are a numerous body in the West Riding of Yorkshire, many of them natives, and many from Ireland and the West of England. An able workman will earn great wages, and, if industrious and steady, is certain to make his way in the world; but it is to be lamented that comparatively few are found of this description. The majority are idle and dissolute, owing perhaps partly to the laborious nature of their occupation, which too often induces habits of drunkenness, and partly to their working in numbers together, a circumstance always injurious to morale.[30]

They were notoriously independent, and had successfully resisted the large-scale introduction of shearing frames to the industry in Yorkshire. They were also attempting, when the wave of Luddite machine-breaking commenced, to have the semi-obsolete sixteenth-century statute against gig-mills upheld. They were unsuccessful because they could not prove that the gig-mills actually in use were the same as those prohibited under the law of Edward VI.

The Select Committee of 1806, backed by the large manufacturers who did not want any outdated restraints on their capitalist enterprise, had recommended repeal of the Acts of Edward VI, and parliament had taken this advice in 1809, giving the master clothiers what the croppers saw as freedom to make fortunes at their expense. The croppers, on the one hand, maintained that finishing by machinery damaged the texture of fine cloth. The masters, on the other hand, believed – as Earl Fitzwilliam, the Whig Lord Lieutenant of the West Riding, had long before pointed out to the then Home Secretary, Lord Pelham – that 'the business done by the croppers is *better* done, as well as cheaper by machinery than by hand'.[31]

The Yorkshiremen were of an essentially different character from the Midlanders, too. They were descendants of the Brigantes, who had harried the Roman occupying forces long after other British tribes had succumbed to imperial rule and adapted to its civilising influences. And on to this fierce ancient independence had been grafted the Viking tradition of warring self-assertion, giving the northerners a propensity to rise in defiant opposition to authority that is still evident to this day. As Elizabeth Gaskell observed: 'Even an inhabitant of the neighbouring county of Lancaster is struck by the peculiar force of character which the Yorkshiremen display . . . Their accost is curt; their accent and tone of speech blunt and harsh.'[32] The average Midlander does not share these belligerent mannerisms.

Lord Fitzwilliam, faced with the rising tide of opposition and law-breaking, had, even in 1802, urged on by Benjamin Gott, described the shearmen as 'the tyrants of the country', and said that their power and influence had 'grown out of their high wages, which enable them to make deposits that puts them beyond all fear of inconvenience from misconduct'. He considered that the masters, by often giving in to workers' demands, had 'lost all superiority. The journeymen are now masters.'[33] He thought the solution might be to flood the industry with gig-mills and cropping machines, and thus cut the ground from under the feet of the workers, but most local manufacturers wisely held back from such provocative action. Such expressions as the Lord Lieutenant's can only have reinforced the government's initial scepticism about the judgement and efficacy of local law enforcement officers, who always imagined their own districts to be the most vulnerable and beyond purely local control, and repeatedly pleaded for government help in the form of more troops.

Meanwhile, cotton machinery at Rhodes' mill at Tintwistle, near Stalybridge, was totally destroyed in a raid there. Cheshire had also been drawn into the machine-breaking territory. Frame-breaking in the Midlands reached its climax, in terms of numbers, in January, when more than two hundred frames were destroyed, mostly in Nottinghamshire, where there was an alarming acceleration towards the end of the month. On the 23rd, a Wednesday, twenty-two frames were smashed at Lenton. On the Friday night, twenty-six machines were smashed at Clifton and fourteen at Ruddington; on the following day, forty-five were destroyed at Bagthorp and Underwood, three at Basford and one at Bulwell.[34] At

Clifton, the frame-breaking was accompanied by theft of articles from some premises, but a letter from 'General Ludd' afterwards denounced the thieves, who, it said, were nothing to do with the true Luddites. Claiming to be 'a friend to the pore and Distrest', the writer said that one of the strangers had been punished for his villainy by being 'hang'd for 3 Menet and then Let downe againe'.[35]

The incident at Basford led to a suspicion of collusion between William Barnes, a framework-knitter, in whose house the frames were standing, and the gang of saboteurs. Two soldiers of the Royal Berkshire Militia, Henry Huggins and Thomas Osgood, stated on oath that when they arrived at Barnes's house, having been sent there at the request of a frame *owner*, Mr Hadden, to guard his frames, Barnes roundly abused them, saying he wanted no soldiers in his house and telling them to 'go to hell'. He went outside twice for about five minutes at a time, and on returning indoors the second time, he was followed in by about twenty men disguised with handkerchiefs over their mouths and armed with pistols and sticks. The two soldiers were overpowered and disarmed, and the gang then smashed three of the six stocking-frames on the premises before departing. The three frames broken were Mr Hadden's; the three left alone were Barnes's own property.[36] Barnes was subsequently arrested and charged with having, 'with divers other persons at present unknown, wilfully, maliciously, and feloniously, broken, destroyed, and damaged two frames'.[37]

The Lord Lieutenant of Nottinghamshire was now thoroughly alarmed. On 5 February he wrote to the Home Secretary:

> You are no doubt informed that the West Riding of Yorkshire is now imitat-ing the bad example of this County and thus that part of Yorkshire, Nottinghamshire, Derbyshire and Leicestershire are in a state of insurrection, for one can scarcely call it by any other name. Sooner or later, I fear, recourse must be had to the severest measures as the only means of checking what may ultimately endanger the State, and I throw it out for your consideration whether it will not be expedient in a short time to declare Martial Law in the Counties above alluded to, unless a better disposition manifests itself.[38]

The local authorities and the manufacturers and middle classes of England were in a state of increasing alarm and apprehension, tormented by uncertainty as to the intentions of the workers, who had clearly demonstrated their power, and mindful of the bloody excesses which had occurred across the Channel only twenty years earlier. Yet the Home Secretary told the House of Commons on 14 February, during a debate on the Frame-Breaking and Nottingham Peace Bills, that 'while he deeply lamented the occurrence of these acts of lawless violence, he had the satisfaction to state to the House that the disturbances had been gradually diminishing; and, for more than a week, had altogether subsided'.[39]

Mr Ryder had already drafted in to the north of England large numbers of troops to reinforce local regiments. In addition to the two thousand soldiers in Nottinghamshire by the end of 1811, Huddersfield, soon afterwards, had a thousand men billeted in the town's thirty-three public houses. The *Leeds Mercury* reported the further arrival in Nottingham of the Royal Buckinghamshire Militia, 'in 38 waggons, they having left Woodbridge barracks, in Suffolk, at 7 o'clock on Friday evening last . . .'.[40] The strong military presence was no more popular in industrial England than an army of occupation, which is what it amounted to in the Huddersfield area in particular. Landlords who, perforce, accommodated the soldiers were not adequately recompensed, and the soldiers, being a long way from home, did nothing for the morality of the areas they were stationed in.

The army was unsuccessful, in any case, in bringing an early end to machine-breaking. The marauding nocturnal gangs easily evaded the troops, and the question was being posed whether the ordinary soldier's natural sympathy with the economic distress of the workers and their families was actually contributing to the ability of the gangs to dodge less-than-zealous military patrols (which were to display a fairly consistent inclination in the future to arrive late at scenes of disturbances).[41] Some Luddites were themselves members of their local militia, and there was some fear that drafted troops would transfer their allegiance to the local rebels. The soldiers were moved around often, to prevent them from forming sympathetic alliances with the people among whom they were billeted.

The Luddites borrowed a few military devices in their efforts to evade detection. Raiding gangs went out in the hours of darkness with masked or blackened faces. They were identified among themselves, in Yorkshire at least, by number rather than by name, and they communicated by means of prearranged signals, such as shots fired into the air, rather than with shouted orders and general commotion.

The Home Office had persuaded itself that the Luddite movement was merely an activity confined to the lower orders of a local industrial population, quite incapable of mounting an insurrection against the government. It was a matter for the local authorities and the military to sort out. Nevertheless, during the course of 1812, there were more troops in the troubled areas of the Midlands and north of England than Wellington had under his command in the Peninsular War. Nearly thirteen thousand men, both cavalry and infantry, were distributed across the region as the army mobilised; they became, in effect, a police force in the industrial heart of England. This part of Britain, *The Times* reported, had every appearance of 'a state of war'.[42] The Yorkshire journalist Frank Peel summed up the situation in characteristically rhetorical prose: '. . . the soldiers who were wanted to fight our battles abroad had to be retained at home to keep down sedition and rebellion in our midst'.[43]

So what are we to make of the argument that the Luddites had political motives for their actions? The chief proponent of the political conspiracy theory is E.P. Thompson, whose influential book *The Making of the English Working Class*, first published in 1963, challenged the long-standing assumption of purely economic motives and branded the common historical view of the Luddites as the 'enormous condescension of posterity'.[44] Luddism, he says famously, 'was a *quasi-insurrectionary movement*, which continually trembled on the edge of ulterior revolutionary objectives'.[45] On the other side of the fence stand numerous historians who have maintained that the Luddite movement was aimed solely at improving the living conditions of the textile workers and their families. F.O. Darvall, for instance, wrote categorically in 1934:

> There is no evidence whatever of any political motives on the part of the Luddites. There is not one single instance in which it can be proved that a Luddite attack was directed towards anything deeper than disputes between masters and men, between workmen and their employers.[46]

Recent historians who have generally supported this traditional view include E.J. Hobsbawm and M.I. Thomis.

There seems little room for compromise between the two positions. The question is simple: did the Luddites, or did they not, have political as well as economic motives in destroying property? The answer is a little harder. We shall need to keep the question carefully in mind as we progress through the history of events, but perhaps it is not too soon to propose a partial answer. There are certainly no grounds for suspecting any political agenda in the minds of the Midland framework-knitters who, in some respects, are entitled to be regarded as the only authentic Luddites. Their campaign originated and continued out of dire need, and when men's backs are to the wall, their first priority is their daily bread. A Luddite song of the period emphasises the economic motives of the machine-breakers and gives no hint of more ambitious designs:

> Chant no more your old rhymes about bold Robin Hood,
> His feats I but little admire.
> I will sing the achievements of General Ludd,
> Now the hero of Nottinghamshire.
> Brave Ludd was to measures of violence unused
> Till his sufferings became so severe
> That at last to defend his own interest he rous'd
> And for the great work did prepare.
>
> Now by force unsubdued, and by threats undismay'd,
> Death itself can't his ardour repress.
> The presence of Armies can't make him afraid
> Nor impede his career of success.

Whilst the news of his conquests is spread far and near
How his Enemies take the alarm,
His courage, his fortitude, strikes them with fear
For they dread the Omnipotent Arm!

The guilty may fear, but no vengeance he aims
At the honest man's life or Estate.
His wrath is entirely confined to wide frames
And to those that old prices abate.
These Engines of mischief were sentenced to die
By unanimous vote of the Trade,
And Ludd who can all opposition defy
Was the grand Executioner made.

And when in the work of destruction employed
He himself to no method confines.
By fire and by water he gets them destroyed
For the Elements aid his designs,
Whether guarded by Soldiers along the Highway
Or closely secured in the room,
He shivers them up both by night and by day
And nothing can soften their doom.

He may censure great Ludd's disrespect for the Laws,
Who ne'er for a moment reflects
That *foul Imposition* alone was the cause
Which produced these unhappy effects.
Let the haughty no longer the humble oppress,
Then shall Ludd sheath his conquering Sword,
His grievances instantly meet with redress,
Then peace will be quickly restored.

Let the wise and the great lend their aid and advice
Nor e'er their assistance withdraw
Till full fashioned work at the old fashion'd price
Is established by Custom and Law.
Then the Trade when this ardorus contest is o'er
Shall raise in full splendour it's head,
And colting, and cutting, and squaring no more
Shall deprive honest workmen of bread.[47]

CHAPTER THREE

Local Responses and Government Reactions

Colonel Ralph Fletcher, a magistrate of Bolton, Lancashire, was among the first to voice his conviction that the Nottinghamshire machine-breakers had set a dangerous example to northern manufacturing districts where machinery was held at least partly responsible for the economic distress of workers.[1] The literate among aggrieved Yorkshiremen were reading almost daily accounts of fresh Midland outrages in the pages of the *Leeds Mercury* and other newspapers, as well as reports that the hosiery masters were in some cases ready to give way to the knitters' demands. Between November 1811 and January 1812 inclusive, Midland hosiery workers smashed an average of around 175 frames per month. F.O. Darvall says that an average of two hundred frames per month were broken between November and February.[2] This appears to be a slight exaggeration but, at any rate, the number of smashed frames represents about 2 per cent of all those estimated to have been in operation in the three Midland counties at the time. Scarcely a day went by during January when there were not reports of more machine-breaking in Nottinghamshire and Derbyshire. No doubt commercial travellers, too, brought up-to-the-minute accounts of new developments. It is more than probable that the news provided inspiration to disaffected workers in the woollen and cotton industries.

The mill-owners, hard hit by the effects of Napoleon's Continental System and the British government's Orders in Council, especially after the American Non-Intercourse Act, cut working hours and reduced wages. Many workers were unemployed and food prices were high. At the beginning of 1812 one-fifth of the population of Lancashire was said to be in need of charitable relief. The depression of trade passed down through the social system to the remaining hand-workers in the woollen and cotton industries. The hand-loom weavers in the north, like the 'poor stockingers' of the Midlands, were among the lowest paid workers in the industrial population. The Yorkshire croppers had at one time been among the most prosperous of textile hand-workers, but they too were falling prey to merciless market forces. They were fighting a losing battle against natural progress. In 1806 there had been only

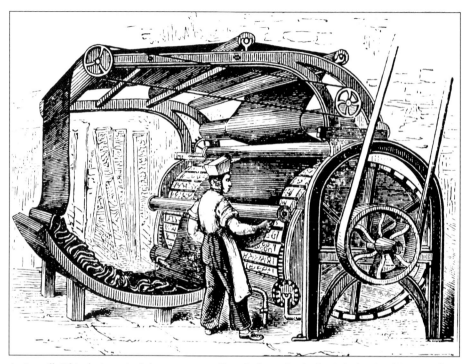

A gig-mill. This device raised the nap on woollen cloth mechanically. It had existed in some form since the sixteenth century, but was not widely used at first in the Yorkshire woollen industry.

five gig-mills working in the north of England. Within a decade, the number rose, in spite of all opposition, to seventy-two. The number of shearing frames increased in the same period from about a hundred to well over a thousand.[3]

Weavers in Scotland fought long legal battles for a minimum wage, and won. But frustrated Lancashire workers soon adopted Luddite methods, though with less organisation and single-minded determination than was shown by the Midlanders and the Yorkshiremen. In the last weeks of 1811 and the first weeks of 1812 rumours began to circulate about links between the Midland rioters and disgruntled workers in the north. A stocking salesman from Nottingham, a Mr Williamson, was reported to have met a committee of workers in Manchester in November.[4] Colonel Fletcher reported information from a 'respectable channel' that delegates from Nottingham had been administering oaths to workers in Bolton.[5] Frank Peel stated that a Nottingham Luddite, George Weightman, came to Yorkshire and spoke to croppers at the Shears Inn near Heckmondwike. There is absolutely no evidence to support this claim, but according to one J. Mayer, writing from Manchester: 'Already we have plenty of Nottingham,

Carlisle and Glasgow delegates, who are holding private meetings *every night* and instigating ours to riot and confusion.'[6]

There were also suspicions of conspiratorial meetings between Luddite 'delegates' from Nottingham and weavers in Stockport, where threatening letters were received by mill owners who had power-looms on their premises. Peter Marsland, a Stockport manufacturer who had made some technical improvements to the steam-loom, which was perceived as a threat to the employment of weavers, reported in February an attempt to burn down his mill.

No such contacts have been proven beyond reasonable doubt, the allegations coming almost exclusively from paid spies and criminal informants. It is difficult to be certain who originated a geographical error which has become self-perpetuating. F.O. Darvall, the historian of popular uprisings in the period, refers to the main area of knitting-frame destruction as *north-west Nottinghamshire*.[7] E.P. Thompson is among others (including George Rudé) who have repeated this mistake,[8] and he says elsewhere: 'Anyone who knows the geography of the Midlands and the north will find it difficult to believe that the Luddites of three adjoining counties had *no* contact with each other.'[9] He means, presumably, Nottinghamshire, Yorkshire and Lancashire, but the sentence is misleading. The area of the chief Midland county infected by Luddism was actually *south-west* Nottinghamshire. The northern limit of violence against stocking- and lace-frames was around Mansfield. The error is by no means trivial. 'North-west Nottinghamshire' suggests physical adjacency with Yorkshire, whereas in fact there was a geographical gap of around 40 miles, as the crow flies, between the northern extremity of machine-breaking in the Midlands and the southern limit in the north of England. Forty miles was a more significant distance in those days than it seems now, and the distance between Nottingham and Manchester – 70 miles – even more so. Machine-breaking did not affect north-west Nottinghamshire or the mining and steel region around Sheffield, Rotherham and Barnsley, now South Yorkshire. The effective gap was between the Mansfield area of Nottinghamshire and what is now the southern area of West Yorkshire around Holmfirth.

Northern Luddism took place in a separate region, as well as in a different industry. This fact makes more debatable any probability of a sympathetic and organisational link between the two. (The known links between the Yorkshire shearmen and those in the West Country are a different matter. Though the distance between them was greater, they were working in the same industry and shared precisely the same problems.) The framework-knitters worked in relative isolation in a widely scattered and largely rural cottage industry. Concerned wholly with their own problems, they had little to gain by urging similar action on a small group of workers in a completely different industry in another part of the country.

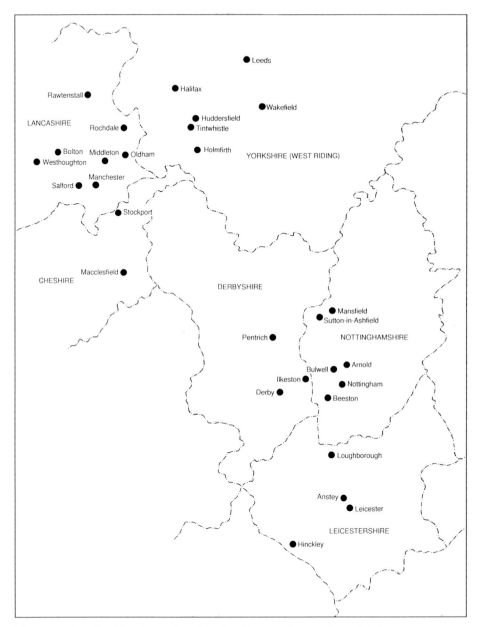

The geography of Luddite riots and machine-breaking. (Old county boundaries)

The Stockport and Manchester areas were already hotbeds of social and industrial unrest, and food riots were common there. The workers who embraced Luddite tactics were not confined to the weavers whose livelihoods were threatened by the introduction of power-looms. There was undoubtedly a stronger Jacobin presence in Lancashire than in either Yorkshire or the Midlands, reinforced by a large community of immigrants from Ireland. Several correspondents in 1808, during disturbances that affected Manchester, Stockport, Bolton, Blackburn, Rochdale, and other towns, had advised Lord Hawkesbury, Home Secretary in the Duke of Portland's administration (and subsequently Earl of Liverpool), that Irish weavers, in the words of the magistrate R.A. Farington, were 'the foremost and most turbulent in all the proceedings'.[10] The Irish, agitating for full Catholic emancipation, and more prone than the English to form illegal combinations and join secret societies, were identified with Jacobinism, and 'Jacobins' were the bogeymen implicated in all civil disturbances at the time, as 'Communists' have been in the twentieth century.

The high degree of secrecy maintained by workers and their families throughout the troubled region made it well-nigh impossible for the authorities to find out exactly what *was* going on, and to decide how best to deal with the situation. The difficulty of obtaining information was a constant refrain in communications with the government. 'The grand difficulty', the Duke of Newcastle told Mr Ryder,

> is the almost impossibility of obtaining information respecting the movements and intentions of the rioters; everything is so well organised amongst them, and their measures are conducted with so much secrecy, added to which, that no one dares to impeach for fear of his life, that it is scarcely possible to detect them.

Revd R. Hardy, JP, wrote from Loughborough ten days later, '. . . we find the class of men to whom we are obliged to look for information, in general very unwilling to give it'.[11]

The Lord Lieutenant of Cheshire, Viscount Bulkeley, recommended to the Home Secretary that John Lloyd, a solicitor and clerk to the Stockport magistrate, Revd Charles Prescott, should be employed as a spy to investigate contacts between the Midland framework-knitters and the northern cotton weavers. This suggestion was adopted, and Lloyd became a zealous spymaster and persecutor of suspected agitators and machine-wreckers, extracting information by threat and sometimes, rumour had it, by torture. General Maitland, in command of the troops in the north-west, admitted that much of Lloyd's work was 'out of the strict letter of the law, though, I believe, perfectly in the spirit both of the law and of the constitution'.[12]

Among the first guardians of the law in Yorkshire to take an uncompromising stand against the Luddites was Joseph Radcliffe, a Huddersfield magistrate. Radcliffe, a wealthy landowner, was unstinting in his pursuit of the criminals, and constantly urged the government, through the Lord Lieutenant, to send in more troops. He had no sympathy with the workers' grievances, and made himself so unpopular that there were several threats to his life and at least one real attempt, necessitating a round-the-clock military guard at his home, Milnsbridge House, where a room used for interrogating suspects became known as the 'sweat room'. Radcliffe asked the local commanding officer for 'ten privates and a non-commissioned officer to be here night and day'.[13] It came to the point where he left his house only when it was absolutely necessary, and his daughters never walked beyond the grounds without receiving insults. Few people, either among the workers or the authorities, seemed to like or trust Radcliffe. The Luddites did not trust him to give them justice in any circumstances. The solicitor-spy, Lloyd, accused him of talking too much. Radcliffe was jealous of Lloyd's success in apprehending suspects. General Maitland considered Radcliffe pompous and neurotic, and indeed his increasing rage and vindictiveness contributed eventually to the development of a nervous tremor, which made his spidery handwriting extremely difficult to decipher. His later letters were mostly written by his clerk, Jonas Allison.[14]

The Home Office was bombarded with confusing and contradictory advice from the provincial guardians of law and order. The Duke of Newcastle had called for martial law to be imposed, and suspected foreign interference. He wrote to the Home Secretary on 20 February: 'I think it right to inform you that it is known that there are orders at Birmingham for arms for the rioters; and it is as far as I can learn certain that delegates are sent from hence into all the great Towns in this Country. The disturbances at Leeds were planned from hence, as I learn.' But he added cautiously: 'I cannot pretend to vouch for the entire authenticity of all that I have mentioned in the latter part of this letter. I can only add that I am strongly induced to believe them.'[15]

The two Bow Street officers, Conant and Baker, denied the 'state of war' impression mentioned in *The Times*, at least as far as Nottingham was concerned, reporting in February that 'this place has been in the most perfect quiet ever since we have been in it'. One frame, they said, had been broken at Attenborough a few nights earlier.[16] Conant was scornful about the rumours of arms from Birmingham. There was no evidence of it, he said, dismissing the informant as 'credulous'.[17] His doubts were seemingly borne out subsequently, when a mob in Sheffield, during a food riot on 14 April, attacked a military armoury and, instead of seizing the weapons there, destroyed most of them. It seems that 198 firearms were broken, the young men involved being urged on by the crowd to smash them. Only 78 muskets were stolen.[18]

Revd John Becher, a magistrate of Southwell and friend of Byron, and a well-known Poor Law reformer, wrote a long and well-argued letter to the Home Office in February in which he analysed the cause of the troubles, and reckoned that more than a thousand frames had been destroyed, with a total estimated value of £10,000. He saw the problem purely as an industrial/economic one, without political implications.★ Having recorded his Tory gentry's dismay that the lower orders had sufficient time on their hands to talk about politics, and his observation that the attractions of working in trade in the towns had led, among other inconveniences, to the 'difficulty of procuring servants', his analysis of the situation, though somewhat verbose, is one of the most carefully reasoned and understanding of all submissions made to the Home Office on the subject. Southwell was outside the area of great Luddite turmoil, so Mr Becher was able, no doubt, to take a more detached view than his colleagues with more sorely pressing responsibilities. Whether his recommendation of frame-rent regulation would itself have been sufficient to satisfy the knitters is another matter.[19]

William Nunn, a lace manufacturer, believed the solution to the problem was wondrously elementary:

As many Hundred Letters have been sent sign'd 'Ludd' threatening the Lives and to burn and destroy the Houses, Frames and Property of most of the principal Manufacturers *through* the Post office, and very few letters are sent through that means but on these occasions, were you to direct Mr. Connant [sic] or those in whom you place your confidence, that when such Letters come, the Person within to open them, and by signal give Notice to others without to follow them, you would in a few days find out the Committee: directly opposite is a Hair Dressers shop where women, boys or men might be station'd, or any others, as three long streets command a Sight of the Office, again if Thirty one-Pound Banknotes all mark'd were to be sent to . . . the Sir Isaac Newton in a Bag, with Directions to send them to Ludd and his Men, they would immediately get into circulation through the Butcher Baker etc. get the five Banks when they come in (which they would do in a few days), to make each Person write his name and place of abode on them and send them to the Magistrates who would send for the Parties all together and examine them, it would immediately be found who the acting men were.

For those who are demolishing in the Villages, a man or two should be placed at the top of a house in each, or on a Hill by the Roadside with Rockets when a party of these Men were in a Village, send up one or more of the Rockets giving a particular Light which would give the alarm to the other on Watch the Soldiers on Guard in the neighbouring Towns to push

---

★ Mr Becher's letter is quoted in full as Appendix I.

forward to the Rocket, giving the Signal where the Rioters are: the horse along the Roads, the Foot over the Fields, a sufficient Number would be secured to stop the whole: leave a few Men in each adjoining Village to detect such as might escape: martial law being proclaimed and every Man order'd to be in by eight or nine 'Clock at Night.

If you would send Mr. Connant six more men by tonights mail, all may be quieted in a week, and all well as soon as the Leaders are taken.[20]

From Yorkshire, a magistrate named Taylor at Horbury wanted the obnoxious shearing frames in the area to be destroyed in order to placate the shearmen,[21] while an elderly magistrate named Walker at Birstall delivered himself of the opinion, in a letter to Earl Fitzwilliam, that all the troubles could be put down to 'young boys larking about in the hills with fireworks'.[22]

Darvall appears to have exaggerated in saying that the neighbourhood of Leeds, like those of Nottingham and Manchester, was 'a seething mass of distress and discontent, liable at any moment, in the bitterness of its apparently insoluble disputes, to break out into disorder'.[23] In spite of the facts that there was a known strong Jacobin presence in Leeds, and that about half the shearmen in Yorkshire worked there, Luddism never gathered force in Leeds any more than in Bradford, the wool town *par excellence*, which does not feature at all in the Luddite story. The reason was that the introduction of gig-mills had been successfully resisted there for some years, and local mill owners were simply not installing new machinery on any significant scale at the time. The owners of machinery throughout the troubled areas were certainly alarmed for the safety of their property, but rumour and false reports seem to have resulted in an impression of ordinary citizens being afraid to go out at night, just as modern television reporting raises public fears by giving – however unintentionally – a hair-raising impression of the current crime rate.

Draconian new laws were passed in 1812 to deal with Luddism, which some saw simply as an alarming and widespread new crime wave. The Luddites were not merely disgruntled workers turning to theft and vandalism. Their actions had specific aims, but machine-breaking was sometimes accompanied by other crimes, and it is clear that ordinary criminals took advantage of Luddism as a cover for their activities. The *Nottingham Journal* was alert to the differences between genuine Luddites and those who adopted 'the *nom de guerre* "Ned Ludd's men" as a cloak for the commission of almost every crime'.[24]

There was also, no doubt, some occurrence of the now well-known phenomenon of 'copycat crime'. There were local destructive attacks on farm machinery in the period of Yorkshire Luddism, in the spring and summer of 1812. Some workers with grudges against their employers simply jumped on the bandwagon. There was no evidence of any ideological campaign. A shopkeeper named Sykes came up for trial in May 1812 after announcing to one of his neighbours that he was one of General Ludd's men and demanding arms. The jury was persuaded that it was only a prank by one who was the worse for drink, and the defendant was acquitted.[25]

It was, ironically, the magistrates of Leicestershire, the textile county least afflicted by machine-breaking, who, with the enthusiastic support of the Treasury Solicitor, Henry Hobhouse, urged on the Home Secretary a Bill to make machine-breaking a capital offence,[26] and it was this proposal that Spencer Perceval's government acted upon, after continuing incidents of destruction in Nottinghamshire and Derbyshire towns and villages. The Frame-Breaking Bill was introduced to the House of Commons on 14 February 1812. The Bill was drafted to provide for the 'exemplary punishment of persons destroying or injuring any stocking- or lace-frames, or other machines or engines used in the frame-work knitted manufactory, or any article or goods in such frames or machines'. It made no reference to gig-mills, shearing frames or power-looms, and was directed solely and specifically at the Midland framework-knitters.

Although several Members of Parliament in a thinly attended House expressed themselves reluctant to support a premature move to extreme measures, and some wanted a committee of enquiry to be set up before resorting to hasty remedies, the Bill passed its first reading by forty-nine votes to eleven. At the second reading, three days later, Sir Samuel Romilly adopted his by-now traditional role in leading the opposition to any further increase in the severity of the criminal code. He argued that the terror of death would not be greater than the terror of transportation, and that the Bill would be self-defeating, for the liability to such punishment would deter witnesses from coming forward, with the result that criminals would not be punished at all. Samuel Whitbread, Sir Francis Burdett and Richard Brinsley Sheridan, in one of the final acts of his political career, were among a few others who voted against the Bill. William Lamb, the future Prime Minister and Viscount Melbourne, demonstrating his intellect by declaring that 'the fear of death had a powerful influence over the human mind', was among those who supported the Bill. Only 111 members passed through the division lobbies, and the second reading was carried by ninety-four votes to seventeen. The third reading in the Commons was on 20 February.[27]

It was during the second reading in the House of Lords, on 27 February, when Lord Holland (Recorder of Nottingham) and Lord Grenville, the former Whig Prime Minister, were among those opposing the Bill, that Lord Byron rose to make his impassioned and famous maiden speech. The Byron family seat at Newstead Abbey, between Nottingham and Mansfield, was situated at the heart of the most troubled hosiery manufacturing district, and the poet had seen for himself the miseries of the local working population. 'I have traversed the seat of war in the Peninsula;' he said, 'I have been in some of the most oppressed provinces of Turkey; but never, under the most despotic of infidel governments, did I behold such squalid wretchedness as I have seen since my return, in the very heart of a Christian country.'* Byron was against the Bill because of its 'palpable injustice, and its certain inefficacy', as he had told Lord Holland in a letter two days earlier. 'The few words I shall venture to offer on Thursday will be founded on these opinions formed from my own observations on the spot.'[28]

'Is there not blood enough upon your penal code', Byron demanded of the assembled peers,

> that more must be poured forth to ascend to Heaven and testify against you? How will you carry the Bill into effect? Can you commit a whole country to their own prisons? Will you erect a gibbet in every field, and hang up men like scarecrows? . . . When a proposal is made to emancipate or relieve, you hesitate, you deliberate for years, you temporise and tamper with the minds of men; but a death-bill must be passed off-hand, without a thought of the consequences.

The House listened in silence as Lord Byron reached his great peroration. Suppose the Bill were passed, he said,

> . . . suppose one of these men, as I have seen them, – meagre with famine, sullen with despair, careless of a life which your Lordships are perhaps about to value at something less than the price of a stocking-frame; – suppose this man surrounded by the children for whom he is unable to procure bread at the hazard of his existence, about to be torn forever from a family which he lately supported in peaceful industry, and which it is not his fault that he can no longer so support; – suppose this man – and there are ten thousand such from whom you may select your victims – dragged into court, to be tried for this new offence, by this new law; still, there are two things wanting to convict and condemn him; and these are, in my opinion, twelve butchers for a jury, and a Jeffreys for a judge!

Byron was warmly congratulated on his speech by persons on both sides of both Houses of Parliament, and Sir Francis Burdett told him that it was the best speech by a Lord since 'the Lord knows when', but Byron's eloquence and logic were lost on the majority of their Lordships, and had no influence on the final outcome. The noblemen of England were deeply entrenched in their support for capital punishment. The Lord Chancellor, Eldon, considered that terror of

---

* Byron's speech is printed in full as Appendix II.

the gallows in the minds of all men was sufficient reason in itself to retain the death penalty. On the motion for the third reading, on 5 March, the Bill was passed without division.[29]

It was already a capital offence, under the notorious Black Act, to go about armed and in disguise, or to write a threatening letter. If desperate men were willing to risk the savagery of the law in those respects, they were hardly likely, one might think, to be deterred from their campaign against losing their livelihoods. As Coleridge remarked some years later, 'what man who saw assured starvation before him, ever feared hanging?' Indeed, these men thought they might as well be hanged for a sheep as a lamb, and turned their thoughts to murdering the capitalists instead of destroying the implements of exploitation. A popular rhyme soon gained currency:

> Welcome Ned Ludd, your case is good,
> Make Perceval your aim;
> For by this Bill, 'tis understood
> It's death to break a Frame –
>
> With dexterous skill, the Hosier's kill
> For they are quite as bad;
> And die you must, by the late Bill,
> Go on my bonny lad! –
>
> You might as well be hung for death
> As breaking a machine –
> So now my lad, your sword unsheath
> And make it sharp and keen –
>
> We are ready now your cause to join
> Whenever you may call;
> So make foul blood run clear and fine
> Of Tyrants great and small![30]

Even while the Frame-Breaking Bill was going through its readings in parliament, knitting-frames were smashed in Nottingham and in Derbyshire, and shearing frames in the Huddersfield district. The *Nottingham Review* reported a local incident on 21 February:

> This morning, about five o'clock, a number of men entered in at the chamber window of Mr. Harvey, West-street, Broad-lane, in this town, and while some of them secured the family, others proceeded into the workshop, and

demolished five warp lace-frames, which were employed in making two-course-hole net: they were all very valuable frames, and one of them was 72 inches wide . . . Two frames were left unbroken, and it is supposed they were saved thro' a neighbouring woman calling out 'Murder'; and who had a pistol fired at her to make her cease her noise. Mr. H. had two loaded pistols and a blunder-buss in his house, the former of which the Frame-breakers took away; and as they were descending from the window, it was thought by persons who saw them, that the nightly piquet was receiving them to conduct them to prison; but it turned out to be about 25 of their companions, armed and dressed in soldiers great-coats, one of whom was dignified with a large staff, and, it is supposed, he was the commander of the party.[31]

In Yorkshire armed men with blackened faces broke into Joseph Hirst's premises at Marsh and held up a man and two boys, then smashed up seven frames and twenty-four pairs of shears. They moved on to James Balderstone's house at Crosland Moor and held Mr Balderstone and his wife at gunpoint while smashing a frame and eight pairs of shears.[32] All the machinery in the dressing shop of William Hinchcliffe at Leymoor was destroyed on the eve of Byron's speech.

A heavy hammer made by Taylors of Marsden, and believed to have been used by Yorkshire croppers to smash shearing machinery. It was nicknamed 'Great Enoch' after its maker.

A local firm of iron-founders, Enoch and James Taylor, whose foundry was at Marsden, near Huddersfield, was building shearing frames for local employers, and they were putting skilled croppers out of work. Yet neither the Taylors nor their premises were ever attacked. The Taylor brothers also made sledge-hammers, and some of these were utilised by the Yorkshire machine-breakers, who nicknamed the implements 'Great Enoch' after their maker. 'Enoch made them; Enoch shall break them,' the motto went, as the heavy hammers wrecked the machines. Nevertheless, it is curious, to say the least, that a local firm making profit from the very machinery that was threatening the croppers' jobs should have been immune from attack. Even the murder of the proprietors would hardly have seemed surprising in the circumstances of the time. One of the attackers at Hinchcliffe's shop was alleged to have shouted 'Let's kill him!', but was dissuaded by another, and several victims of machine-wrecking and arms raids spoke of being threatened with having their brains blown out if they did not keep quiet. So why were the Taylor brothers left alone? Both the brothers and other members of the Taylor family were well known to be free-thinking radicals. It may be that a leading Luddite with Jacobin sympathies, such as George Mellor, protected them. Mellor, twenty-two years old, has generally been identified as the leader of the Luddites in the Calder Valley area of Yorkshire.

Local magistrates, manufacturers, merchants and others met at the George Inn, Huddersfield, on Thursday 27 February to consider means of preventing further depredations, and resolved to offer a reward of a hundred guineas for information leading to any conviction for the recent attacks.[33] But no such information was forthcoming. There was a profound hostility among the working people of the north, as in the Midlands, to the capitalist employers and the magistrates who supported them. General Grey, commanding the troops in Yorkshire, reported that 'even the more respectable portion of the inhabitants' were 'in unison with the deluded and ill-disposed populace with respect to the present object of their resentment, Gig Mills and Shearing Frames'.[34] In the Midland hosiery industry, many of the masters, who were themselves struggling to survive against competition from the wide frame cut-ups of less scrupulous manufacturers, quietly approved of the Luddites' results, even if they did not entirely acquiesce in their violent methods.

On 14 March large crowds gathered in Stockport and raided provision stores in the town, then went to the house of Peter Marsland in Heaton Lane and broke his windows, after which they threw stones at the windows of his mill across the river. Then they attacked several factories on the south side of the town, pausing on the way there to break the windows of the house of the local constable, John Birch. Finally they broke into John Goodair's mill at Edgeley, where they cut up warps and destroyed looms, before moving on to his house in

Huddersfield.

AT A GENERAL MEETING

OF THE

MAGISTRATES,
Merchants, Manufacturers,
And Inhabitants

Of Huddersfield, and its Vicinity,

Convened by Notice, to be holden at the House of Mr. John Townsend, the George Inn, in Huddersfield, aforesaid,

On Thursday, the 27th. Day of February, 1812,

The following Resolutions were agreed to:

IT appears to this Meeting, that a violent and determined Spirit of Insubordination has gained much Ground amongst the Workmen employed in various Trades and Manufactures, and particularly amongst the Shearmen, and that the same is organised and supported in a Manner, not only Alarming to Trade in general, but to the Peaceable Inhabitants of this Town and Neighbourhood in particular.

THAT we cannot sufficiently deprecate all Attempts to limit the ingenuity of our Artificers, the employment of our Capital, and to prescribe the mode in which the different operations of our Trade shall be conducted, and particularly those now making in this Neighbourhood, for the Destruction of the Machinery used in the finishing of Woollen Cloth.

THAT the Destruction already Committed upon this kind of Machinery in this Neighbourhood, and the Threats of future Depredations, evidently proceed from an illegal Combination of Desperate Men; And We conceive it the duty of all Men to suppress, as much as lies in their power, such Vicious and Unlawful Combinations, and to assist and use their utmost endeavours, to detect and bring to Justice, not only the Perpetrators, but such as Countenance and Support them.

THAT a Subscription be immediately entered into, for the purpose of procuring Information of the Proceedings of any illegal Combination, and of liberally Rewarding any Person, giving such Information as may lead to the Detection and Conviction of any such Offenders.

THAT the Management of this Subscription be under the Direction of a Committee, any Five of whom shall have power to act, as Occasion may require.

In Pursuance of the above Resolutions,

A Subscription has been entered into, and the Committee hereby offer a Reward of

One Hundred Guineas,

To any Person or Persons who will give Information, so as to lead to the Conviction of any of the Parties recently concerned in Destroying the Dressing Frames of Mr. Joseph Hirst, of Marsh; Mr. James Balderson, of Crosland Moor; and Mr. William Hinchliffe, of Ley Moor, all near Huddersfield; and also the same Reward will be given to any Person or Persons, who will give *Private Information* of the intention of the Depredators to commit any further Mischief, so as such Information shall lead to the Apprehension and Conviction of any of the Offenders, and *Inviolable Secrecy will be observed.*

A reward poster printed at Huddersfield in February 1812. It notes a 'violent and determined Spirit of Insubordination . . . particularly amongst the Shearmen . . .'.

Castle Street. They set fire to the house and made a bonfire of Mr Goodair's furniture in the garden. While they were at their destructive work here, the military arrived, and the Riot Act was read by Charles Prescott. When the crowd refused to disperse, the cavalry charged them with drawn swords, and infantrymen advanced with fixed bayonets. Many people were wounded, and some of the ringleaders were arrested and committed to Chester Castle to await trial.[35]

The mob was led by two men dressed as women, who were referred to among the crowd as 'General Ludd's wives'. This large-scale riot included attacks on food shops, and confirms the strong connection between Luddism and the frequent food riots of the period. Women, tenacious when it came to feeding their children, were often the instigators and leaders of such riots, and were thought less liable to arrest and prosecution than men. The 'Bloody Code' was generally perceived as being more lenient towards women. (Later in the summer a food riot in Leeds was led by a woman who called herself 'Lady Ludd'.)

There was a spate of machine-breaking in villages in the Huddersfield area between 5 and 15 March, culminating in an attack on the premises of Francis Vickerman, a cloth finisher at Taylor Hill. Vickerman had a cropping shop with ten shearing frames, and had earlier received a letter threatening not only the machinery but his life – 'we will poll [sic] all down some night and kill him that Nave and Roag'.[36] At about 8.30 p.m. on 15 March a gang of men forced an entry into the premises and smashed the ten frames and thirty pairs of shears. Household furniture was also smashed, as well as all the windows in the dressing shop, and an abortive attempt was made to burn the place down. The gang departed hurriedly when shots were fired by well-placed look-outs to warn them that soldiers were approaching. The gang was led by George Mellor and William Thorpe, both cloth-dressers from Huddersfield.

Meanwhile, Revd Hammond Roberson, vicar of Liversedge and a zealous enemy of the Luddites, had written to Radcliffe on 9 March that he had 'good reason to think we should have had a visit from these Croppers if we had not been prepared – as we are. I almost wish they would make an attempt. I think we should give a good account of them.' [37]

Radcliffe had asked the Lord Lieutenant to beg the Home Secretary for more troops to be sent to the area, and Lord Fitzwilliam received, for once, a prompt government response from the Under-Secretary of State:

Whitehall, 14 March 1812

Sir,
I have been honored this morning with your Letter of the 12th Inst. with its Inclosures – and I am to acquaint you by Mr. Sec. Ryder's Directions that

the necessary orders have been given for stationing 2 Troops of the 2nd Dragoon Guards at Huddersfield. – Should the Magistrates think it necessary to call to their aid an additional military Force I am to request that their application may be made to Lieut General Grey Commander in the York District.

I have the honor to be
Sir
your most obedient
& faithful servant
J. Beckett[38]

Two days after the attack on Vickerman's in Yorkshire, eight men were brought before Sir John Bayley at Nottingham Assizes charged with machine-breaking. Six were convicted and the other two acquitted. The guilty men were William Carnell, aged 22; Joseph Maples, 16; Benjamin Poley, 16; Benjamin Haycock, 22; Gervas Marshal, 17; and George Green, about 22. All six were sentenced to transportation – Carnell and Maples for fourteen years; the others for seven years.[39]

The sentences were greeted with outrage in some quarters, not for their savagery, but quite the opposite. Judge Bayley's leniency was deplored by Joseph Radcliffe, among others. Having the death penalty at his disposal, the judge, it was alleged, had failed to implement it. In actual fact, however, the men were not legally liable to the death penalty unless burglary were proved against them as well, which it was not. The Act making machine-breaking a capital offence did not receive the royal assent and become law until 20 March. Nevertheless, Radcliffe thought that Bayley had given 'great Encouragements to the Luddites who call him their friend and me their Enemy'.[40] Even so, the foreman of the jury, a Mr Byrnny, received a threat in biblical tones from a representative of 'General Ludd': 'Remember, the time is fast approaching When men of your stamp Will be brought to Repentance, you may be called upon soon. Remember – your a marked man.'[41] The two witnesses, John and Elizabeth Braithwaite, upon whose evidence Carnell and Maples were convicted, were forced to leave the area for their own safety, after receiving a reward of £50 each.[42]

A manufacturer named George Smith at Huddersfield received, in the same month, an ominous undated letter signed in the name of 'the General of the Army of Redressers, Ned Ludd, Clerk'. After threatening Mr Smith that if he did not dismantle his shearing frames, three hundred men would be sent to do it for him and would, for good measure, burn his buildings to ashes and murder him if he should have the 'Impudence to fire upon any of my Men', the letter went on to refer to 'that Damn'd set of Rogues, Percival

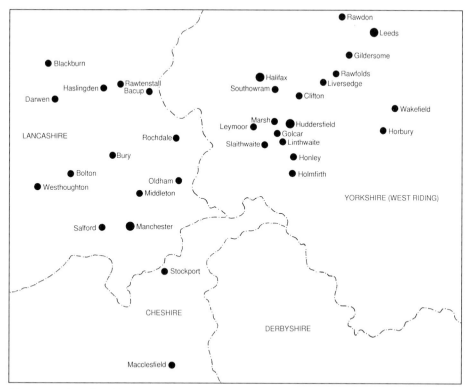

The geography of Luddite riots and machine-breaking in the northern counties, 1811–16. (Old county boundaries)

[sic] and Co to whom we attribute all the Miseries of our Country. But we hope for assistance from the French Emperor in shaking off the Yoke of the Rottenest, Wickedest and most Tyranious Government that ever existed.' There were, the letter added, '2782 Sworn Heroes bound in a Bond of Necessity either to redress their Grievances or gloriously perish in the Attempt in the Army of Huddersfield alone, nearly double sworn Men in Leeds'.[43]

Missives of this kind, which were at least semi-literate, naturally reinforced the opinions of many of those in authority who feared there was more to the Luddite outbreaks than mere economic opposition to machinery. The educated radical then, as always, came under immediate suspicion as being the prime mover and leader of the illiterate rabble. A lurid letter was addressed at about the same time to 'all Croppers, Weavers &c & Public at large', and signed 'General Ludd Commander of the Army of Redressers':

Generous Countrymen. You are requested to come forward with Arms and help the Redressers to redress their Wrongs and shake off the hateful Yoke of a Silly Old Man and his Son even more silly and their Rogueish Ministers, all Nobles and Tyrants must be brought down. Come let us follow the Noble Example of the brave Citizens of Paris who in sight of 30,000 Tyrant Redcoats brought A Tyrant to the Ground. By so doing you will be best aiming at your own Interest. Above 40,000 Heroes are ready to break out, to crush the old Goverment and establish a new one.

Apply to General Ludd Commander of the Army of Redressers.[44]

Clearly these two letters were by the same author, but who was he? George Mellor, perhaps? No one was ever sure.

On 20 March, in the early hours of the morning, a sizeable mob attacked the premises of William Radcliffe at Stockport. Radcliffe was the inventor of a steam-powered dressing machine, and used power-looms in his mill. The attackers broke windows and attempted to set fire to the warehouse by throwing in lighted torches of cotton waste dipped in pitch, tar and turpentine. But the men were driven off by the military, and little damage was done. John Lloyd promptly announced a reward of £200 for information leading to the conviction of the 'Principals concerned in this diabolical crime'. On the same day, a letter, ostensibly from Nottingham, was sent to Joseph Radcliffe:

Take notice that a Declaration was this Day filed against you in Ludd's Court at Nottingham, and unless you remain★ neutral judgment will immediately be signed against you for Default, I shall thence summon a jury for an Enquiry of Damages take out Execution against Both your Body and House, and then you may expect General Ludd, and his well Organised Army to Levy it with all Destruction possible.

And I am Sir your –
Solicitor to General Ludd.

★ PS you have Sir rather taken an active part against the General But you are quiet and may Remain so if you Chuse (And your Brother Justices also) for him, but if you Either Convict one, or Countenance the other side as you have Done (or any of you), you may Expect your House in Flames and, yourSelf in Ashes in a few days from your next move.[45]

Three days after the Stockport attack, during the night of 23/24 March, a large-scale raid took place at Rawdon, near Leeds, when more than thirty machines were smashed at the firm of William Thompson & Brothers. On the next night the premises of Dickinson, Carr & Shann in Leeds came under attack, when the factory was entered and 'eighteen pieces of fine cloth, dressed by machinery, torn and cut into shreds'.[46]

After Easter, more attacks occurred in the Huddersfield area, when shearing frames were wrecked by small gangs attacking three workshops at Honley and Snowgate Head, Holmfirth. The machinery smashed in these raids included that belonging to George Smith, the recipient, a few weeks earlier, of the threatening letter quoted above. A few days after this, on the night of Thursday 9 April, a more ambitious attack was made on Josiah Foster's mill at Horbury, near Wakefield. Three hundred men were reported to have been involved in this raid. (Foster himself thought there were six hundred.) Many men were seen crossing Grange Moor from the Huddersfield direction, while others converged on the mill from the Wakefield side. This was clearly a carefully planned and coordinated operation, although many in the crowd were only sympathetic onlookers, not active Luddites. The latter, at any rate, wasted no time in achieving their object of breaking up gig-mills and shearing frames, while Mr Foster's three sons, ejected from the adjoining house in their nightshirts, were forced at gunpoint to witness the destruction of their father's property, valued at about £700.[47] After the attack a copy of the constitution of the United Britons, an old underground republican movement, was found at Foster's mill – allegedly dropped by one of the Luddites.

John Wood's cropping shop at Longroyd Bridge in the Colne Valley. This contemporary drawing shows wool-finishers at work. The cropping boards are shaped to match the curved blades of the cropping shears, which one man is seen using. The man in the left background is raising the nap with teazels in a frame called a 'nelly'.

The jubilant Yorkshire shearmen soon had their own anthem, which, it has to be said, displays a somewhat higher literary quality than the verses of the Midland men:

> Come cropper lads of high renown,
> Who love to drink good ale that's brown
> And strike each haughty tyrant down
> With hatchet, pike and gun.
>
> Who though the specials still advance
> And soldiers nightly round us prance,
> The cropper lads still lead the dance
> With hatchet, pike and gun.
>
> And night by night when all is still
> And the moon is hid behind the hill,
> We forward march to do our will
> With hatchet, pike and gun.
>
> Great Enoch still shall lead the van.
> Stop him who dare, stop him who can.
> Press forward every gallant man
> With hatchet, pike and gun.
>
> *Chorus*
> Oh, the cropper lads for me,
> The gallant lads for me,
> Who with lusty stroke the shear frames broke,
> The cropper lads for me.

CHAPTER FOUR

Yorkshire Climax

The climax of Luddite activity in the Yorkshire woollen industry came on the night of 11/12 April 1812. According to the local journalist Frank Peel, Rawfolds Mill was chosen as the target of an organised attack at a secret meeting in March at the Crispin Inn, Halifax. Rawfolds Mill, on the River Spen at Liversedge, near Dewsbury, was a water-powered four-storey building owned by William Cartwright, whose business was the dressing of woollen cloth by machinery. The choice between Rawfolds and a similar mill at Ottiwells was made by the spin of a coin. At the same meeting, John Baines, an ageing Halifax hatter and a republican disciple of Tom Paine, told the assembled workers that only the overthrow of the 'bloody aristocracy', which had bled white the nation and reduced the people 'to the condition of galley slaves in the land of their birth', would bring about 'the glorious triumph of democracy'.[1] Mr Cartwright, Elizabeth Gaskell tells us,

> was a very remarkable man, having, as I have been told, some foreign blood in him, the traces of which were very apparent in his tall figure, dark eyes and complexion, and singular, though gentlemanly bearing. At any rate, he had been much abroad, and spoke French well, of itself a suspicious circumstance to the bigoted nationality of those days. Altogether he was an unpopular man, even before he took the last step of employing shears, instead of hands, to dress his wool.[2]

Mr Cartwright had anticipated a Luddite attack on his premises for some time. In February a cart-load of shearing frames for delivery to Rawfolds had been ambushed and destroyed by a gang of men as it crossed Hartshead Moor. Cartwright, who was also a captain in the Halifax Militia, took what he considered to be appropriate precautions. He had slept in the mill's counting house for several weeks, and some of his loyal employees also spent nights in the building. These men were reinforced by soldiers, armed with muskets and ammunition. A guard dog was kept on the ground floor. An alarm bell was installed on the roof so that a local detachment of cavalry could be warned of an impending attack. On the mill's staircase were positioned vicious rollers with metal spikes, and at the top of the mill, a carboy of acid was kept in readiness.

On the night of Saturday 11 April Luddites from a wide area of the West Riding converged on a pre-arranged rendezvous, the stone obelisk near Mirfield commonly known as the 'Dumb Steeple', then in the grounds of Sir George Armitage. They were variously armed with muskets, pistols, hatchets, sticks and hammers. By the time the men set off over the moor towards Rawfolds, more than two miles away, they numbered well over a hundred, although estimates of the number varied. Three hundred is thought to be an exaggeration, and a figure nearer a hundred and fifty is more likely. Their leaders appear to have been George Mellor and William Thorpe. These two organised the men into companies, numbering them off in military fashion, and marched them over the moor and down towards the riverside mill, where they arrived in the early hours of the morning. They were then formed into lines, thirteen abreast.

Mr Cartwright had gone to bed at twenty-five minutes past midnight. Five soldiers were in the building, as well as half a dozen of his employees. Hardly had the owner laid his head on his pillow before shots were heard some distance away – apparently as signals – and then the dog began barking. Mr Cartwright got up immediately. Neither he nor his men had time to get dressed before the ground floor windows were smashed and muskets were fired. One of the

Rawfolds Mill. A nineteenth-century drawing of Cartwright's premises at Liversedge: a steam-driven factory employing shearing machines.

workmen tried to ring the bell, but the rope broke. All the armed defenders except one quickly returned the rioters' fire and successfully prevented them from entering the building. The exception was a young soldier of the Cumberland Militia who refused to fire at men for whom he evidently had some sympathy. Two other soldiers were reluctant to fire, but did not disobey their orders to do so. Cartwright ordered two of his men to get up to the roof and ring the alarm bell by hand. The rioters were hammering violently at the doors of the mill to cries of 'Bang up, lads!' and 'Damn the bell, get to it and silence it!' Cartwright's men hurled down large stones from the roof, which caused the assailants to draw back from the doors. Flashes in the darkness from the Luddites' muskets showed the defenders where to aim their weapons. Suddenly, amid all the commotion, one of the attackers was hit by musket-fire, and then another. The rioters' attempts to smash their way into the mill ceased, and they retreated in hasty disarray, leaving some wounded behind to escape as best they could.

The small army of Luddites, despite their planning, had been taken by surprise by the mill's defence. Cartwright was the first manufacturer to defend his premises so vigorously, and the assailants had not expected armed resistance. The attack had lasted for about twenty minutes. No one defending the mill had been injured. Although those inside were afraid at first to open the doors, a few local people soon arrived on the scene and shouted reassurance from outside. Among the arrivals was Revd Hammond Roberson, who came armed with a sword as if he were the mad archangel himself. The windows of the mill had been smashed and the doors and walls riddled with gunfire. The ground outside was littered with abandoned weapons and implements, and spattered with the blood of wounded men, most of whom had managed to get away. Two were left behind, and one of them, writhing in a pool of blood, was said to have cried out, 'For God's sake shoot me – put me out of my misery.'

About half an hour after the attack had ended, a detachment of cavalry arrived on the scene, and the two seriously wounded Luddites were taken on litters to the Star Inn at Robert-town, a village just over a mile to the south, where they received medical aid. It was alleged afterwards that Cartwright had at first refused to help the dying men unless they revealed the names of accomplices. One of them was 24-year-old Samuel Hartley, a former employee at Rawfolds and a private in the Halifax Militia, who had been made redundant by machinery; and the other was 19-year-old John Booth, a saddler's apprentice from Huddersfield. One of Booth's legs was shattered, and amputation was necessary without delay, but the victim had already lost so much blood that he died at six o'clock that morning. Hartley had been shot in his chest, piercing a lung, and survived only until three o'clock on the Monday morning. Both men had been interrogated before their deaths by Revd Roberson, among others, and there were suspicions that they had been tortured, because of nitric acid stains on the bedclothes. Cartwright said the acid had been used to cauterize their wounds. When the coroner's inquest 'assembled upon the dead bodies', as the *Leeds Mercury* quaintly put it, a verdict of 'justifiable homicide' was returned on both men.[3]

There were unsubstantiated rumours that two other men died from their wounds later. Cartwright himself had noticed that there were 'very heavy' traces of blood in different places. Revd Patrick Brontë, vicar of Hartshead-cum-Clifton, is said to have turned a blind eye when he saw, soon afterwards, men digging in a corner of his churchyard, less than two miles from Rawfolds Mill. He would have known they were not bodysnatchers if there had been no recent burial in that part of the ground, so they were assumed to be burying, illegally, a Luddite who had died while in hiding after being wounded. After this time Mr Brontë regularly carried a loaded pistol, which he is said to have fired from his bedroom window each morning.

Meanwhile, the Recorder of Leeds, Mr Hardy, took his chance at the Borough Sessions on 13 April to condemn the Luddites' short-sightedness:

I cannot omit this opportunity of expressing my regret, that circumstances should have arisen, which have rendered it necessary to put in force an act passed in the present Session of Parliament, for the better preservation of the public peace, and for preventing and suppressing those outrages which have originated in a neighbouring county; but which have unhappily extended to this: outrages which have for their object the destruction of property employed in machinery. These discontents have manifested themselves in a manner at once dangerous to the public peace, and subversive of the public prosperity; because it is only by the aid and extension of machinery, that this nation can preserve its manufactures and commerce. When any new machinery is introduced, it most probably, for a time, has the effect of lessening the demand of labour in that particular department, and may occasion some temporary distress; but persons so affected by it should recollect, that every acre of land is mortgaged and all the personal property of every individual, is pledged for their support. The nation is bound to provide for them. These deluded men, are most grossly deceived, if they imagine that their efforts to put down machinery can ultimately succeed: they will indeed, bring down upon themselves more aggravated distress, and one is at a loss, whether to feel more indignation at their outrages, or surprise at their folly. If these persons could be indulged in their experiment, and could root out all the machinery in the kingdom, the result of the experiment would prove most fatal, and demonstrate the fallacy of their reasoning. We have heard much of the restrictions under which commerce has laboured, and still labours; but if these men could succeed in their design, the commerce of this country would suffer a paralysis from which it could never recover. It requires no prophetic spirit to foretell, that notwithstanding all the organisation of which they boast, their muster roll of numbers instead of names, they will be foiled in their endeavours. They may indeed protract for a time, the return of tranquillity, and by new outrages till up the measure of their guilt. They will, they must be subdued, and after the outrages they have committed, and the warnings they have received, it cannot be expected that mercy will be found in the footsteps of that justice which must sooner or later overtake them. If the measure now adopted by the Legislature should not be sufficient to arrest this alarming evil, other measures must be resorted to, commensurate with the exigencies of the case, even though it should be necessary (which God forbid), to put this part of the country, for a time, under military law.[4]

On the following day a petition was presented by Earl Fitzwilliam, Lord Milton and Mr Wilberforce to the Prince Regent and both Houses of Parliament on behalf of the West Riding clothiers, against the Orders in Council. Lord Milton told parliament that if the petitioners believed that the Orders in Council were in the interests of national honour or welfare, they would willingly submit to the peculiar privations to which they were subjected, but they were convinced of the contrary. The commercial Decrees of France were harmless with respect to their trade, but as soon as the Orders in Council were issued they found that trade much abridged. America, however, was still open to them, but that resource had been rendered precarious, and reasonable apprehensions were to be entertained that it would soon fail altogether.[5]

The young soldier of the Cumberland Militia who had refused to fire at the Rawfolds Mill attackers was court-martialled and sentenced to be flogged for disobeying orders. He was originally sentenced to three hundred lashes – a virtual death sentence – but this savage retribution was reduced to twenty-five lashes through the intervention of Mr Cartwright.

News of the verdicts on the two dead Luddites spread rapidly throughout the north, and there were widespread riots, as far apart as Sheffield and Carlisle. A Lancashire manufacturer, Thomas Garside, gave his opinion to the Home Secretary that the uprising in the north of England was 'the most desperate and best organised conspiracy that the world has ever witnessed'.[6] William Cartwright, who is said to have injured his leg quite badly on his own spiked rollers as he went upstairs after the attack, was later awarded a small sum of money by the government for his spirited defence of his mill, but he had been reduced almost to bankruptcy, and a public subscription for him raised £3,000, chiefly from fellow mill owners, whose best interests had been served, he claimed, 'by my successful stand against a lawless and Blood-thirsty Banditti'.[7]

One cannot but wonder what support for Cartwright there would have been if he had resorted to using the carboy of acid to repel the invaders, which he was obviously prepared to do if he considered it necessary. A Glasgow magistrate and cotton manufacturer, Henry Houldsworth, wrote to the Home Secretary some years later deploring a 'diabolical mode of violence' in local incidents which, by the use of vitriol, had left many 'lingering in their beds or pining through the streets blind and disfigured, rendered for life equally burdensome to themselves and to the community'.[8] But this was a case of violence by other workmen, not upon workmen by their employers.

The funerals of Hartley and Booth, at Halifax and Huddersfield respectively, attracted large crowds of sympathisers, many dressed in mourning, and several of whom openly expressed their regret that the attack on the mill had failed. Revd Jabez Bunting, minister at the local Methodist chapel, refused to conduct Hartley's funeral, and the service was taken by his assistant. Booth was buried hastily at six o'clock the following morning, in order to pre-empt similar demonstrations of unity at Huddersfield, and the crowd that turned up for the ceremony, originally set for noon, was disappointed.

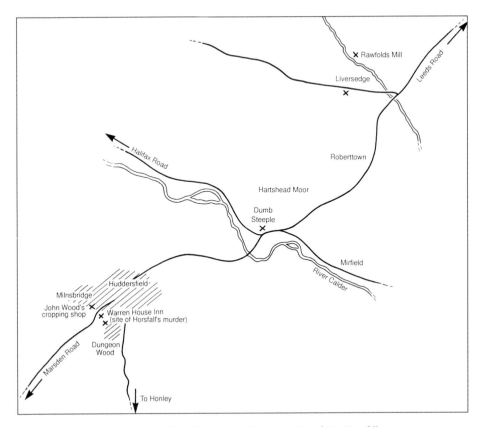

Sketch map of the vicinity of the Rawfolds raid and the murder of Mr Horsfall.

A Luddite fellow-traveller signing himself 'G.D.' subsequently alleged, in a letter addressed 'Dear Brothers and Sisters' and left at the post office at Dobcross, on the edge of Saddleworth Moor near Oldham, that the failure of the attack at Liversedge was 'oing to Halifax Luds not coming up as they were apointed'.[9] Another account said that a contingent from Leeds had arrived late and taken no part in the attack. A Huddersfield cropper, Benjamin Walker, testified later that when a group of workers at John Wood's cropping shop at Longroyd Bridge were discussing the events at Rawfolds Mill afterwards, George Mellor had said that 'the method of breaking the shears must be given up, and instead of it, the masters must be shot'.[10] Notices were appearing on doors in the area calling for 'vengeance for the blood of the innocent'. On 18 April, as William Cartwright was riding through Bradley Wood on his way home from Huddersfield, where he had been giving evidence at the court martial of the reluctant soldier, shots rang out in an attempt on his life, but the would-be assassins missed their target. Cartwright's horse shied, but he managed to stay in the saddle and ride away, escaping unhurt.

The local fanatics, enraged at the murder of their two companions, then turned their attention to William Horsfall, the owner of Ottiwells Mill at Marsden, who not only was one of the pioneering employers of machinery (flatly refusing to abandon it despite repeated threats), but was also chairman of a Huddersfield Committee for the Suppression of the Outrages, and had stated publicly, and somewhat recklessly, that he was 'ready to ride up to his saddle-girths in Luddite blood'. He was a signatory to a letter to the Huddersfield magistrate, Joseph Radcliffe, following a hastily arranged meeting after the attack on Vickerman's premises, asking for the Home Secretary to send Bow Street officers to assist in detecting 'the perpetrators of such dangerous and unlawful acts'.[11] And his passionate hatred of the machine-breakers was so well known that children mocked and taunted him in the streets, calling out, 'I'm General Ludd!' Mr Horsfall had protected his mill by building a defensive wall of stone across the front, pierced with apertures through which a cannon could be fired. He had even purchased a wheeled cannon for that very purpose.

Mr Horsfall, who was about forty years old, invariably went to the weekly market at Huddersfield on Tuesdays, and he was there until about five o'clock on 28 April. He then departed for home, via Crosland Moor, stopping briefly for refreshment at a public house known as the Warren House Inn. Riding on, he had gone barely three hundred yards before shots were fired at him. Mr Horsfall was hit and fell forward on his horse's neck, then he managed to raise himself slightly and cry out 'Murder!' Other travellers on the road came to his aid, but he was bleeding profusely, and fell from his horse with his feet caught in the stirrups. He was taken back to the Warren House and a surgeon was called, but the shots had damaged the femoral artery in the victim's right thigh, and by

Ottiwells Mill, Marsden. This old photograph shows the defensive wall built by William Horsfall with apertures through which a cannon could be fired. The mill has long since been demolished.

nine o'clock on Thursday morning, Mr Horsfall had died of his wounds. All he had been able to tell anyone about his attackers was that he had seen four men with firearms.

One witness said that he had seen four men running away from the scene of the crime.[12] Colonel Campbell, the military commander at Leeds, who was himself attacked while riding home one night, reported that the dying Horsfall had been reproached by a gathering crowd with being an oppressor of the poor.[13] While Horsfall was lying at the Warren House poised between life and death, a Committee for Preventing Unlawful Depredations on Machinery and Shearing Frames met in secret at the George Inn at Huddersfield, and drafted to the Home Secretary a memorandum proposing the immediate imposition of martial law.[14]

It is perhaps worth a brief diversion at this juncture to glance at one or two points of interest about the vicinity in which the cathartic events at Rawfolds took place. The so-called Dumb Steeple near Mirfield, where the Luddites gathered for their march on the mill, is thought to have been a boundary marker

The 'Dumb Steeple' at Mirfield, so called presumably because it 'says nowt'. It originally had a ball finial on top, and was the rendezvous for the Luddites who gathered to raid Rawfolds Mill.

of the medieval Kirklees Priory, a small Cistercian nunnery, where Robin Hood, on his death-bed, is traditionally supposed to have shot his final arrow from a window to determine his burial place. The obelisk, which originally had a ball finial atop the stepped square pier, now stands by the roadside at a spot called Cooper's Bridge, on the north bank of the Calder, where nowadays heavy traffic thunders past on the road between Leeds and Huddersfield. At the time of the Luddites, it stood in a field belonging to Sir George Armitage. On the higher ground above it, at Roe Head, Charlotte Brontë became a pupil, and then a teacher; one of her friends here was Mary Taylor. Mary's father Joshua was a mill owner, related to the Taylors of Marsden and sharing the radical and republican views associated with that somewhat notorious family. His mill had a history of Luddite troubles and he had been bankrupted by the post-Napoleonic War depression. Charlotte Brontë was a frequent guest at the Taylors' home, the Red House at Gomersal, where she heard much about the Luddites, reinforcing her father's accounts, which led to her use of the period as the background to her novel *Shirley*. She used Cartwright as the model for her character Robert Moore, the mill owner, and Roberson for the clergyman Helstone. Rawfolds

Mill became Hollow's Mill. The accuracy of Miss Brontë's understanding of the circumstances, and her description of the attack on the mill, helped by her research in the reports of the *Leeds Mercury*, is generally accepted, but the portraits of the real personalities by her biographer, Mrs Gaskell, have an even greater veracity, not being moulded to the needs of fiction.

★　★　★

The day before the murder of Horsfall, an attempt had been made on the life of a Nottingham hosier, William Trentham. Trentham was alleged to have docked twopence a pair from the wages of women workers, and to have challenged them to 'tell Ned Ludd'. The women were said to be under very strong temptation to turn prostitutes, so extreme was their poverty.[15] Trentham was shot at, while standing at the door of his house in Kaye's Walk, by two men. His wounds were not fatal, but a reward of £600 was offered for information leading to apprehension of the assailants.[16] They were never caught. A suspect named Farborough was questioned but then released, and in early June the Nottingham town clerk had to advise the Home Office that the authorities there had '*NO* Intelligence of the Persons who attacked Mr Trentham nor any hopes of obtaining any'. Mr Coldham added that the passing of the Bill to make frame-breaking a capital offence had 'operated a very mischievous effect upon the mind of the Mass of the People by teaching them that to render their plan of Intimidation complete they must strike at the Life of Man and that they may now as safely Do this as they could before Destroy Frames'.[17]

In Yorkshire, meanwhile, the zealous Hammond Roberson wrote from Healds Hall on 30 April to Mr Cartwright, saying that he was 'decidedly of opinion that the troops in this neighbourhood are too few':

> There is not an inhabitant in all this Neighbourhood, that I know of, that is at all alive to the situation of the country, or rather, perhaps, *that is able* and that *dares*, to take any decisive part in directing the operations of the Military besides myself. Were it possible for me to devote my whole time to the Military I would do my best, and might do something: but I am called upon to act in a *great variety of ways*, this weakens the effect of my best exertions in any particular direction.[18]

Thefts of arms and money in West Yorkshire were occasionally attended with half-hearted attempts at murder. The *Leeds Mercury* reported one such attack:

> About twelve o'clock on Monday night last, three musket balls were fired thro' the windows into the house of Mr. Wm. Milnes, who is a Constable at Lockwood, near Huddersfield; the windows were then broke to pieces with large sticks, and the persons who committed this atrocious act, immediately

made off. It appears that Mr. Milnes had incurred the displeasure of the Luddites by the vigilant discharge of his duty as a Constable. Similar depredations have also been committed at the house of an Excise Officer at Elland; he had several pistols in his house which he was compelled to deliver up. These atrocities have become so common in this neighbourhood, that they now excite little attention.[19]

The day after Horsfall's death a letter was addressed to 'Mr Edward Ludd, Market Place, Huddersfield', apparently from Nottingham:

By Order of Genral Ludd . . .

I am reqested to express the hye sence of honer entertaned of the meretoreous movments you and your forses have so gallently mad in the neberood of Hudersfeld to secure the rites of our pour starving fellow creturs.

I am also desired to say that they lament with extrem regret the fate of the two *brave boys* who galantly spilt theire blod in a lodible cose at Rawfolds. They further learn with pleser that a noble attempt was made about a mile from Huddersfeld though without suckses [two words are illegible here] the Hytown *machenry man*.

The Genral further athorises me to say that he trusts to the attachment of his subjects for the avenging of the death of the two brav youths who fell at the sege of Rawfolds. He also wishes me to state that though his troops heare are not at present making any ostensable movments that it is not for want of force – as the orgenisation is quite as strong as in Yorkshire – but that they are at present only devising the best means for a grand attack and that at present thay are dispatching a few indeviduals by pistol shot on of which fel last nite.

I am further otherised to say that it is the opinion of our general and men that as long as that blackgard drunken whoreing fellow, called Prince Regent and his servants have anything to do with government that nothing but distres will befale us there foot-stooles.

I am further desired to say that it is expected that you will remember that you are mad of the same stuf as Gorg Guelps Juner and corn and wine are sent for you as wel as him.

Peter Plush
Secretary to General Ludd[20]

This letter, ostensibly a message of approval and encouragement from 'General Ludd' to his representative in Yorkshire, may have been intended more as a broadside to alarm the authorities and reinforce the perception of a powerful organised link between Luddites in the Midlands and the north. It looks suspiciously like the work of a literate person who deliberately resorted to misspelling to further disguise his identity. The shot which 'fel last nite' refers, presumably, to that which wounded Mr Trentham.

On the day of Horsfall's funeral at Huddersfield parish church, four days after his death, Cartwright sent eleven pairs of shears to Wakefield to be sharpened. They never came back, and were subsequently discovered in a field, smashed beyond repair.[21]

Early in July, a report from Chester appeared in *The Times*: 'On Friday a Luddite, of the name of Barrowclough, charged with the atrocious crime of *twisting in*, was brought from the edge of Yorkshire to the New Bayley prison, in a post-chaise, escorted by a party of dragoons.'[22] Joseph Barrowclough had been arrested at Holmfirth by Lloyd's men, who had a warrant from the Manchester and Salford magistrate, Revd Hay. Barrowclough was a carpenter and a corporal in the local militia, and he was hurriedly whisked away to Stockport, as one of Lloyd's spies had reported that Barrowclough was a mine of information about Luddite activities. The prisoner was questioned by Lloyd himself and by Mr Allison, solicitor for the Huddersfield Society for Prosecuting the Luddites. Barrowclough turned informer, and told his interrogators that the coming revolution, or the 'marriage feast of Mrs. Ludd', had been postponed until 24 July 1814, which would be, he said, the twenty-fourth anniversary of the beginning of the Luddite system. Arms and ammunition were being stored, roads were being mined, and French officers were drilling Luddite volunteers. Pressed for more detail, Barrowclough gave the sites of numerous arms depots in fields around Holmfirth, and named the murderer of William Horsfall as Samuel Haigh, a 34-year-old labourer of Totties (a location near Holmfirth), who was promptly arrested and sent to York Castle under armed guard. General Maitland, apprised of this alarming intelligence, wasted no time in organising thorough searches by his troops of the Holmfirth fields. No arms came to light – not a single musket, nor even a heavy hammer or rusty sword.

Barrowclough also alluded to Luddites quoting a verse from the Old Testament among themselves, and calling themselves 'the Godly': 'Thus saith the Lord God; Remove the diadem, and take off the crown: this shall not be the same: exalt him that is low, and abase him that is high.'[23] Mr Hay, the magistrate, wrote to Joseph Radcliffe (who was furious that the man had been spirited out of his jurisdiction) that he thought Barrowclough was 'somewhat light in his upper regions',[24] and in this diagnosis he was undoubtedly correct.

A man apprehended in another connection, however, proved much more useful. The efforts of the West Riding authorities to track down all the murderers of William Horsfall had met with no success during the several months which had elapsed since his death. A cloak of secrecy was maintained in the local community, although many Luddites and their sympathisers must have suspected, even if they did not know, who was responsible. But no name was betrayed until a 25-year-old cloth dresser of Longroyd Bridge, Benjamin Walker, succumbed to the temptation of the £2,000 reward offered for information, as well as grasping the opportunity to save his own neck. He was one of several men who had been arrested on suspicion of being involved in the attack on Rawfolds Mill, and after four days of interrogation by John Lloyd, he broke down and turned King's Evidence.

Major-General Acland, General Maitland's second-in-command, advised the Home Secretary from Huddersfield on 22 October that there were strong grounds for believing the murderers of the late Mr Horsfall had been discovered:

> Two men by name William Thorpe and Thomas Smith have been this day committed to York Castle by Mr. Radcliffe as accomplices with George Mellor (already at York Castle) on the evidence of Benjamin Walker, who says he was the fourth concerned with the men already stated, that Mellor and Thorpe were the two men who actually fired the pistols, neither Smith nor himself fired.[25]

Mellor, Thorpe and Smith were clapped in irons with other prisoners at York to await trial. Walker was taken, for his own safety, to Chester Castle.

General Maitland, in command of the situation in more ways than one, was anxious to discontinue the use of Special Constables. He was aware that they were causing great offence in the local communities by knocking up householders in the dead of night and forcing them to quarter troops, and by their dubious methods of extracting information. A man named Charles Faith had been threatened with 'swinging' unless he supplied names. James Starkey, a 22-year-old carpet weaver from Millbridge, was coaxed, by men posing as Luddites, into suggesting how Cartwright's mill might be destroyed. As soon as he innocently supposed that a barrel of gunpowder might do the trick, he was arrested and charged with inciting two soldiers of the Stirlingshire Militia to blow up the mill. It took all the efforts of Revd Roberson, Starkey's parish priest, to get him off.[26]

CHAPTER FIVE

Rumour and Repression

While these events were unfolding in the Midlands and Yorkshire, the flames of revolt were being fanned in the cotton towns of Lancashire and Cheshire. There were disturbances, including food riots, but not machine-breaking, at places as far apart as Wigan and Newcastle-under-Lyme, with a particular concentration in the Manchester–Oldham–Rochdale area. On 20 April, a riot occurred at Daniel Burton's mill at Middleton. Power-looms were in use here, too, weaving calicoes, and the introduction of machinery had cut the workforce by half. The crowd that gathered was reckoned to number several thousand, and the attack again began with stone throwing. The military arrived on the scene and succeeded in driving off the rioters, three of whom were killed in the affray.

Next morning, the mob reassembled, and was eventually joined by over a hundred men armed with miners' picks and muskets with fixed bayonets. They carried a straw effigy of 'the renowned General Ludd whose standard-bearer waved a sort of red flag . . .'.[1] The mill was too well defended for the Luddites to be able to carry out the threat, made in an anonymous letter, to 'Destroy Both Dressing Machines and Steam Looms'.[2] Men intent on wrecking machinery in large steam-powered factories were at an obvious disadvantage compared with their counterparts in the Midlands, whose targets were a few machines in houses or small workshops, often in rural situations. So the crowd set fire to Mr Burton's house before again being dispersed by the military, but five more rioters were killed in exchanges of gunfire. A few days later, the company issued a notice that 'D. Burton and Sons have determined not to work their looms any more'. It was reported that 'The loss sustained by Mr. Burton, in the destruction of his house and furniture, is between two and three thousand pounds, no part of which will be allowed by the insurance offices, being the result of a civil commotion.'[3]

In terms of the dead and injured, this incident was the most disastrous episode in the entire machine-breaking campaign. Only two of the dead rioters were identified as workers in the cotton industry. The others included coal-miners, a baker, a joiner and a glazier. A senior officer of the Oldham militia was informed that while this riot was in progress, delegates among the 'revolutionary Jacobins' were in the roads and local public houses collecting signatures on a document headed with a rebellious oath and summoning signatories to attend a general rising on 4 May.[4]

Three days later, the premises of Wray & Duncroff at Westhoughton, near Bolton, came under attack. This large cotton mill, which had more than 170 steam-powered looms, had been threatened several times before, and an earlier attack had been mounted, evidently at the instigation of an *agent provocateur* employed by the magistrate, Colonel Fletcher. John Stones (ingeniously disguised by the code-letter 'S'!) had organised an arson attack on the mill for 9 April, but had failed to recruit enough men. Stones had persuaded the more gullible among the alleged members of a secret committee of local workers that radical leaders in London, such as Sir Francis Burdett, were only waiting for the northerners to rise, and together they would achieve a revolution. Colonel Fletcher then reported that the attack had been postponed because preparations for a simultaneous rising in the capital were not complete! Stones was said to have arranged secret meetings on Bolton Moor, at which he organised weavers into groups under 'captains' with names such as 'Oliver Cromwell' and 'Sir Francis Burdett'.[5]

The attack on 24 April evidently took the authorities completely by surprise, and the mob managed to set fire to the mill. Captain Bullen of the Scots Greys had received a call for assistance and had taken a party to the mill; finding no one there he had returned to Bolton with his men under the impression that the alarm had been a hoax. But the mob gathered later, during the afternoon, and broke the mill's windows, then threw heaps of straw inside and set it alight, causing around £6,000 worth of damage. The authorities, with spies and informers employed by Colonel Fletcher and Joseph Nadin, Deputy Constable of Manchester, active among the disaffected sections of the populace, wasted little time in arresting those they believed responsible for these outrages.

Meanwhile, the *Leeds Mercury* reported that James Haigh, a cloth-dresser of Dalton, near Huddersfield, had been arrested on suspicion of involvement in the attack on Cartwright's mill:

> This man, who appears to have received a wound from a musket-ball in his shoulder without being able to give any satisfactory account of the cause of that wound, has undergone several examinations before Mr. Radcliffe, of Milnsbridge, and was on Thursday committed to York Castle.[6]

Haigh had claimed that he had fallen down a quarry, but the wound was not consistent with such an accident.

The spies working for Fletcher, Lloyd, Nadin and the military commanders obtained a good deal of evidence about the administering of illegal oaths among the cotton workers. It was known as 'twisting in', and involved, according to one account from an informer in Yorkshire, swearing to 'Punish by death aney trater or trators should there aney arise up amongst us'.[7] There was also – again only on the evidence of spies and informers – a password for recognition of fellow-Luddites, which necessitated raising

> your right Hand over your right Eye – if there be another Luddite in Company he will raise his left Hand over his left Eye – then you must raise the forefinger of your right Hand to the right Side of your Mouth – the other will raise the little finger of his left Hand to the left Side of his Mouth & will say What are you? The answer, Determined – he will say what for? Your answer, Free Liberty – then he will converse with you and tell you anything he knows . . .

When the critical date of 4 May passed without incident, General Maitland wrote to the Home Office: 'For my own part, I am a total disbeliever that either such rising was seriously intended or that they were in a state of organisation to admit of it.'[8]

In that first week of May, the government introduced a Bill to parliament to make the administering of illegal oaths a felony punishable by death. Sir Francis Burdett and Samuel Whitbread were among the Members who opposed the Bill, arguing that the evidence was insufficient to justify legislation increasing the number of capital crimes still further. Whitbread pointed out that the taking of an unlawful oath would now be equivalent in law to murder. Meanwhile, a report to the Home Office alleged that a gaoler at Lancaster Castle had searched a cloth-worker and found in his pocket a letter from William Burdett, Sir Francis's brother, intimating support for a workers' committee in Bolton. At the same time, a prisoner at Chester had been interrogated and had said that the royal family was to be deposed and a 'New Commonwealth' established, with Sir Francis Burdett at its head.[9]

Burdett's was not the only name to be taken in vain by paid spies and revolutionary propagandists. William Cobbett and Major John Cartwright were invoked, too, as imminent leaders of the masses towards some vaguely imagined Utopian republic. Perhaps a few of the more revolutionary-minded activists misunderstood the parliamentary reform ideas this radical trio held in common, and deluded themselves into believing that one or all of them would support a general uprising if it had a chance of success. In fact, nothing could have been further from the truth. Radical reformers Burdett, Cartwright and Cobbett were, but militant revolutionaries they were certainly not. Cartwright had been urging the Nottinghamshire knitters to give up machine-breaking and put their energies, instead, into solving their economic problems by achieving parliamentary reform. Burdett had only recently been in the Tower for sedition, but he was a wealthy baronet whose chief pleasure in life was fox-hunting with the Quorn. Cobbett was in Newgate at the height of the Luddite revolt, but wrote his famous *Letter to the Luddites* to dissuade them from their violent methods. None of the three had the least idea of overthrowing established authority by force.

Back in 1810, when Sir Francis Burdett had been committed to the Tower by a warrant of the Speaker of the House of Commons for publishing a seditious libel in Cobbett's *Political Register*, a mob had attacked the Prime Minister's house in London. And it was none other than Spencer Perceval who, in his capacity as a lawyer, had prosecuted Cobbett for libelling Tory peers. Cobbett himself, residing in Newgate, wrote to a friend in America summing up the situation:

> A considerable regular army is assembled in that part of England for the purpose of opposing and putting down the people who have risen; and a law has been passed inflicting the punishment of death in certain cases, where the punishment before was transportation. To give you some idea of the sufferings of the poor people, it will be quite sufficient for me to state these facts: that the weekly wages of a working man does not upon an average throughout England, exceed 15*s*; that the price of a bushel of wheat is, upon an average, 18*s*; that the price of a bushel of potatoes has been for some time past, upon an average, 8*s* 6*d*.[10]

The Prime Minister, Spencer Perceval, had been sent a letter in February from 'Genl. C. Ludd' at 'Shirewood Camp', saying that the 'Bill for Punish.g with Death, has only to be viewd. with contempt and opposd. by measures equally strong; and the Gentlemen who framd. it will have to repent the Act: for if one man's life is sacrificed! blood for blood! Should you be calld. upon, you cannot say. I have not given you notice of de-.[11]

At about 5.15 p.m. on Monday 11 May, the Prime Minister walked into the lobby of the House of Commons to attend a committee hearing on the Orders in Council which had aroused storms of protest from British manufacturing industry. As he crossed the lobby floor, a man approached him, raised a pistol and fired at point-blank range into the left side of the Prime Minister's chest. Mr Perceval staggered forward, gasping 'Murder!', then fell on his face to the floor. A doctor was sent for while Members of Parliament and attendants carried Perceval into a small room in the Speaker's chambers and laid him on a sofa, but by the time a doctor arrived, the Prime Minister was dead.

The assassin had made no attempt to escape. He stood with the pistol in his hand until he was arrested and disarmed, and when committed to Newgate and questioned, admitted that he was the man who had shot Mr Perceval. 'My name is John Bellingham,' he said. 'I know what I have done. It was a private injury – a denial of justice on the part of the government.' Nevertheless, the immediate assumption in the country was that Bellingham was a northern merchant with Luddite sympathies, and that his motive was revolutionary. The assassination of Spencer Perceval was applauded by noisy mobs in Lancashire and Cheshire, and celebrated with a bonfire by framework-knitters in Nottinghamshire.

It turned out, however, that Bellingham was a madman. He had run up enormous debts through a failed business venture in Russia, where he had ended up in prison, and had nurtured a bitter resentment against the British government for failing to help him and compensate him for his losses. He was determined to take his revenge on someone. It just happened that the Prime Minister was on the spot at the critical moment.

A friend of Joseph Radcliffe wrote to him from London a few days after the assassination, agreeing that more troops were needed 'in your part of the country', despite the fact that 'all the Soldiers that can be spaired [sic] are sent to Portugal'. He then added that

> some people think [Bellingham] must at times have been insane; tho' that did not appear on his trial . . . I have been in company this morning with an upholsterer, who was several times in Bellingham's company; who solemnly declared to me, that he never discovered one iota of derangement in his behaviour. Lord Lievson (or Levison) Gower who had been Ambassador in Russia was very fortunate in coming into the House of Commons a few minutes before Bellingham took his stand in the Lobby, or he would have been the victim, or if Mr Rider [sic] had appeared to him first, he would have been shot; which I think of itself is a proof of insanity.[12]

Nevertheless, Bellingham's plea of insanity was rejected on the grounds that he was fully aware of the nature of his act, and he was hanged outside Newgate within a week of his crime.

In Yorkshire, meanwhile, the mill owner Benjamin Gott had received an anonymous letter. Gott was not only the biggest woollen manufacturer in Leeds, but he carried out his own finishing on the premises, rather than putting it out, as most did, to specialist workshops. Gott's mill had suffered from industrial relations problems since 1802, and he was heartily disliked by the croppers. The letter was ostensibly a warning from a well-wisher:

> No doubt you are Informd as to the proceedins of the Ludites But feariful you Should Not to the Extent is the Caws of My trublin you thus = a friend of Mine ad it from a Man that was Theair and on Sunday Night at Rounda wood to the Number of 400 thay theair Decreed the Death of 2 and with Great Diffecalty He Extorted from the Man that you was one = Be Carful of your Self for a few Weeks = alter your usal walks to your Busness . . .[13]

Although Bellingham's motive had come as an anti-climax to the more extreme Luddites, plenty of rumour of insurrection was reaching the government around this time – rebellion was imminent; a mass escape of prisoners from York Castle was about to take place. A prisoner at Chester talked of insurrection, and one at York said that an armed body in Huddersfield might rise and overthrow the government. Another, entirely ignorant of the republican principles he purported to espouse, declared that when the revolutionary blow was struck in the capital, Sir Francis Burdett should become king of England!

Thousands of people in Stockport were ready to 'rise against the government when needed', according to information received by Colonel Fletcher. A spy in his employ, named Bent and referred to in correspondence as 'B', reported that a general rising of the people would take place at some date to be fixed on, and that half a million men were ready to rise in the north and Midlands.[14] Thousands in Sheffield were 'ready to promote riot, insurrection and revolution', according to other reports.[15] The whole object of the Luddite organisers, it was alleged, was to create such disturbances in the provinces that troops would be drawn away from the capital and thus make a successful rising possible there. The alarming spread of disturbances throughout the northern counties seemed to some to confirm rumours that the working classes were indeed bent on revolution.

Thefts of arms and ammunition were certainly a new development after Rawfolds, and created a fresh sense of alarm among some of the enforcers of law and order. On the night after Horsfall's murder, Clement Dyson, owner of the shearing frames which had been smashed at Dungeon, found between twenty and thirty men at his door demanding arms, and his terrified wife passed out to them a gun and a pistol. A witness from Skirgate, near Halifax, testified during a trial for burglary that one member of a gang who had beaten at his door had shouted, 'General Ludd, my master, has sent me for your arms.' Similar raids occurred in many West Riding villages during May and June, although the arsenal of arms thus accumulated cannot have been sufficient to pose any serious threat to order on anything more than a local scale.

Luddites and revolutionaries, however, were not the only ones collecting arms from the local inhabitants. The military, too, were busy rounding up private weapons so that they were not available to the criminals, and an arsenal of many hundreds of muskets, pistols, blunderbusses and swords was soon under strong guard in Huddersfield. Nevertheless, General Grey told the Home Secretary that the entire British Army would be inadequate to meet the requirements of the West Riding of Yorkshire alone.[16] The owners of the weapons resented confiscation by the soldiers as much as theft by the Luddites. Either way, it left them without the means of protecting themselves.

After the death of Perceval, the Prince Regent invited the 2nd Earl of Liverpool to form an administration, and Lord Liverpool appointed as Home

Henry Addington, Viscount Sidmouth, whom Lord Liverpool appointed Home Secretary. He presided over the savage repression of Luddites in all areas from 1812 onward.

Secretary Henry Addington, Viscount Sidmouth. The change in cabinet personnel marked a turning point in the Tory government's response to the Luddites. The vacillation of the Home Office under Richard Ryder, which *The Times* characterised as 'the sink of all the imbecility attached to every Ministry for the last thirty years',[17] was at an end.

Before the month was out, Special Commissions of Assize sat in Lancaster and Chester to try more than a hundred people arrested and charged for riots and assaults during April at Stockport, Middleton, Westhoughton and other places. At Lancaster, before Baron Thompson and Mr Justice Le Blanc, there were fifty-eight defendants, of whom twenty-eight were convicted. Eight of these were sentenced to death and thirteen to transportation. Among those hanged outside the walls of Lancaster Castle on 12 June was a boy of sixteen, Abraham Charlson, who cried out for his mother to help him, 'thinking she had the power to save him', and a fifty-four year-old woman, Hannah Smith, who was convicted of stealing potatoes.[18] At Chester, before Judges Dallas and Burton, forty-seven prisoners were tried, and twenty-nine convicted. Fifteen of these were sentenced to death, and eight to transportation. In the event, only two of the death sentences at Chester were actually carried out, the victims being Joseph Thompson, thirty-four, and John Temples, twenty-seven, both weavers convicted of stealing. In both places, the various crimes included arson, theft during the riots, and administering illegal oaths. Few of the convicted were machine-breakers. Three of those condemned to death at Chester but subsequently reprieved were convicted of attacks on machinery. One of them, James Crossland, was a shoemaker. Another man, William Walker, who called himself 'General Ludd' and was convicted of inciting a mob to disorder, turned out to be a coal-miner. M.I. Thomis is not quite accurate when he says: 'All those charged with machine-breaking offences belonged to the occupations concerned in the operation of the machinery destroyed.'[19] As well as the shoemaker at Chester, a waterman was later convicted at York of machine-breaking and other crimes, and John Booth, who would have been charged if he had not been killed in the attack of Rawfolds Mill, was a harness-maker's apprentice.

Sir Francis Burdett told the House of Commons soon afterwards that he was shocked by many of the executions at Lancaster:

> Women executed for stealing potatoes, and children, as he might call those of sixteen years old. Executions of this nature appeared to him much more likely to produce disgust than any beneficial example. Indeed, if those cases had been laid before the Prince Regent, he had little doubt but that his humanity would have prompted him to extend his mercy to them, as he had done to many who had been convicted at Chester, where but two persons were executed.[20]

Not surprisingly, perhaps, the executions appear to have had an immediate, if temporary, inhibiting effect on the machine-breakers everywhere. Throughout the summer months, although there were food riots, armed raids and continuing threats of death and revolution, no machinery was wrecked, either in the north or the Midlands.

Lieutenant-General the Honourable Thomas Maitland, who had been in command of the military in Lancashire, superseded General Grey in Yorkshire at the beginning of June, and united all the troops in the north under one supreme command. Grey had not been sufficiently up to the task, in Joseph Radcliffe's opinion, tending towards defeatism and lethargy, and failing on occasion to despatch troops to protect threatened premises. Grey protested that he did not have the men to spare. Even if he had ten times as many under his command, he said, he could not supply 'separate guards for every individual who may be under apprehensions for the safety of his property'. When General Grey asked for leave of absence to get married, the opportunity was taken to replace him.[21]

Maitland, nicknamed 'King Tom', was an altogether more cool-headed character than most of the politicians and local authorities, not to mention other army officers. He was not given to hysterical outbursts like that of the Foreign Secretary, Viscount Castlereagh, who informed parliament, during a debate on the Preservation of the Public Peace Bill, that 'all the army of the empire could not afford protection and safety to the King's faithful subjects against their depredations, as the law at present stood'.[22] Among those who supported his Lordship in defending the government's Draconian new measures was William Wilberforce, whom Cobbett castigated, with some justice, as one who cared more for the condition of slaves in the colonies than for the fate of workers in his own country.

By June 1812 hundreds of troops were stationed in each of the larger Yorkshire towns – Leeds and Bradford, York and Hull, Sheffield and Wakefield, Huddersfield and Halifax. They came from Hampshire and Kent, the south of Devon and the north of Wales. Maitland cooperated with the new Home Secretary, Sidmouth, in organising the planting of spies among the northern workers' committees, and an elaborate dossier on suspected Luddites and sympathisers in the West Riding of Yorkshire was gradually built up at the Home Office. But Maitland understood that low wages and the price of bread and potatoes were matters of greater urgency to working families than any political ambitions. Weavers' wages, he pointed out, had fallen from thirty shillings to ten shillings a week, and for that pittance 'they must work six days in the week and hard'.[23] He believed that the present condition had originated, and now existed, 'without either, any definite Object, or distinct End'.[24]

Members of the public were being enrolled as armed special constables to maintain law and order under the Watch and Ward Act, but this system of law

A weaver's cottage at Almondbury, near Huddersfield, showing the characteristic windows on the upper floor which gave maximum light for hand-loom weaving.

enforcement was very unpopular in some places, particularly Huddersfield. The Vice-Lieutenant of the West Riding, Sir Francis Wood, maintained that the disaffected members of the population outnumbered the peaceable,[25] and there was widespread conviction that the system would not work. The Clerk of the Peace at Wakefield told the Home Office that, as the local powers of defence were connected with the insurgents, the enforcement of the Watch and Ward Act, 'so far from aiding, would be putting arms into the hands of the most powerfully disaffected'.[26]

The army was fighting a losing battle in attempts to prevent Luddite riots. Detachments of troops marching about were noisy and conspicuous, while the gangs of machine-breakers, with blackened faces, adopted guerrilla tactics, moving along country tracks familiar to them but unknown to soldiers from outside the area. No one informed on the saboteurs, and the troops heard about an attack only when it had already caused a local commotion, and usually arrived at the scene too late, when the frames had been smashed and the attackers had vanished into the night.

Attempts by the military to overcome these handicaps included the formation of a unit of shock troops under the command of Captain Francis Raynes of the Stirlingshire Militia. These men, based in the Pennine foothills east of Stockport, moved about under cover of darkness, and were never in the same place on consecutive nights. Captain Raynes's orders from Major-General Acland were to

> act according to circumstances, and quarter himself where he may chuse: he will remain no two nights in the same place; but is to keep in a constant state of movement; dividing his party, or keeping it together, as he may find it expedient: in short, the party is to be fixed no where . . . Captain Raynes will never state where he is going; and should always move in the night . . . Captain Raynes will never let the officers, special constables, or any of his party, know where or when he intends moving.[27]

Raynes also established a network of paid informers in some of the trouble centres in Cheshire and Lancashire, and employed a system of ambushing suspects on the road. He would

> send two men in plain clothes, in advance; the first being desired, on meeting any person or persons, to let them pass, but give a signal to the second, by whom it was conveyed to the soldiers in the rear, who were marching in small bodies of six or eight; they, on receiving the signal, immediately closed up, and the travellers, whoever they were, found themselves in the midst of the soldiers, before they suspected we were near. By this method, and observing the most profound silence, we avoided the noise usually attending the march of troops. We interrogated every one, and not unfrequently, on these patrols, apprehended those of whom I had information.[28]

Among the first acts of the new government was the repeal of Perceval's Orders in Council, a step intended to relieve the strained relations with America and help the export market – a move Spencer Perceval's government had failed to implement despite persistent appeals from industry. But the change of heart, on 23 June, came five days too late. On 18 June the United States had declared war on Britain. Her ports remained firmly closed to British shipping, and a further strain was added to Britain's severely stretched financial and military resources.

One of Lord Liverpool's earliest statements as Prime Minister perpetuated the myth that the cause of all the trouble in the Midlands hosiery and lace industries was 'new machinery'. He told parliament that legislation was required to protect it.[29] Ironically, machine-breaking had almost entirely ceased in the Midland counties at around the time it had begun in Yorkshire. And thefts of arms and

Robert Banks Jenkinson, 2nd Earl of Liverpool, who became Prime Minister after the assassination of Spencer Perceval. After the portrait by Sir Thomas Lawrence.

ammunition appeared to have replaced machine-breaking in the north. A Mr Walker wrote to Earl Fitzwilliam about an arms raid at Clifton, near Brighouse, on 13 July, when 'an armed banditti' searched a village 'a mile in length for arms and took away six or seven, without attempting to touch other property, firing repeatedly into houses and at individuals who attempted the least resistance with a promptitude and apparent discipline that no regular troops could exceed'. A Justice of the Peace took statements from two Clifton residents, Joshua Goldthorpe, a cordwainer, and John Wilkinson, a cardmaker, who both testified to being knocked up in the middle of the night by armed men who threatened to blow their brains out if they did not hand over their arms, and warned them not to look out of their windows at them as they departed.

The misunderstandings about machinery were given further credence by the report of a Secret Committee appointed by the House of Lords to enquire into 'the Disturbed State of certain Counties'. It referred to the rioters as 'at first principally those thrown out of employ by the use of the new machinery', as well as to a 'new machine' which enabled the manufacturers to employ women, 'in work in which men had been before employed'. The driving force behind all the rioting, this Secret Committee solemnly reported, appeared to be – a Secret Committee!

> . . . and . . . this Secret Committee is therefore the great mover of the whole machine; and it is established . . . that delegates are continually dispatched from one place to another, for the purpose of concerting their plans; and that secret signs are arranged by which the persons engaged in these conspiracies are known to each other.[30]

The Lords' report observed that the outrages had spread into Derbyshire and Leicestershire, 'where many frames were broken', and that the 'spirit of riot and disturbance had extended to Ashton-under-Line, Eccles and Middleton . . . Wigan, Warrington . . . and the contagion in the mean time had spread to Carlisle and into Yorkshire'. It spoke of 'men of desperate fortunes, who have taken advantage of the pressure of the moment, to work upon the inferior class', and warned that the views of some of those involved 'have extended to revolutionary measures of the most dangerous description'.[31] Both Houses of Parliament had set up Secret Committees, in fact, and the Commons' committee also came to the conclusion that the Luddites had established an extensive armed organisation. Lord Sidmouth introduced a Bill on 23 July to give increased powers to local authorities in preserving public order.

In Yorkshire on 22 July the parish clerk of Holmfirth, John Hinchcliffe, was shot and badly wounded at Thong, where he was in business as a clothier. Hinchcliffe had told the rector, Revd Keeling, that he had been approached in

REWARDS.

WHEREAS, two Villains did, on the Night of Wednesday the 22nd. Day of July Instant, feloniously SHOOT at and WOUND *John Hinchliffe*, **of** *Upper Thong*, **in the West Riding of the County of York, Clothier, with intent to MURDER him, of which Wound he lies in a dangerous state.**

A Reward of 200 Guineas

will be given to any Person who will give such Information, as may lead to the Apprehenfion and Conviction of either of the said Villains.

AND WHEREAS, John Scholefield Junior, of Nether-Thong, in the said Riding, is strongly suspected of being concerned in the said Murderous attempt, AND HAS ABSCONDED.

A Reward of Twenty Guineas

IS HEREBY OFFERED TO ANY Person, who will apprehend the said John Scholefield, and lodge him in any of his Majesty's Prisons, and give Information thereof, or give such Private Information as may lead to his apprehenfion; *and Invictable Secrecy will be Observed.*

The said John Scholefield is by Trade a Cloth-Dresser, about 21 Years of Age, 5 Feet 10 Inches High, Brown Hair, Dark Complexion, rather stout made; commonly wears a Dark coloured Coat, made rather short, and Lead coloured Jean Pantaloons.

The above Rewards will be paid upon fuch Information, Apprehenfion, and Conviction as above mentioned by

Mr. John Peace, of Huddersfield,

in the said County of York, Treasurer to the Huddersfield Association.

Notice posted in the Huddersfield district offering a reward for the apprehension of the men wanted for shooting John Hinchcliffe.

May by a cropper with whom he was acquainted, John Schofield, who had offered to 'twist him in', since they needed a body of men at Holmfirth, as elsewhere, ready to rise and overturn the government. Mr Keeling had passed this information on to the parish constable, John Blythe, who had then threatened Schofield with arrest. It appeared that Hinchcliffe had been shot as an informer, and Schofield *was* arrested.

Meanwhile, the Bill for making illegal oaths a capital offence was progressing through parliament. It originally proposed the death penalty for both the giving and the taking of oaths, but by the time it became law on 9 July as Act 52 Geo. III c. 104, it had been amended to make death the penalty for *administering* an oath, and transportation for life the penalty for *taking* one. Furthermore, it offered indemnity to those coming forward within the next three months to confess that they had taken illegal oaths and swear allegiance to the Crown.

A spy informed Captain Raynes that a meeting in Stockport had broken up because the Luddites thought there was a traitor among them – one William Cooper, also known as 'Bill Strapper'. They had decided afterwards that he must be 'put out of the world as an informer, according to the tenor of the oath by which they were bound'. When another man was found horribly burnt and disfigured, near Cooper's house, it was thought at first that he had been murdered, but when Captain Raynes was called to the scene, he realised that the dead man, identified as Samuel Crabtree, was the victim of an accident. One of a party which had gone to murder Cooper, he had put a loaded pistol into his pocket, where it had 'accidentally gone off, several bullets having entered his back, and the fire communicating with a quantity of powder he had about him, produced the dreadful appearance the body assumed'.[32]

At Lancaster on 27 August the trial took place of thirty-eight men who had been arrested in a Manchester public house by Joseph Nadin and his officers ten weeks earlier. The charge was that they had taken part in administering an illegal oath to Samuel Fleming, an unemployed weaver. But it was shown that Fleming was actually a spy in Nadin's service, and had been sent specially to get himself 'twisted in'. And as his was the only evidence against them, all the prisoners, who became celebrated as the 'Manchester Luddites', were acquitted. Only seventeen of them were textile workers.[33]

By the end of August, around a thousand people had taken advantage of the offer of immunity from prosecution for oath-taking. But half of them had come in at Stockport, according to the magistrate Mr Prescott, and the rest, somewhat tardily, from Manchester, Bolton and the surrounding areas. General Maitland calculated, from the number of men claiming indemnity, that oath-taking must have been taking place on an enormous scale. But it soon turned out that those who were confessing came almost exclusively from that part of north-west England where Captain Raynes and his zealous commandos had been continually harrying the local population. Major-General Acland was informed by Mr Prescott that five hundred had taken the oath of allegiance within a week.[34] It must have been clear to anyone with an eye to see that a great many gullible and illiterate men and boys had been duped into believing that the whole working-class population of the country was secretly taking the Luddite oath in preparation for a great rising, and that fear of the consequences was now driving them to confess, whether they had really taken an oath or not. Very few Yorkshiremen came forward, and none from the Midlands.

Further alarming news reached the government from Chelmsford, Essex, when Sergeant Lawson, a deserter from the 1st Royal Surrey Militia, confessed to Brigade-Major Chamberlain that he was involved in a plot to set up a republic and assassinate Lord Castlereagh. Lawson said that he had taken the Luddite oath in Lancashire, and had seen a letter from Talleyrand, the leader of French opposition to Napoleon, addressed to Lord Lovat, whose secretary Lawson had been, he said, and whom he named as one of the leaders of the imminent rising in Britain. The letter had begun, he said, with the words 'My Beloved Couzin'. Lord Lovat, Lawson explained, was raising a Catholic force in Dublin to join the Luddites. His army was being paid for with huge quantities of forged banknotes. Lawson was questioned by Maitland's second-in-command, Acland, who swallowed this story hook, line and sinker, and sent Lawson directly to the Home Office, where not only the Home Secretary and his Permanent Under-Secretary were taken in, but several other government officials. On 21 September Lord Sidmouth issued a warrant for the arrest of Lord Lovat and twenty-one others named by Lawson, on charges of high treason. But 'Lord Lovat' and his accomplices existed only in Lawson's fertile imagination. The Home Office papers relating to this con-man's 'confession and allegations' refer to him as 'a fabricator of false intelligence'. Lawson made off to Ireland before he could be again apprehended.[35]

Urged on by those local magistrates and dignitaries who were alarmed by such false reports and insufficiently cool-headed to weigh the evidence calmly and judiciously, the government was undoubtedly over-reacting to the situation. The organisation of local government did not breed great confidence in those whose duty it was to maintain the public peace, but the government, whatever its own view of the situation might have been, could not ignore urgent appeals from its own appointees to high civil office, not to mention its high-ranking military officers, many of whom genuinely feared the breakdown of law and order and issued constant warnings of insurrection and armed uprising. The government had to give these officials support in carrying out their duties and maintaining their authority. And, as E.P. Thompson has admitted, it is impossible to know how far the authorities were 'themselves deluded by conspiracies which their own informers engendered'.[36] It became part of the government's interest to propagate the myth of imminent revolution in order to justify its repressive measures.

Spies and informers would have given their masters the information they wanted to hear, no doubt enhancing a rumour here and exaggerating a suspicion there, until magistrates and others absorbed such alarming apprehensions of massive and well-organised armed uprisings that they were easily able to persuade the parliamentary secret committees that there was a real threat to national security in these troubled areas. The reports of secret oath-taking very much reinforced the sense of alarm already created by threatening letters and arms raids. Secret societies had long existed among radical working men in the north, and had been encouraged by the passing of the Combination Acts and other repressive measures, which forced men to do in secret what they would otherwise have done openly. The members talked vaguely of revolution, no doubt, but had no means of bringing it about without the active support of influential national figures, which they did not have. Illegal union meetings, not necessarily rebellious in nature, took place by night in fields and on moors, or in the private rooms of taverns like the Bay Mare in Leeds; the Shears Inn at Liversedge; the St Crispin at Halifax; the Good Samaritan at Salford; the Sir Isaac Newton's Head at Nottingham. E.P. Thompson illustrates a rough printed ticket, said to admit the holder to secret Luddite meetings in Lancashire, bearing the words: 'Enter. No general but Ludd means the poor any good.'

The Shears Inn, near Heckmondwyke. It was once a meeting place for local croppers, and the present inn sign shows machine-breakers at their work of destruction.

The sharing of ritual and mystic secrets induces a comforting sense of fraternity and has a natural attraction for the more insecure sections of society. Weavers in Manchester, Stockport, Bolton, Bury and other cotton towns in the north-west, and workers in Sheffield, Leeds and other Yorkshire towns, readily joined societies formed in defiance of the Combination Acts, and oaths of loyalty and obedience were universal among them. The spy Bent reported one version to his masters in which each member was required to swear that, rather than betray the society's secrets, he would have his head and hands cut off.[37] This is usually dismissed as a wholly fictitious invention by Bent, or 'B', himself. It owed something, possibly, to the more bizarre rituals of the Freemasons. A more common version of the Luddite oath, given below, was dictated from memory by Thomas Broughton, a Barnsley weaver who, having been a Luddite, turned informer. Variations on this version exist, usually more verbose than this one, but it is, as Broughton himself testified, in 'substance and matter of fact', the oath that northern Luddites were required to swear.

> I —, of my own free will and accord, do hereby promise and swear that I will never reveal any of the names of any one of this secret Committee, under the penalty of being sent out of this world by the first Brother that may meet me. I furthermore do swear, that I will pursue with unceasing vengeance any Traitor or Traitors, should there any arise, should he fly to the verge of Statude.★ I furthermore do swear that I will be sober and faithful in all my dealings with all my Brothers, and if ever I declare them, my name to be blotted out from the list of Society and never to be remembered, but with contempt and abhorrence. So help me God to keep this my Oath inviolate.
> Signed ....

One Thomas Wood made a deposition to Mr Prescott that he had been accosted at Mottram by two men, one of whom he knew as John Hamer of Stockport, and persuaded to go with them to Manchester. They told him that

> there was to be a revolution, and that all who were not for it, would be killed; and those who were for it, were to take an oath, which he produced and read over to examinant, who repeated it after him, and kissed a book given to him by Hamer, who also gave him a copy of the oath, and told him to *twist in* as many as he could.[38]

There is no real evidence, however, of any close association between these ostensibly republican groups and the machine-breaking Luddites. Oath-taking

★ The word *Statude* appears to have been a corruption of the original phrase, which was *Nature* in one version and *Existence* in another.

did not take place to any significant extent among the Midland framework-knitters, while in Yorkshire, the Mayor of Leeds, William Cookson, had told Lord Fitzwilliam in 1802: 'Very few of the cloth workers are supposed to attend these meetings. They are composed of the labouring poor of all descriptions.' Whereas members of these nocturnal radical clubs excited themselves with talk of overthrowing the government, the croppers' organisation was 'directed steadily to their own immediate concern'.[39]

The sinister aspects of oath-taking were somewhat over-rated by the author of one well-circulated warning against the practice:

> The tendency of this oath is to banish truth, honour, and humanity from the breasts of men, and to introduce in their room, falsehood, malice, revenge and cruelty; and ultimately, if not checked by the strong arm of the law, to convert this highly civilized and truly Christian country into a vile horde of savages and barbarians.[40]

CHAPTER SIX

Gravenor Henson and the Framework-knitters' Union

Alternatives to terrorism were all the while being tried by those representing the framework-knitters. Notwithstanding the Combination Acts, trade unions throve in Nottinghamshire, albeit illegally, throughout the Luddite period. The prominent figure in negotiations on behalf of the knitters was Gravenor Henson,★ a Nottingham man who had started his working life as a stockinger, and had risen by his own efforts to become an employer in lace-making and leader of the local trade union, which he had formed as the Union Society of Framework Knitters (subsequently renamed the Society of Mechanics).[1] A forceful and dogmatic character, he was characterised by William Cobbett, much later, as a man whose 'offensive conceit' and 'vulgar ignorance' would injure 'any cause he meddled with'.[2] (In October 1807 John Gravenor Henson had been ordered by the Nottingham magistrates to pay regular sums to the parish of St Mary, for the maintenance of a female child he had fathered on one Elizabeth Bradwell.[3]) He had become a thorn in the flesh of the Midland hosiers, and at this time he was busy attempting to secure an Act of Parliament to regulate the hosiery trade and prevent abuses.

Henson was publicly critical of the Luddites, whose activities were an embarrassment to him in his efforts to alleviate the distress of the knitters. His Bill for 'Preventing Frauds and Abuses in the Framework Knitting Manufacture and in the Payment of Persons Employed Therein', introduced to the House of Commons by Peter Moore, MP for Coventry, aimed at setting minimum standards in the quality of knitted goods, maintaining fair payment for work

---

★ Although modern authors almost invariably spell Henson's first name *Gravener*, it is printed as *Gravenor* in his own book. Henson himself sometimes wrote his own name as Gravener, but on the assumption that his publisher and printer checked the spelling, I have followed their version.

according to a standard price-list, abolishing 'truck' payment, and allowing frame-rents to be regulated by local magistrates. The committee which drew up this programme resisted pressure to petition for a Minimum Wage Bill on the grounds that, although governments had taken steps to regulate wages in the past, 'the writings of Dr Adam Smith have altered the opinion, of the polished part of society, on this subject'. Any attempt to persuade the government to fix wages would now, it was feared, be like trying to 'regulate the winds'.

In the spring and early summer of 1812 Henson and his colleagues had been frantically busy drumming up support for the petition from all corners of the country and getting it through parliament. Thomas Large wrote to the Committee's secretary, Thomas Latham, from Leicester on 8 April:

> This place is a thousand times Worse, than we expected to find it, there is not half a dozen good fellows in the Town those principally are composed of Sherwood Lads, If i had not been assisted by a fellow prentice, and some of his acquaintence we should never have got a meeting, and even then, I was compelled to pay the cryer, out of my pocket, the meeting did not exeed 100 men – there is 2300 frames in town, With much persausion we raised a committee, they promise to do their best, and damned all the rest . . . The Committee give us such a bad account of Hinkly, we think it prudent not to throw away time and expence after it . . .[4]

Mr Large was apt to break into verse in his official correspondence, and did so on this occasion:

> Of all the places e'er my Eyes did see
> Oh! Leicester, Leicester, none e'er equaled thee
> They can't step forward, don't possess the means
> Slaves in every sense, even Beans
> Once their food, and fill'd the Lads with courage
> Are Substituted by bad water porrage
> Here socks, and sandals, cut from top to Bottom
> I'll bring a sample, for by GOD! I've got 'em.[5]

Large was in London with Henson a fortnight later, and was incensed by a shopkeeper in Cheapside who

> has got such tales about Ned Ludd, stuck in his window, and two stocking-frames at work close to the shop door a large drawer full of guineas, half guineas, and seven shilling pieces in the window, all to attract notice, and he sells the damed'ist Rubbish of Framework goods we ever saw in our Lives.[6]

Henson wrote from Nottingham to Latham who was in London, regarding
signatures for the petition and samples of various kinds of work which were
being prepared as evidence in support of the Bill. He ended his letter with a
postscript: 'Roper, Greensmith, and Bowler desire to be remembered to you,
they want to know if London is improved in Smell.'[7]

On 21 May Henson himself wrote from London to Roper, the Committee's
treasurer, who resided at the Sir Isaac Newton's Head in Glasshouse Lane,
Nottingham:

> One Person is sufficient to remain here when the Bill is in Parliament at least
> till the Third Reading – Why the Devil dont you send the Silk Stockings; are
> you asleep! Mr Keck★ leaves Town for Leicestershire to morrow and will not
> be in Town before the Kings Birth Day. Lord how negligent you are, If you
> cannot send all send some Damn the Trade they seem determined on their
> own Destruction: They are the most backward dilatory, *unwilling to do good*
> race of Men on Earth: Send if you can but I confidently hope they are now
> on the Road; send them Blast them either send them or burn them, If they
> do not arrive instantly they will be of no use, If any Man in the Trade refuses
> to do his Duty in the making of Articles for the Recovery of his Trade Knock
> his Teeth down his Throat instantly.[8]

Thomas Large was one of the framework-knitters who had given evidence to
the Select Committee appointed to consider petitions to the House of
Commons; its report was published at the end of May. The Committee
concluded that there were, indeed, 'many fraudulent practices and abuses', and
that they could only be remedied by the interference of the Legislature. Large
had told the Committee about fraudulent goods in the lace trade:

> Describe what you mean by 'fraudulent goods'?
>   The first is single press.
> Shortly and clearly state to the Committee what you mean by 'single
> press'.
>   By single press we mean a kind of lace that is only looped once; by being
> only looped once it is rendered loose in its texture, and when washed,
> what should be a hole is filled up by the looseness of its texture, or nearly
> so.
> Does it preserve its appearance when washed?
>   No.
> What has been the effect of manufacturing this lace?

★ George Keck was MP for Leicestershire.

We consider the effects as throwing numbers of frames out of employment that formerly were employed on good lace; what I mean by good lace is, double press or lace double looped.
Is the consumption of single press lace much diminished?
Very much so.
Were any agreements ever entered into among the journeymen manufacturers at Nottingham, not to manufacture this single press lace?
Yes.
Have you any written agreement of that sort in your possession signed by a great number of persons?
I have, signed by most of the lace manufacturers in Nottingham.
What were the causes that prevented that agreement being duly performed?
We consider the cause was this; some of them found it very profitable to introduce this lace in the market, they sold this kind of lace for the best lace; by that means they had very extraordinary profit on that kind of lace.[9]

One Samuel Baker wrote to Roper from Great Yarmouth to say that many members of the Royal South Lincoln Militia were framework-knitters who would contribute towards defraying the expenses of getting the Bill through Parliament: '. . . at these Distressed times I conceive that we Soldiers can as well afford to Lend a helping hand, as some others that are not in the Army'.[10]

Henson, meanwhile, had gone to Dublin:

I had considerable difficulty during the afternoon in finding the Persons I wanted, owing to the Difference between the Pronouncing the Street I wanted and the Spelling of it, it being wrote Malpas, and pronounced Maypas, I was taken to Marlborough Strt (pron. Maybor) and Mapert Strt, and at last I was forced to be drove to *Frances Street*, I there found a Person that knew me . . . There is a Corporation of Hosiers (Framework-knitters) in Dublin, granted by James the 2nd similar to that in London . . . The Framework-knitters here are not much benefited by this Charter as it is like the English Charter in a dormant state: The Framework-knitters of Dublin have very good regulations among themselves, but they are most shockingly oppressed by bad English Goods; 10 years since there were 700 Hands here now there is not above 200 They very much wish for this Bill.[11]

But a few days later, the secretary of the Dublin knitters wrote to Roper at Nottingham to say that those who had framed the Bill had had no right to include Ireland and that the word Ireland must be expunged from the Bill:

A typical Midland framework-knitter's cottage, with long mullioned windows on the upper floor. This one is at Crich, Derbyshire.

. . . we do not practice any of those evils which you so loudly and justly complain of, No Sir, we have no cut up work or fraudulent work made of any description the evil Originated with your Selves We have no Coults nor Women working with us, each Man must Serve his Regular Seven years before he will be Allowed to get Journey work, therefore Sir, we have nothing to petition for as Mr. Henson so Streanously Sought for . . .[12]

The petition in support of the Bill finally contained the signatures of more than ten thousand Midland framework-knitters. Many manufacturers were also in favour of the proposed measures, and donations to the cause included what was acknowledged as 'my Lord Birons handsome subscription'.[13]

Henson informed the Nottingham committee on Friday 26 June that the Bill had received its first reading late the previous night. Mr Vansittart (Chancellor of the Exchequer) and Lord Castlereagh (Foreign Secretary) were in favour of regulating the trade, and the Bill was to be read a second time on Monday:

Large and me, in company with Mr Keck, went to the Secy of States Office for the Home Department, and had an Interview with Lord Sidmouth, who assured us that it was the Inclination of the Prince Regent to give our Manufacture every encouragement in in [sic] his Power, that he had no Doubt that the Prince Regent, would wear our Stockings, Ornamented and give encouragement to that Fashion . . . Lord Sidmouth said repeatedly Success to your 'Manufacture'. Therefore my Lads there's no opposition in the Lords.[14]

Lord Sidmouth bought six pairs of figured silk hose and a cotton shawl for his daughters, and some stockings were to be presented to the Prince Regent for his own use – 'make them Womens 26 Inches long', Henson wrote, 'they will fit best, I cant explain the reasons why here'.[15]

However, while Henson and his colleagues were occupied in making amendments to the Bill for the third reading, they were informed that the hosiers of Leicester were proposing a counter-petition, objecting to the prohibition of cut-ups and other clauses. Henson remained confident, nevertheless, that the Bill would be supported. Vansittart himself had drawn up the clause prohibiting payment in goods, and Castlereagh, Sidmouth and the Prince Regent were all thought favourable to the measures being proposed. 'We have only Dr A Smiths Disciples to contend with, whose principles are execrated all over the Kingdom.'[16] A few days later, however, Henson had to inform Nottingham that:

Mr Hume★ opposed our Bill on Dr A Smiths grounds of letting Trade alone, Genl Tarlton moved the House to adjourn, there not being Forty Members present, they ran out of the House when our business came on like wild fire: A Letter has come from Mr Hooley of Nottm Hosier to D.P. Coke protesting against our Bill, G Coldham Town Clerk is employed against us by the Hosiers of Nottm who have addressed a circular Letter to the Members.[17]

The Framework-Knitters' Committee was forced to make many emasculating amendments to the Bill, deleting the clauses which the hosiers objected to most, before it could go forward for the third reading. Then, on 14 July:

Dr Sir

It is with extreme regret, I have to inform you that the Committee of the House of Commons, have come to the decision of Reporting that the Clauses of our Bill which relate to *Hosiery* ought [to] be erased They have reported in Fafour of the Hosiers to their utmost satisfaction notwithstanding every effort we have made The Cause as it respects Hosiery is completely lost, We are *very reluctantly* I assure you preparing a Bill to extend to Lace, and the Prohibition of Payment in Goods: The Committee have in the most unfeel-ing manner but not without a Division decided against us, on the foolishest *lying* evidence that was ever given.

I am Sir Yours

G. Henson [18]

The leaders of the lace-makers in Nottingham asked Henson and Large to remain in London on their behalf and see the Bill through. It passed its third reading in the Commons on 21 July. 'The Ministers were for the Bill only 12 in the House when it Passed all the Patriots went away as usual.'[19] The Bill went to the Lords three days later, where even what remained of it was thrown out. Its chief opponent was Lord Sidmouth.

The Nottingham MP Daniel Coke wrote to Henson a few days later that he rejoiced to hear that a public meeting of knitters had been very peaceable, all things considered. He hoped that the same disposition would continue, because all future relief to be expected from parliament would, in his opinion, depend upon that circumstance.[20] But the machine-breakers soon took up the initiative again. Their response was not immediate. Events abroad were having a beneficial effect on British trade. October 1812 was the month of Napoleon's enforced retreat from Moscow. His army, severely depleted at Borodino in September,

★ Joseph Hume, the radical Scottish MP.

now suffered defeat by the Russian winter, and limped home, losing huge numbers from hunger and exposure on the way. The emperor's Continental System broke down, and British textile manufacturers were again able to supply a growing export market.

In November and December, however, a new spate of frame-breaking began in Nottinghamshire, where things had been relatively quiet for six months or more while the north of England had taken over the lead in violence against machinery. There were only isolated incidents at first, but on New Year's Day 1813 – a Friday – ten frames were destroyed at Melbourne in Derbyshire, and two days later, three silk frames in Nottingham. A week after this, another frame was smashed up in Nottingham, and then a few at Wymeswold in Leicestershire.

We ought to be aware that, whatever the hardships suffered by the stockingers and lace-makers in the Midlands, where violence against machinery was more persistent and lasted much longer than in the north, it was only a small minority of working men who became actively involved in machine-breaking. We have no means of assessing the extent to which the men of violence had the moral support of workers throughout the industry. It is certainly obvious that no local community was prepared to betray its Luddite members to the authorities, but that is not to say that all framework-knitters approved of violence against property. Clearly, if the operators of 25,000 stocking-frames had risen in unison in 1812 to force the hosiers and the government into redressing their grievances, the outcome would have been different. But Luddism was a campaign instigated

Coat of Arms of the Nottinghamshire stocking-makers' union, which grew out of the efforts of Gravenor Henson and others on behalf of the framework-knitters.

and carried out by a tempestuous minority, not by a mass movement. The majority of fellow-workers *may* have given the campaign their passive approval, but most of them and their families probably either suffered in silence or had sufficient means to get them through the years of crisis in one way or another. Felkin mentioned his own grandfather, William Felkin, who died in his ninety-fourth year in 1838. He had been a bound orphan apprentice; had built his own cottage at the age of thirty-eight; and bought his own frame for £25, which he worked at for thirty-five years before selling it for £10.[21] He was doubtless more typical of the stoical Midland framework-knitters than the rampant young men who, more impulsive than Hamlet, took arms against a sea of troubles.

CHAPTER SEVEN

Trials and Tribulations

Attacks on machinery had not entirely ended in Yorkshire, though they were by now much more isolated. A Luddite attack was reported in Halifax during September, and at Elland, near Huddersfield, a soldier guarding premises had his fingers chopped off with a broadsword when he tried to resist a gang of saboteurs.[1] The undercover operations of Captain Raynes and his men had been transferred, by this time, to the Yorkshire country between Leeds, Huddersfield, Halifax and Wakefield.

Towards the end of 1812, preparations were well advanced for the trial by a Special Commission at York of the three men charged with the murder of William Horsfall, and of sixty-one other prisoners being held in York Castle on charges ranging from burglary and administering illegal oaths to taking part in the raid on Rawfolds Mill. A trial of this sort had been in prospect since mid-May, and by the end of October Lord Fitzwilliam was urging on the government the need for early 'detection, conviction and punishment', which could alone 'avert the evils of further Lud outbreaks during the dark winter nights'. He was much concerned that the dark nights would afford further opportunities for the machine-breakers before the trials in the spring could make an example of Horsfall's murderers and the Rawfolds raiders. 'Hitherto', he wrote on 26 October, 'the whole band of Luddites of our Riding have escaped untouch'd: their system of Oaths & terror apparently renders them intangible: an appearance much to be lamented, that is productive of most serious evils . . .'.[2]

Meanwhile, the *Leeds Mercury* reported a resurgence of Luddism at Huddersfield, but cited instances of robbery with violence in the area, rather than machine-breaking.[3] *The Times* told what had happened:

The spirit of Luddism, which was thought to be extinct, has again appeared and raged with more than usual violence. Last Sunday night, about a quarter past nine o'clock, a number of men armed with pistols and short guns, one of them with the lower part of his face covered with a black handerkerchief, entered the house of Mr. W. Walker, of Newhall, near Huddersfield, cloth manufacturer, and after taking from him a gun, a pistol, and powder horn, demanded his money, and obtained from him about £15 in notes, the whole

of which they offered to return him, except one, if he would give them a
guinea in gold: not being aware of this decoy, he took out a small purse, con-
taining five guineas, which they immediately seized, and took all the gold,
without returning the notes. The chief then proceeded to ransack his papers,
while others of the party presented their pieces at Mr. Walker, and after cau-
tioning the family, on pain of death, not to quit the house for two hours after,
they departed.

The same gang on the same night proceeded to the house of a shopkeeper,
at Far Town, from whom they took a gun, some silver, and notes to the
amount of £20, together with a pair of silver tea tongs, and two silver tea
spoons: not content with this booty, they went into the cellar, and seized a
bottle of rum and some provisions. From thence they went to a farmer's
house, near Fixby; four men entered, two of them armed with blunderbusses,
a third with a gun, and the other with a pistol; their first demand was for
arms, but on being told that the family had neither arms nor money, they
ordered 'Enoch, Captain, Serjeant, and Hatchetmen' to enter; but on
promising to find them some money, they retired at the word of command.
Here they received £5. They next proceeded to the house of Mr. James
Brook, of Bracken Hall, in Far Town, where, after conducting themselves in
an outrageous manner, they took his watch, a pound note, and four shillings
in silver.

From thence they marched to John Wood's, where, after breaking the
doors and windows, and rummaging the house, they called over the numbers
from one to nine, and went away . . .[4]

The ever-vigilant magistrate Radcliffe had asked the Home Office to ensure that
the Special Commission would not be presided over by Judge Bayley, and
General Acland similarly believed there was sufficient evidence for the
conviction of Mellor 'if tried by any Judge but Bailey [sic]'.[5] The judges
eventually appointed were Sir Alexander Thompson, Baron of the Exchequer,
and Sir Simon Le Blanc, who had both presided over the earlier trials at
Lancaster. 'I am very glad to hear', Radcliffe wrote, 'that there is no chance of
the prisoners being tried by Judge Bailey [sic].'[6]

That the government was looking for Byron's 'twelve butchers for a jury and
a Jeffreys for a judge' is chillingly proven by discussions which took place over
the Christmas period between Henry Hobhouse, the Treasury Solicitor, who
was arranging the trial, and various others, regarding the executions and disposal
of the corpses of the three accused of murder. General Acland considered that
the three should be hanged at the murder site itself, near Huddersfield. But it
was essential to avoid the possibility of a sympathetic crowd making martyrs of
the three and organising a mass funeral procession. Gibbeting, though still a legal

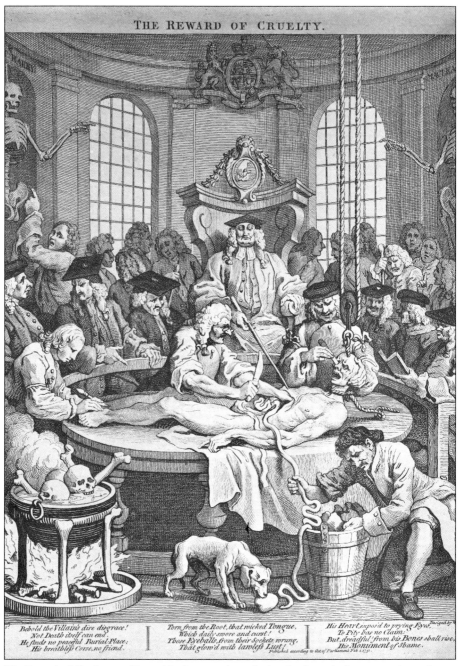

The Reward of Cruelty was Hogarth's dire warning of what lay in wait for executed murderers. Mellor, Thorpe and Smith were among those ordered to be dissected after hanging. This, or hanging in chains on a gibbet, was the mandatory sentence for those convicted of murder.

option, seemed similarly out of the question. The obvious answer was for the judge to opt for the alternative exemplary punishment and order the bodies to be handed over to surgeons for dissection. But there was some doubt as to whether any surgeon in the district would dare to outrage local sensibilities by taking on the job. Acland thought dissection at Leeds was the answer. Although there was no officially recognised medical school there, surgeons had occasionally before been granted the corpses of criminals executed after the York Assizes. 'I conceive the bodies may be consigned to the infirmary at Leeds for dissection,' Acland wrote, 'and will be most acceptable to the medical practitioners there.'[7]

These macabre exchanges of views took place one week before the opening of the trial. Thus the fate of at least three Luddites was already sealed. This was to be a show trial, staged as an awful warning to workers throughout the land; and all the prisoners, though many of them were neither cloth workers nor machine-breakers, were to be treated as Luddites by association.

On Saturday 2 January 1813 the roads into York brought large numbers of working people, by cartload, horseback, or on foot, to attend the trials. The crowds came mostly from the south-west – from the industrial towns and villages of Lancashire and the West Riding – and converged on the Assize Courts at York Castle, where the Special Commission was soon in session. Twenty-three men were sworn in as members of the Grand Jury. Their foreman was the Hon Henry Lascelles, subsequently Earl of Harewood, and one of the members was none other than Joseph Radcliffe, JP.

The first case before the court was that of four men, three of whom were coal-miners, charged with various burglaries in July. J.A. Park, leading counsel for the prosecution, made it transparently clear in his opening address that all the defendants before the Special Commission were to be treated as Luddites by association, whatever their crimes, and regardless of whether or not they had any professional grievances against machinery. 'It is quite impossible', he said,

> that any man, from the most remote corner of the kingdom, can be otherwise than apprized of the dreadful disturbances that have been taking place in one district of this county for a considerable period of time, amounting almost to a state of actual rebellion; and the prisoners at the bar are charged as being a part of the gang implicated in those disturbances.

The four, all in their thirties, were found guilty on clear evidence, and sentenced to death, although the jury recommended mercy in the case of one, John Lumb, who was finally reprieved and transported for life. The court was then adjourned until Wednesday, 6 January.

On that day, the court was even more packed when George Mellor, William Thorpe and Thomas Smith were brought up from the county gaol to answer the main charge of murder and other charges of capital crimes, including machine-breaking and attempting to destroy Rawfolds Mill. So many people had crowded into the courtroom that officers of the court had difficulty getting to their seats. These defendants, all cloth-finishers in their twenties, were the Luddites proper. Smith was an apprentice. The three pleaded Not Guilty. Their defence was in the hands of Henry Brougham, the future Baron Brougham and Vaux and Lord Chancellor of England.

Mr Park outlined the case in his opening address, describing events on the evening of Horsfall's murder, and saying that both Horsfall and Henry Parr, a farmer who was riding some distance behind Horsfall when he was shot, had seen four men at the scene of the crime. Mr Parr testified that he had been on the road about a hundred and fifty yards from the corner of Mr Radcliffe's plantation near Dungeon Wood when he had heard gunfire and seen four men dressed in dark clothes in the plantation, and had then heard Mr Horsfall cry out 'Murder!' as he fell forward on his horse. When Parr galloped up to his aid, Horsfall, with blood gushing from his side, asked him to go straight to his brother Abraham, a local curate, which Parr did, leaving Horsfall in the care of two local boys until he could be conveyed to the Warren House Inn. Mr Parr said he did not know the three men in the dock, and he was not asked to identify the man he alleged had climbed on to a wall before running away, and to whom he had shouted, 'What, art thou not content yet?'

The Assize Court building (now Crown Court) at York Castle. Designed by the Yorkshire architect John Carr, it was relatively new when it became the scene in January 1813 of the Special Commission to try accused Luddites.

Mr Rowland Houghton, the Huddersfield surgeon who had attended Mr Horsfall at the Warren House, said he had found wounds to the victim's thighs, belly and scrotum, and that the cause of death was a shot which had pierced the femoral artery in the right thigh.

There was an excited murmur of anticipation in the courtroom when Benjamin Walker, the chief prosecution witness, was called. He said that he, Mellor and Smith worked at John Wood's finishing shop at Longroyd Bridge, and Thorpe worked at Fisher's shop not far away. There had been much discussion among the men at Wood's after the attack on Cartwright's mill, and it was then that Mellor had made his remark that breaking the shears must be given up, and the masters must be shot. They had 'lost two men, and they must kill the masters'. On the day of the murder, Mellor had asked Walker if he would 'go with him to shoot Mr Horsfall'. Walker was given a loaded pistol by Mellor and told to go to Radcliffe's plantation. Smith and Thorpe were present, and Walker and Smith, who also had a pistol, went to the plantation together. Walker claimed that he had not wanted to go at first, and on the way had suggested to Smith that they turn back. Smith had replied, 'Nay, let us go to the place and try to persuade them not to do it, for if we do not go we shall be shot.' When Smith had spoken to the others, however, he had been told they would be shot if they left. Mellor and Thorpe were to fire first, and if they missed the target, Walker and Smith were to fire. Walker reported:

> I do not know what Mellor and Thorpe did, I could not see them for the wood. We heard pistols go off, and Smith and I fled back into the wood, and were joined directly by Mellor and Thorpe. I then saw Mellor's pistol, and Thorpe gave me his, saying he would not carry it any further. Mellor damned Smith and myself, and said we should have shot however it had been. On receiving Thorpe's pistol, I observed the cock was gone down, and the barrel was warm. I never saw Mr Horsfall.

The four men escaped into Dungeon Wood, Walker added, hid their weapons, and dispersed. At Wood's shop next day, Mellor had made them all, including other workers who knew about the deed, swear on the Bible to keep silent, on pain of death. Joseph Snowden, another employee of John Wood's, confirmed the taking of the oath, by himself and several others who had been told what had happened. Mellor had 'brought the men into the shop, by twos and threes to receive the oath'. (It was Snowden who had read in the newspapers about the £2,000 reward and told Walker about it, Walker himself being illiterate.)

Joseph Mellor, George's cousin, was called to testify that Mellor and Thorpe had been to his house at Dungeon Wood Bottom that evening. Joseph Mellor himself had not returned home from the market when they arrived, but his wife, Martha, stated that the time of their arrival was 6.15 p.m. They left again at 6.30. Horsfall had been shot just after six o'clock. Joseph Mellor had arrived home at seven, and his young apprentice, Thomas Durrance, had told his master that the two men had left pistols in the house. Joseph Mellor and the boy had then hidden the pistols under some straw in the barn. Neither Martha Mellor nor Durrance could identify Thorpe as the man with Mellor, and Martha was the only witness who identified Mellor himself with any degree of confidence. The father of the two boys who had been left with the wounded victim testified that he had seen four men in dark clothing running towards Dungeon Wood a few minutes before his boys came to tell him that Mr Horsfall had been shot.

The case for the defence rested entirely on the three prisoners' alibis. A motley procession of witnesses, including a watchmaker, a blacksmith and a cobbler, said that they had seen George Mellor in Huddersfield at various times ranging from about 5.30 to 6.45 p.m. Smith was allegedly seen eating a meal at six o'clock and was in Wood's shop around seven. A woman named Frances Midwood said that she had seen Thorpe in Fisher's workshop at 5.10 p.m. She had gone back and forth there for water until she heard the news of Horsfall's murder, and swore that during the whole of that time Thorpe was there. This was confirmed by a shoemaker, Abraham Pilling, who had seen Midwood and Thorpe shortly after six, and had himself spoken to Thorpe.

After the summing-up by Mr Justice Le Blanc, the jury retired to consider its verdict, and took only twenty-five minutes to find all three defendants guilty. They recommended mercy for Smith, but this was refused. The judge asked the three men if they had anything to say before he passed sentence on them. They all briefly protested their innocence before the judge made the customary remarks about the wickedness of the prisoners and exhorted them to use the time remaining to them to make their peace with the Almighty. He then sentenced them to be hanged by the neck until dead, and their bodies to be 'delivered to the surgeons to be dissected and anatomized, according to the directions of the statute'.

The suggestion has been made that the killing of Horsfall was 'a political assassination, not a common murder'.[8] But this is absurd, and there can be no possible mitigation of the crime on any grounds. It was inspired by hatred, not by political judgement or expediency, or for the common good. The murderers had not sat down calmly and considered the consequences of their actions. If they had, they would have realised, perhaps, that the murder of an individual in a position of authority invariably leads to savage reprisals by the system the victim represented, and achieves nothing. The murder was a revenge killing, and the killers had the classic example of Jean Paul Marat, less than twenty years earlier, to look to for their lesson. The fact that in Marat's case it was the victim who was the radical makes no difference. George Mellor deluded himself in the same way as Madame d'Armans had done, sacrificing his own life, and arguably those of others who were innocent of any serious crime, for no useful purpose whatever. If the Luddites *had* carried out any killing that could legitimately be considered as assassination, it would lend some much-needed force to the argument that they had political motives.

No time was to be wasted in carrying out the Law's decree. While Batley, Fisher and Swallow, the three men given death sentences a week earlier, lingered in the condemned cells, the three convicted of Horsfall's murder were brought out in chains to be hanged outside the castle walls on Friday morning, two days after their trial. Troops lined the approaches to the castle and guarded the vicinity of the scaffold, lest any attempt should be made to rescue the prisoners. The three prayed as they were prepared for the drop by the hangman, but none confessed himself guilty of the murder, and at 9 a.m. the three young men were, as the saying was, 'launched into eternity' in front of a large crowd of silent onlookers. They died after a few seconds' convulsions. The corpses, after hanging for the customary hour, were taken down and delivered to the York County Hospital, which was guarded by the military for some days afterwards to prevent any attempt to recover the bodies.[9]

There was one curious sequel to the story of Horsfall's murder. In the 1860s an old man named John Nowell, of Farnley Tyas, near Huddersfield, who had been a close friend of the Taylor family in 1812, claimed that Enoch Taylor, and not William Horsfall, had been the intended victim on the night of 28 April. Taylor and Horsfall, he said, used to ride home together from Huddersfield market, but Nowell himself, among others, had been responsible for delaying Taylor in the town on that particular date, so Horsfall had left alone. It was Enoch Taylor 'whose life they most wished for', according to Charles Hobkirk, a local historian, who interviewed Nowell on the subject in 1867. It is difficult to know how much credence to give to this story. Possibly it was due to faulty memory in an old man who, more than half a century earlier, had overheard discussions about killing Taylor which had then been over-ruled. But it does add a further dimension to legitimate doubts about the evidence of Walker, the thoroughness of investigations into the murder, and the conduct of the trial.[10]

On the day following the executions of Mellor, Thorpe and Smith, the trial of those charged with the attack on Cartwright's mill commenced. There were fourteen in prison accused of this crime; all croppers, ranging in age from nineteen to thirty-two. Two others, William Hall and Joseph Drake, turned King's Evidence, and along with Walker, testified for the prosecution. When Walker described how the raiding party had been formed into lines and numbered off, he said that he himself had answered to the number thirteen, in the company armed with guns, led by Mellor. Six of these accused were discharged without prosecution, including the youngest, nineteen-year-old

Charles Cockcroft. Three others were acquitted. Five men were convicted and sentenced to death. They were Thomas Brook, Jonathan Dean, James Haigh, John Ogden and John Walker. As well as Haigh's shoulder injury, it was shown that Dean had also been wounded in the attack, having been shot in the hand. Counsel for the prosecution suggested that news of the machine-breaking riots in Nottinghamshire, which the defendants had read about in local newspapers, had incited them to act in imitation of the Midland Luddites.

Six other men were convicted of machine-breaking and/or burglary, and given death sentences. These were James Crowther, William Hartley, James and Job Hey, John Hill and Nathan Hoyle. None of them was a cropper, but they had all worked in the woollen trade except Job Hey, who was a waterman. Nathan Hoyle, a weaver convicted of burglary, was forty-six, and the oldest of all the men sentenced to death. These six, and the five condemned for the Rawfolds attack, together with the three awaiting execution, made fourteen to be hanged. Their executions were fixed for Saturday 16 January. Mr Park is said to have asked the judge, Lord Thomson, if the fourteen were to hang together on one beam. 'Well, no, sir,' his Lordship is alleged to have replied, 'I consider they would hang more comfortably on two.'

There were still more men to be tried on various charges. They included Samuel Haigh, the man originally named by Barrowclough as having murdered Horsfall. He was indicted for stealing arms, but discharged on bail. John Schofield, the 21-year-old cropper charged with maliciously shooting John Hinchcliffe at Upper Thong, was acquitted. It appeared that Hinchcliffe had been 'encouraged', during questioning by Lloyd, to 'remember' that Schofield was one of those who had fired at him.[11]

The two oldest men held in the cells at York Castle were Samuel Harling, a 69-year-old hawker, charged with threatening the life of Joseph Radcliffe, and John Baines, a 66-year-old hatter of Halifax, charged with administering an unlawful oath. Harling was discharged without prosecution, notwithstanding that he had called Radcliffe a 'damned rascall' who would not live long, for he (Harling) would 'give him a pill' (i.e. a bullet). But Baines was sentenced to seven years' transportation beyond the seas. He was clearly considered the really dangerous man, though he was not a Luddite. Lord Thomson took care to point out that if the oath Baines and others had administered to one Macdonald (who was a government *agent provocateur*) had been taken a few days later than it was, they would have been given a mandatory death sentence. 'No person', he remarked to the court, 'who seriously reflects on the infinite mischief which may result to society, from men combining in unlawful associations, under the sanction of an oath, can consider these punishments in the least degree too severe.'[12] But the prosecution witnesses, Macdonald and Gosling, were constables in the employ of Mr Nadin, who had sent them to Halifax specifically to get the oath administered to them. Macdonald had said his name was Smith, and after he had taken the oath, told Gosling, 'I ha' gotten twisted in.' Rede, the York Castle historian, indignantly asked:

> Now when such men as these, who live by perfidy and duplicity, who make hypocrisy their trade, and practise treason upon traitors, when such fellows give evidence as to the acts of others, should it not be received with caution? and when they detail their *own* actions, do they deserve implicit credit?[13]

As it was, Baines's son John, William Blakeborough, George Duckworth, Charles Milnes and John Eadon were likewise sentenced to transportation for seven years for administering oaths. Baines's youngest son, Zachariah, was also tried for the same offence, but acquitted on account of his tender age – he was fifteen.

On 16 January the fourteen condemned men were executed behind York Castle – the largest number ever hanged there in one day. There was a large crowd of solemn spectators, as before. The hangman, John Curry (aka William Wilkinson), who had himself been sentenced to death twice for stealing sheep, and only escaped the second time by agreeing to become Yorkshire's executioner, hanged seven of them together at eleven o'clock, and the other seven at half-past one. The victims prayed and some sang a hymn as they were prepared for the drop, but not one confessed to the crimes for which he had been sentenced. Some accused Walker and the other informers of being the most guilty among them. They died 'praying most loudly', Colonel Norton reported, 'but I do not think at all repenting the Crime . . . I do not think any of them had a proper sense of the Crime they died for, I mean any of the eight I call Luddites.'[14]

Some of the bodies were claimed by relatives who took them away for burial, and they were accompanied by many sympathisers along the road from York. At Greetland, however, Revd Thomas Jackson refused permission for interment in the burial ground of the Wesleyan chapel, on the grounds that the men were not Methodists. This decision was upheld by the local magistrate. Near riots were caused by a similar Methodist refusal of burial at Holmfirth. Captain Raynes had been ordered to keep a close eye on the funerals. 'The object of this', Acland told him, 'is not to prohibit their fair and decent burial; but to ascertain, as far as may be, the temper of the country upon the subject.' Raynes's impression was that a 'sullen silence prevailed, occasionally interrupted by acknowledgments of having done wrong: not, it appeared, from a sense of the enormity of their crimes; but because they had failed in accomplishing their object.'[15]

England's criminal code, the most barbarous in Europe at that time, had maintained its awful reputation. Rarely, if ever, had a modern government of this country orchestrated, so skilfully and cynically, a more brutal act against its own citizens – seventeen hanged and seven banished from their homeland, chiefly on the evidence of paid spies and turncoats out to save their own skins at the cost of others' lives. Moreover, the law making machine-breaking punishable by death had been misappropriated in order to hang these men. The Act referred only to machinery used in framework-knitting. Manipulation of existing legislation was a common occurrence during the period of the so-called Bloody Code, and explains why no one can be certain exactly how many capital crimes there were. The original Black Act of 1723, for instance, referred to men going about armed and in disguise, but this was soon interpreted by the courts to mean armed *or* in disguise. It is universally agreed that there were over two hundred capital crimes. Some say the number was probably nearer three hundred.

The conduct of the trial for Horsfall's murder does not bear close scrutiny. None of the three executed for the crime was identified by the only eye-witness, Parr, and only Mellor was identified with certainty by anyone who saw them afterwards. There were clear contradictions between the story told by the unreliable Walker and other accounts. There is no real evidence to suggest that the three convicted men were innocent (although one wonders why the witnesses who came forward with alibis for them were not afterwards prosecuted for perjury), but even by the standards of the time, Smith, *at least*, ought to have been reprieved, and the modern Court of Appeal would have to overturn all the convictions as 'unsafe'.

Mr Park's conduct of the prosecution was much criticised. L.T. Rede, the contemporary historian, wrote that

> Mr Park, who has been as remarkable for his unexpected success as for his intemperate zeal and ill-timed severity, has set an example in these cases that have been too readily followed on different occasions since; an example that might have met universal approbation in the days of Judge Jeffreys, but that ill accords with the feelings and opinions of the present day.[16]

Several mysteries about the murder will probably never be answered satisfactorily, but we might reflect briefly on the possibility that more than four men were involved. Ben Walker had told his parents about the shooting, and Lloyd spirited Mrs Walker away as a vital witness whom he was anxious to protect from being 'tampered with'. According to Lloyd, in a letter to Beckett at the Home Office, Mrs Walker accused Joshua Haigh of being one of the murderers. Haigh was a 27-year-old cropper, who was arrested for taking part in the raid on Rawfolds Mill but was discharged without prosecution. Now, Walker originally told Radcliffe that Mellor had fired twice, Thorpe once, and either Smith or himself once; but then changed his story, saying that only Mellor and Thorpe had fired. The *Leeds Mercury* reported that 'all four fired'. Horsfall was hit four times. Were these cloth dressers – whoever it was that fired – such expert shots that no one missed the target? Moreover, both Walker and the *Mercury* report said that the men were armed with pistols, but the fatal wound was caused, according to the surgeon, by a musket ball.[17]

Four men were seen by Horsfall himself and by other witnesses, but Walker thought that he and Smith could not be seen from the road because they were hidden in the plantation, some distance from Mellor and Thorpe. Were more than four men present, and if so, was Joshua Haigh one of them? Alternatively, if there *were* only four men there, was Haigh one of them, and either Smith or Thorpe, unidentified by prosecution witnesses, entirely innocent? Is it possible that the informer Barrowclough, who accused Samuel Haigh of being Horsfall's killer, confused Samuel with Joshua?

Mellor had said in prison, in reference to Ben Walker, that he would 'rather be in the situation he was then placed, dreadful as it was, than have to answer for the crime of the accuser, and that he would not change situations with him for his liberty and £2,000'. Of the sixty-four men brought before the Special Commission, fewer than half were cloth-dressers. Of the twenty-four convicted of various crimes, eight were croppers, and all of them were executed. Of the sixteen men in other trades, nine were executed. There were said to be fifty-seven fatherless children as a result of the executions, not to mention young widows. A Quaker evangelist, Thomas Shillito, visited some of them afterwards, and tried to comfort them. He called on the informer, Ben Walker, too, and found him 'raw and ignorant' and overcome with self-condemnation. Others referred to Walker's pale and ghastly countenance.[18] He never got his £2,000, though he tried hard enough. The reason was perhaps that he had not been the first to come forward with useful information. He was reviled and ostracised, and reduced to beggary on the streets of Huddersfield.[19]

Harriet Westbrook, Shelley's wife, wrote to Thomas Hookham at the end of the month: 'I see by the Papers that those poor men who were executed at York have left a great many children. Do you think a subscription would be attended to for their relief?' She offered to start it off with two guineas each from Shelley, herself and her sister.[20]

Public opinion in the Luddite areas was now even more hostile to the authorities than it had been before. The Treasury Solicitor sent instructions to Radcliffe, on 22 January, that the Home Secretary did not wish him to continue tracking down Luddites with the zeal he had shown formerly. The trial and executions had satisfied the Law, and further vindictive acts would only provoke more hostility and resentment.[21] The executions had also, it appeared, had the desired deterrent effect. There was no more machine-breaking in Yorkshire. General Maitland was soon able to report with confidence that 'the spirit of Luddism is completely extinguished'.[22]

Two days after the mass executions, the Prince Regent issued another Proclamation, offering a free pardon to anyone who would confess his crimes before a Justice of the Peace and take the Oath of Allegiance. This time, many Yorkshiremen did so. The wording of the Proclamation (given in Appendix III) makes it clear that this was a government ruse to obtain information which the local authorities were all the while confessing themselves unable to obtain by other means, regarding the whereabouts of hidden arms, etc. Granting immunity from prosecution to an indeterminate number of men was a small price to pay for genuine intelligence about Luddite activities. But neither the quantity nor the quality of information so gained was, it appears, of any great value.

Some recent historians have tended to exaggerate – by sins of omission rather than by intent – the scale of Luddite machine-breaking in the northern counties. By dwelling on events in the north, at the expense of the less exciting or controversial affairs in the Midlands, they tend to give a misleading impression of the different time-scale involved. It is rarely made sufficiently clear that machine-breaking in the north was a very short-lived affair compared with the lengthy, if intermittent, campaign of the framework-knitters. Midland machine-breaking began in March 1811 and continued, on and off, until the end of 1816, a period of five and a half years. Sustained attacks on machinery in the north of England, on the other hand, commenced early in 1812 and were virtually over by May of the same year, although there were one or two isolated outbreaks later. A few months of Luddism in Yorkshire failed to survive the Act making oath-taking a capital offence and the executions of seventeen men for murder and other crimes. This certainly seems to prove beyond reasonable doubt that any threat of revolution emanating from the Yorkshire croppers was all hot air, lacking real substance. If these Yorkshiremen ever constituted a revolutionary mob, they were singularly half-hearted; one might almost say lily-livered. The situation in Lancashire and Cheshire was very similar, although E.P. Thompson has said that Luddism in Lancashire showed 'the highest political content'.[23]

On 28 January someone fired shots into Joseph Radcliffe's home, Milnsbridge House, in Yorkshire. Radcliffe was unhurt, but the attack perhaps helped him to decide to retire to a more distant and peaceful scene, Rudding Park, near Harrogate. Of all the enemies of the Yorkshire Luddites, many of whom had been threatened and/or shot at during the most active period, Radcliffe was perhaps the luckiest to remain alive when it was all over. He remained almost neurotically vindictive to the end. He received more threats and abuse than

Joseph Radcliffe, the Huddersfield magistrate who relentlessly pursued the Yorkshire Luddites and interrogated suspects at his home in Milnsbridge.

anyone else, and if there had been a Luddite 'hit-list', when the more extreme
Yorkshiremen began to think of murder rather than machine-breaking, Radcliffe
would surely have been at the top of it, along with Horsfall. One of those who
had made threats against him was Thomas Riley, a tailor of Crosland Moor, who
was heard by several people on various occasions to advocate the assassination of
this 'tyrant upon the earth'.[24]

On 15 December 1812 Earl Fitzwilliam had written to Radcliffe to say that, if
acceptable to him, he would recommend a baronetage [sic] as a reward for his
services. Radcliffe replied promptly that he would be honoured to accept. But
Lord Fitzwilliam soon received a discouraging response from the Home
Secretary:

> . . . Of Mr. Radcliffe's Zeal & Merits as a Magistrate no doubt can be justly
> entertain'd; but it appears to me, as I must acknowledge to your Lordship, that
> the effect of conferring such a distinction upon Mr. Radcliffe, under present
> Circumstances, & for the reason assign'd, would be to create a Precedent,
> likely to prove inconvenient & embarrassing, on various Accounts, & particu-
> larly to occasion many similar Applications from other respectable Quarters,
> which it might be extremely objectionable to comply with, and invidious, if
> not unjust, to refuse.[25]

Among others who were opposed to a baronetcy for Radcliffe was General
Maitland, but Radcliffe did finally receive the honour in September 1813. An
anonymous correspondent addressed a letter to 'Sir Joseph Ratcliff' [sic] on
12 March 1815, saying that 'Ludding is going to Start here again . . . Ludders
this time Will Die to a man the Determined to have Blood for Blood the Swear
that the Will Shoot thee first old Bellsybub.'[26] But Sir Joseph died of natural
causes, aged seventy-five, in 1819.

Lord Fitzwilliam himself who, along with General Maitland, had remained
one of the more cool-headed of those charged with dealing with the
Luddites, was promptly removed from office when he made protests about the
'Peterloo Massacre' at Manchester in 1819. John Lloyd, the leading spy-master
and interrogator of Luddites in the north, was rewarded financially for his
services by the mill owners. Captain Raynes never received adequate reward
for his part, despite promises from both the government and the military.
After much prevarication, Lord Sidmouth advised him to seek a suitable post
in Scotland, but the Duke of Montrose, colonel of his regiment, told him
there were many applications but few appointments, adding, 'besides, you are
not a Scotchman!' Captain Raynes resigned his commission and in 1817
published an ill-advised and embittered account of his long and abortive
campaign for preferment.[27]

Although Methodist ministers had refused burial to some of those executed, Colonel Norton's impression was that 'they were all Methodists'. Whether they were or not, too much has been made of the Methodist influence on the Luddite Rebellion. It has been seen as an agent of the exploiters as well as a friend of the exploited. By encouraging discipline among the workers, it is said, Methodism favoured the capitalists. In 1811 Methodism had only recently become a separate denomination. Wesley himself had been an ordained member of the Church of England and always considered himself a loyal Anglican. The hold of the established Church on the north of England was weaker than elsewhere, and Wesley's message filled the vacuum left in the rapidly expanding industrial areas. In the West Riding of Yorkshire, especially, many centres of industry had become strongholds of Methodism by the time the Church of England had woken up to the need for new churches in the region.[28]

Wesley's message of salvation for all – not just the 'chosen' or the Tory establishment – had a powerful appeal for poor working-class folk in the north. When the new denomination was fractured by internal divisions, the Methodist New Connexion and the Primitive Methodists became particularly strong in the Midlands and north. The English, however, are famous for double standards. Hypocrisy, as Orwell said, is the English vice. And religion is, to most people, a matter for Sundays only, and has little to do with the working week. The so-called 'Protestant work ethic' arises from other causes; not from the exhortations of preachers. Wesley's condemnations had precious little effect on Cornish wreckers, though Methodism was especially strong in Cornwall. And the philosophy of hard work and discipline was nowhere more fixed than in Leicestershire, where Methodism was *not* so strong!

By the end of 1813 few of the troops who had been drafted in to the north of England still remained there. The local militia were now capable of dealing with such disturbances as still occurred. The credit for turning the Yorkshire shearmen away from violence is given by some, however, not to the military, nor the magistrates, nor even to the terrible example made of the prisoners at York, but to William Cobbett. 'It is beyond all question', Frank Peel asserted, 'that this result was materially hastened by the writings of the famous William Cobbett.'[29]

Cobbett's *Letter to the Luddites* in the *Weekly Register* set out to demonstrate to violent extremists that machinery was not necessarily an evil, and that in the long run it would benefit rather than harm those who were now opposed to it. But the date of this letter was November 1816, and machine-breaking in Yorkshire was a thing of the past long before then. Cobbett had been anticipated by 'Bishop Blaze', who had published a broadside in Manchester as early as May 1812, addressed to 'The Misguided Men who Destroy Machinery', in which he exhorted them to reflect on the long-term benefits brought to *everyone* by new inventions:

The Price of Wages is such in England, that it could not go into any Market with any people in Europe; and only for a few objects in America, if it were not for the superior Machinery which you endeavour to destroy. If you destroy Manchester, Birmingham, Nottingham, Sheffield and other industrious and ingenious towns, you destroy the glory and support of England, and the wonder and envy of the world; and what is still more against your intentions, your wives and children will be left without consolation, without pity, and without bread, and, what is still worse, they will curse you as the cause of their misery.[30]

Cobbett's later message was addressing the hosiery and lace makers of the Midland counties, whose campaign was never against machinery, *per se*, in the first place. Their campaign had resumed within months of the Yorkshiremen's ending.

CHAPTER EIGHT

Midland Dénouement

The long hiatus in machine-breaking, after the ending of violence in the north and the flurry of renewed activity in Nottinghamshire and Leicestershire in January 1813, lasted until April of the following year. The pause was due to several factors which produced some temporary optimism among the working population and throughout industry generally. The defeat of Napoleon in Russia and repeal of the Orders in Council reopened the export market for British goods. Prospects of a record harvest helped food prices, and there was some stabilisation of wages. 'The increase of work and of wages will I should hope,' the Nottingham town clerk wrote to the Home Office on 20 February 1814, 'take from the Workmen all cause of discontent and all occasion for combining to increase their wages.'[1]

Mr Coldham's optimism was misplaced. The Orders in Council were not the only things repealed by parliament in 1814. Part of the Statute of Artificers and Apprentices of 1563 – 5 Elizabeth c. 4 – was also repealed, removing the last important restrictions on the labour market. This legislation was a triumph for capitalist licence. Inevitably, during the first two weeks of April, machine-breaking was resumed. After frames had been smashed at Kimberley and Greasley in Nottinghamshire, a raid at Castle Donington in Leicestershire on 10 April resulted in a dozen frames lying wrecked, and during the following night five more were smashed in Nottingham.

Thomas Morley stated on oath that five or six men had broken into his workshop at Greasley, threatened him with death when he had shouted out 'Murder!' from a window, and had then smashed five frames within about four minutes. The frames were the property of two Nottingham hosiers, Messrs Needham and Nixon, and the raiding gang had said specifically that they were after 'Mr Nixon's frames'. Needham and Nixon had both refused to accede to a demand for an increase in wages of two pence a pair of stockings. The town clerk wrote to inform the Home Secretary that 'the organized System of Combination among the Framework-knitters has begun to act in the former mode of breaking Frames'.[2]

A garrison of dragoons had been removed from Nottingham while a county election took place, but now the immediate return of these cavalrymen, applied for by the local magistrates, was not enough. Mr Coldham was compelled to ask the Home Secretary to send more troops. There was, he wrote, 'every appearance of the system of Frame-breaking recommencing with more than its former activity in this Town'.[3] There was also much alarm at the suggestion that the earlier departure of dragoons had been accompanied by sales of their weapons in the neighbourhood. Officers of the 9th Regiment appear to have accepted that seventy swords had been sold by their men.[4]

On 27 April the mayor of Leicester, William Walker, informed the Home Office that a hosier named Rawson had received a threatening letter, and added that some serious disturbances had occurred at Hinckley, as a result of which the local hosiers had given in to the workers' demands.[5] On the night of Wednesday 4 May an anonymous letter to the police office at Mansfield said that an attack would be made on knitting-frames there on the Friday night. The warning also reached the newspaper office. The militia were put on the alert. In the event, no attack occurred, but a woman in Nottingham next morning was heard to say that 'a great many frames had been broken in Mansfield'.[6] This tends to suggest either that a widely known plot was afoot, and was called off at the last moment because it had been betrayed; or that a new device was being tried – the laying of false information in order to cause the authorities as much inconvenience as possible. As betrayal of Luddite plans was so rare throughout the whole course of the troubles, the latter alternative seems perhaps the more likely. On 8 May four frames *were* smashed at the workshop of William Matthews in Bellar Gate, Nottingham. The cost of repairing them all was put at £80.

A few days later, the Southwell magistrate, Mr Becher, apprised the Home Office of the fact that the 'Union Society, as it is styled, does not conceal its existence', and that 'the principal Leader is stated to be Grosvenor [sic] Henson'. Mr Becher went on:

> Henson does not now work at his trade, but is maintained by the Association at a weekly allowance of about three guineas. In connection with him are many desperate characters, who are strongly suspected of being the Frame-breakers and the Instruments of popular vengeance upon all who, in the language of the Society, are 'denounced'. The names of these ruffians are very carefully concealed; and as their number is small I entertain little expectation of detecting them until they have been emboldened by success and impunity to the perpetration of more frequent or more tumultuous outrages . . .
>
> Mr Nixon . . . feels convinced that the order for demolishing his frames was issued by Henson, and that the evidence which he gave against the Bill for regulating the framework-knitting trade, and his non-compliance with the exorbitant demands of the workmen are the sources of provocation . . .
>
> For my own part I attribute the late as well as the present outrages to those jacobinicall principles with which the inferior orders have been sedulously inoculated by our Nottingham Reformers, who have, in many instances,

become the objects of that secret organisation and malevolent confederacy which they fostered by their pernicious examples, their licentious harangues, and their seditious Press for the attainment of their factious projects . . .[7]

George Coldham was likewise in little doubt that 'the late breakings of Frames were dictated by the executive Committee of the Union'.[8] But Mr Coldham repeatedly regretted in his letters to the Home Secretary that it was 'a most difficult matter to find a Frameworknitter [sic] upon whom we can rely to obtain and give us information. Every Constable as such is known and is more or less a subject of suspicion.'[9] 'It is inconceivable', he repeated later, 'the difficulty there is in getting any Frameworknitters upon whom you can depend to obtain information for you, and no other person can be of the smallest use.'[10]

After the failure of Henson's Bill for preventing abuses, the framework-knitters, under his leadership, had taken legal advice in forming a trade union with a constitution which would evade the terms of the Combination Act. Tickets were printed with a coat of arms and a motto exhorting members to maintain their code of silence: '*Taisez vous*.' The union's branches hired frames, took in work, and let it out to unemployed brethren. It also paid small allowances to those on low wages, under the guise of charity to members who were destitute.[11]

In July two Nottingham knitters, George Gibson and Thomas Judd, were charged in a test case under the Combination Act with 'collecting money for illegal purposes'. Found guilty, they were each sentenced to a month's hard labour. It was the first prosecution under the Combination Act in Nottinghamshire. This, combined with lack of funds, brought about the collapse of the union. Peaceful attempts to solve the knitters' problems having thus broken down, the initiative passed again to the Luddite extremists.

On 26 July several frames were wrecked in raids at Sneinton, just outside Nottingham, and in the town itself. It is perhaps worth noting that these attacks were close to, but not on, the date mentioned by the informer or con-man Barrowclough as the day of the coming revolution, or the 'marriage feast of Mrs Ludd'. But nothing of any significance happened in Yorkshire on 24 July, and if the events in Nottinghamshire had any connection with a revolution, they were more like a whimper than a thunderous uprising.

More sabotage occurred early in September, and in October a raid was made on the house of Thomas Garton, a hosier at Basford. Mr Garton was prepared for an attack, as he had been instrumental in securing the arrest of a local stockinger, James Towle, on suspicion of being involved in a raid on machinery in the previous month. (When Towle was brought to trial at the spring Assizes, he was acquitted.) Several constables were on hand at Basford on this occasion, and there was an exchange of gunfire. Samuel Bamford, one of the assailants, was hit, and as the Luddites retreated, a neighbouring householder, William

Kilby, opened his front door to see what all the commotion was about, and was shot dead by one of the raiders.[12] Mr Kilby was himself a framework-knitter. A subscription was raised by the town of Nottingham and local gentlemen and manufacturers to provide an annuity for his widow, Sarah.

Violence again subsided after this event, and in December the Treaty of Ghent brought an end to the war with the United States, opening once again the most valuable market for British exports of textiles. This gave the authorities fresh hope that machine-breaking was, to all intents and purposes, at an end, and indeed, there was a cessation of violence throughout 1815 and the early months of the following year, except for an isolated attack at Quarmby, near Huddersfield, on 24 February 1816, when the dressing workshop of John Roberts was raided, and four machines and four pairs of shears, valued at £25 17s 6d, were smashed, and windows broken.[13] There had been threats of a revival of machine-breaking in the Huddersfield area in 1815, as we have seen, as well as threats to the lives of manufacturers who used gig-mills and shearing frames. An Irish cropper, Jimmy Rourke, was said around this time to call himself 'General Ludd'.[14] But the Quarmby incident in the following year was the only manifestation of any such intent.

The ending of the Napoleonic wars after Waterloo had left the Midland framework-knitters in a state of limbo, excluded from the general air of prosperity that was returning to the rest of the nation. They were trapped in a static industry, still largely rural, scattered and unprogressive, which left them behind in economic terms, unable to recover the standard of living which, though never high, they had once happily tolerated. Of 1,200 families at Hinckley, for instance – one of the major framework-knitting centres – 600 were out of work in the autumn of 1816, while another 300 were excused from paying poor rates because of their poverty. So the remaining 300 families, bearing the burden of the poor rates, slowly dwindled as they slid helplessly down into the lower states under the economic pressure. The parish then further overstocked the market by trying to help the poor by itself employing them in framework-knitting. The chief concern of a local clergyman was that 'the morals of the lower classes are in danger of being vitiated from want of employment'.[15]

Boys of eight were being used by their hard-pressed parents as winders of yarn for the knitting-frames, and girls of six or even younger for seaming stockings and gloves. Mary Thorpe of Bulwell told a government Commission on the Employment of Children that her younger sister had begun stitching gloves at the age of three and a half: 'She used to stand on a stool so as to be able to see up to the candle on the table.' A child of four could seam five pairs of stockings a day, working from early morning until early evening. Mary said that little children were often kept going until midnight towards the end of the week, in

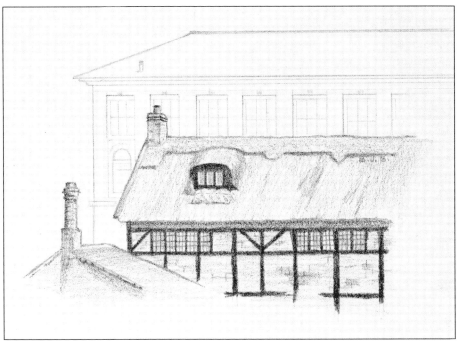

Former framework-knitters' timber-framed and thatched cottages in Bond Street, Hinckley; across the road now stands one of the town's largest modern hosiery factories.

order to get the week's work finished. Mothers would pin them on their knees to keep them working, and if they showed signs of falling asleep, would slap their heads to keep them awake. They received no education except at Sunday School, because that was the only day they could be spared from work.[16]

Revd Robert Hall, the famed Baptist preacher of Leicester, regarded as one of the greatest pulpit orators of his time and a man of very different temper from Cobbett's Tory 'parson-justices', soon added his powerful voice to pleas on behalf of the 'poor stockingers' of Leicestershire:

> The writer well remembers [the county] when it was the abode of health and competence: a temperate and unstrained industry diffused plenty through its towns and villages; the harsh and dissonant sound of the loom was not unpleasant to the ear, mingled with the remembrance of the activity which it indicated, and the comfort it produced . . . But what a contrast is now presented in the languid and emaciated forms, and dejected looks of the industrious mechanic, who with difficulty drags his trembling limbs over scenes where his fathers gazed with rapture . . . A rapid depression of wages, like a gangrene, preys upon their vitals and exhausts their strength.[17]

'It became', another observer wrote, 'a long and widely spread practice to still the cravings of hunger in the adults by opium taken in a solid form.'[18] Henry Heginbotham, the Stockport historian, was told later, by local people who remembered the Luddite years, about the bread they had to live on. One person said: 'The bread generally eaten was nearly black and mixed with barley and rye. The people were frequently a month without tasting wheaten bread.' Another described the typical loaf, which was 'surrounded by the crust, but the middle of it was as soft and sticky as bird-lime, and, in the lower quality of bread, could be drawn from the middle of the loaf with a spoon'.[19]

In mid-May a further outbreak of violence against machinery occurred in the Midlands, when lace-frames were attacked at Loughborough. Then on the night of 8/9 June a dozen stocking-frames were wrecked by a gang at New Radford, and on the 18th, nineteen lace-frames belonging to William Wright and Thomas Mullen were broken up in their workshops. These attacks were a prelude to the approaching climax of the long machine-breaking campaign in the Midland counties – the raid on the factory of Heathcoat and Lacy at Loughborough.

John Heathcoat, a native of Derbyshire, was an inventive frame-smith and mechanic who had made various improvements to stocking-frames and in 1808, at the age of twenty-four, patented a traversing bobbin net lace machine, an ingenious adaptation of the stocking-frame which mechanically imitated hand-made pillow lace. This machine, which became known as the 'Old Loughborough', was 'by far the most expensive and complex apparatus existing in the whole range of textile mechanism'.[20] Heathcoat went into partnership with Charles Lacy and John Boden, and by 1816 they had fifty-five lace-frames at work in their Loughborough premises. But because Heathcoat's rivals were infringing his patent rights, he had cut the wages of his employees in order to reduce his prices.

At midnight on Friday 28 June a gang of sixteen men led by James Towle, with their faces covered or blackened and variously armed with hammers, hatchets and blunderbusses, raided the factory, while a crowd of around a hundred sympathisers watched and kept the street clear outside. A large dog, which leapt at the armed men as they burst through the factory door, was shot. Workmen on the night shift were forced to lie down on the floor by some members of the gang while others set about sabotaging the machinery, to cries of encouragement such as 'Do your duty well', and 'It's a Waterloo job, by God!' One workman, John Asher, was acting as an armed nightwatchman, and he was shot and wounded in the course of the break-in. By the time the attackers had completed their destructive rampage, virtually all fifty-five lace-frames had been ruined, and the work on them burnt. Some of the Luddites had come from Nottingham to participate in the raid, and after the gang's getaway, four men lay low in the long grass of the meadows at Loughborough, waiting for the darkness of the Saturday night to give them cover for their escape back to Nottingham via the banks of the Soar to Barton in Fabis, where they crossed the Trent by the ferry.[21]

John Heathcoat and his partners were faced with the destruction of their machines, worth between £8,000 and £10,000; the hostility of some of their employees, because they were working at lower than standard rates; and one of their loyal workers seriously wounded. They decided to sue the county for damages, and the court of King's Bench eventually made an award of £10,000, with the proviso that the money should be spent locally to help revive the local economy. Mr Heathcoat, who had acquired a water-powered mill at Tiverton in Devon, refused to accept this condition, and he and his partners agreed that they should move their entire business to south-west England.[22]

Heathcoat thought that Luddite knowledge of his acquisition of the premises at Tiverton may have been the reason for the attack, but this seems unlikely. The raiders can hardly have thought to keep him in Leicestershire by destroying his machinery. At any rate, the business moved there, many loyal workers going south with it, and Leicestershire thus lost its valuable connection with the lace trade.

Later in the summer, two arrests were made. James Towle, the knitter from Basford who had been acquitted nearly two years before, through lack of evidence, of taking part in a Luddite attack, was well known to the authorities as a trouble-maker. Now he was arrested and charged again, and this time was convicted at Leicester Assizes and sentenced to death. Samuel Slater, tried at the same time, was acquitted, because his defence counsel called no fewer than fifty-six witnesses who testified to his innocence.[23] Towle, who was widely regarded as a Luddite 'captain' in the Midlands, the equivalent of George Mellor in Yorkshire, refused to name his accomplices while in prison, and went to the gallows in front of Leicester gaol in November 1816, maintaining his silence to the end. He did confess to his own guilt, however, giving some information about how money and arms were collected for each 'job', but denying that the Luddites possessed any arms depot, and that he had ever taken an oath of secrecy.

Towle's corpse was taken back to Basford for burial on 21 November, the day after the execution. (The Nottingham authorities had expected some trouble as it passed through the town, but it was taken through secretly during the night.) A crowd of around three thousand had gathered for the burial, but Dr Wylde, the rector of St Nicholas, Nottingham (another clerical JP), not only refused to conduct the funeral himself, but forbade the parish parson to do it, threatening, according to an informer, to strip off his gown if he did. A local schoolmaster did the job, and someone in the crowd damned Dr Wylde, but another said 'it did not signify to Jem, for he wanted no Parsons about him'.[24]

Watch and Ward.

NOTTINGHAMSHIRE.

NOTICE IS HEREBY GIVEN,

THAT a Special General Sessions of the Justices of the Peace acting in and for the said County of Nottingham, will be holden at the Shire Hall, in *Nottingham*, in and for the said County, on Tuesday the twenty-ninth Day of October Instant, at Ten o'Clock in the Forenoon, to take into consideration, and to determine upon the Expediency of carrying into Effect, the Powers and Provisions of an Act of Parliament passed in the fifty-second Year of the Reign of his present Majesty, intitled " An Act for the more effectual preservation of " the Peace, by enforcing the Duties of Watching " and Warding until the first Day of *March*, one " thousand eight hundred and fourteen, in Places " where Disturbances prevail, or are apprehended," (and which Act has been revived and continued by subsequent Acts) and of enforcing the same within this Parish, Town or Place. Dated this seventeenth Day of October, in the Year of our Lord, one thousand eight hundred and sixteen.

EDWARD SMITH GODFREY,
CLERK OF THE PEACE.

An 1816 notice of local resort to the Watch and Ward Act in Nottinghamshire, following further outbreaks of rioting in the late stages of Luddism.

Meanwhile, in the period between Towle's arrest and his execution, more frame-breaking had occurred in Nottinghamshire. A minor incident in Nottingham on 3 October was followed six days later by a raid on premises at Lambley, when thirty frames were destroyed, and on 2 November four more were wrecked at Bulwell. One story had it that James Towle's younger brother, Rodney, known as 'Bill', had organised a machine-breaking foray in order to show Jem 'that they could do something without him'.[25]

Six months after the raid on Heathcoat's premises – in January 1817 – a Nottinghamshire stockinger, John Blackburn, was arrested for poaching on Lord Middleton's land. He had attacked the gamekeeper who apprehended him. In order to save his own neck, Blackburn confessed to involvement in the raid at Heathcoat's factory. He said he had been offered forty pounds (and his expenses) by William Withers to join the gang being organised to make the attack, and described how he and two other men, Aaron Dakin and John Disney, alias 'Sheepshead Jack', had gone to a granite quarry at Mountsorrel, four miles south-east of Loughborough, where they had obtained one 30 lb and two 12 lb hammers and an iron crowbar, which they had then hidden in a ditch on the outskirts of Loughborough in readiness for the raid on the following night. The three had then slept in a cart on the town's outskirts. Blackburn turned King's Evidence and named his accomplices. Warrants were immediately issued for the arrests of thirteen men. One of them, named Burton, also turned King's Evidence.[26]

The others were brought to trial at Leicester Assizes in April 1817, except for Samuel Caldwell, commonly known as 'Big Sam', who succumbed to a convulsive illness and, being unfit to plead, was not tried until July. The main charge against the chief defendants was attempted murder – shooting the watchman John Asher with intent to kill. Blackburn's evidence described how the gang had gathered in a lane and disguised themselves in various ways 'and all tied their handkerchiefs over their faces. Some changed coats and others turned their own inside out. Slater [had] Big Sams smock frock on – Mitchel his own coat, turned and a Handkerchief over his face.' Blackburn thought that some of the men who had walked to Loughborough had stopped at the Ship Inn at Rempstone:

. . . they had pistols in their inside great coat pockets and heard some of the party after say that a labouring man saw them and fetched either the landlord or his Master to look at them who looked at them over a screen and said something to them wishing to know what their pistols were for they left Rempstone and went on to the Bell at Hoton where Bill Towle was sick is not certain whether this occurred at Rempstone or Hoton Bill Towle had a great coat on – the above named persons went from the lane above mentioned directly to the Factory they met a man going to the factory they threatened if he did not get them quietly admitted he should suffer for it he rang the bell the door was opened and they rushed in – a great dog flew at them and James Towle shot him Bill Towle struck at him first but the Hatchet flew out of his hand – they cried out 'rush forward' deponent staid at the corner of the factory till he heard they were in the room where the Guard was placed while entering the door he heard a Pistol going off and wished to retreat but some one said he would blow his brains out if he did not go forward – which he then did does not know who this was soon after he was placed Sentry at the door of the factory upon their going up to the top shop he was called and placed sentry over the men in the first floor shop whilst there he saw them go into the top shop – Hill armed with pistols went first – Mitchel with Pistols next he was called to go up and went with an Axe and broke some of the frames . . .

Rodney alias Bill Towle was going to pocket some Lace and Hill said 'we are not come to rob but for the good of the Trade if ever I see you up to that again I will blow out your brains' he took it away from him and burnt it on the floor they all broke the frames in turn upon going out of the factory several of them went to shake hands with Asher who was shot whilst deponent was guarding the outer door he told them to be off that he might have a Doctor. . . .[27]

Of those accused and found guilty, six were condemned to death and two sentenced to transportation for life. Caldwell was also sentenced to transportation later. The six given death sentences were William Withers, Thomas Savage, John Amos, Jos. Mitchell, John Crowther and Rodney Towle. Among those attending the trial was Robert Hall. He deeply deplored the sentences, and afterwards 'dwelt with much feeling on the unjust severity of the criminal code, and the glaring inexpediency of intrusting to the judge the power of life and death, and whether the sentence should be carried into full effect, or undergo a commutation'.[28] Revd Hall's passionate opposition to the death penalty made no more impression on the authorities than Byron's, however.

The six condemned were led out to execution in front of the Leicester county gaol at noon on 17 April 1817. A crowd of around fifteen thousand had gathered to witness the hangings, and many joined the condemned men in singing hymns. The victims were described as 'fine-looking young men, in the prime of life, health, and vigour'.[29] The two informants, Blackburn and Burton, were shipped to Canada for their own safety.

There was one further tragedy in that year before the Luddites bowed out and organised machine-breaking virtually disappeared as a means of 'collective bargaining by riot', in E.J. Hobsbawm's graphic phrase.[30] A young man named

Daniel Diggle was convicted at Nottingham Assizes of shooting one George Kerry during a raid at Radford in the previous year, and wounding him with intent to kill. Sentenced to death, Diggle went to the scaffold on 2 April 1817 deeply repenting his association with the Luddites and having disobeyed his parents' commands.[31]

'The Luddites', a Derbyshire JP wrote to John Beckett, 'are now principally engaged in politics and poaching. They are the principal leaders in the Hampden Clubs which are now formed in almost every village in the angle between Leicester, Derby and Newark.'[32] The organisation and, above all, the discipline of the Midland Luddites in themselves argue for interpretation of their campaign as one of precise and limited objectives. The Yorkshiremen were most vociferous and belligerent, regularly taking up arms and threatening lives as well as smashing up machinery in pursuit of at least one of their aims – to prevent the woollen manufacturers from putting them out of work by using machinery. Rede, the historian of York Castle, went so far as to say that the local Luddite mobs

> were made up of men generally unaffected by the evil they complained of – Machinery; men who, being idle and dissolute, uneducated and brutal, had a love of brutality and excess, who found it more pleasant to seize by violence, than to gain by industry; and who, looking on the thing at first as a frolic, got excited by drink and the presence of a number of coadjutors to perpetrate the most dreadful crimes.[33]

This extreme view is not generally supported by the available evidence. The men of Lancashire and Cheshire were the most confused, it seems. Certainly the hand-loom weavers wanted to prevent the increasing use of power-looms, but they were only part of a chaotic tendency to riot and create widespread disturbances for a variety of reasons not connected with machinery at all. The hosiery workers adopted machine-breaking as a method of terrorising unscrupulous hosiers into meeting their specific demands, and, generally speaking, they confined themselves to this object throughout their five-year campaign. Their restraint seems remarkable in the circumstances, in a national climate of general violence and public alarm. Over and over again we read of gangs of Luddites raiding workshops but taking care to smash *only* the frames which were being used to make cut-ups or otherwise undermining the livelihoods of skilled workmen.

Robert Baker, the Bow Street officer, had reported to his superiors as early as February 1812 that the workers in the Nottingham area resented those hosiers who

> paid the underprice, and the unemployed and ill-disposed went about disguised to break the frames belonging to these particular persons, and also all frames that facilitated the work by being made wider than the old ones...

They have seldom made free with other property, altho' opportunities at all times have presented themselves, and in one instance lately at Clifton, some cloths, that one of the framebreakers brought away, were carefully sent back again the following day.[34]

The refusal of the more intelligent Midland Luddite leaders to allow their men to steal goods, and thus provide the authorities with ammunition with which to brand them as nothing but gangs of common criminals, is evident. Men who tried thieving were censured and threatened during the raid on both Heathcoat's factory, and at Clifton in January 1812, according to the claims of those who took part. And George Coldham told the Home Secretary that the framework-knitters had

> exercised great judgement and discretion in the selection of their victims in the town, by fixing upon the property of individuals on some account obnoxious to popular resentment. The last frames destroyed in the town belong to persons who have been in the habit of paying the workman in part or in whole in goods generally inadequate in value to the price of his labour.[35]

The Midlanders were also, on the whole, more efficient than their northern counterparts. As far as we can judge, they usually did what they had set out to do. They were helped, of course, by the fact that they were operating mostly in small towns and villages spread over a wide area of three counties. The Yorkshiremen were hampered by operating in a relatively small area of highly concentrated industrial activity, policed by a large number of troops. The Lancashire Luddites were hampered by the difficulties of gaining access to large cotton mills, and had to attack the buildings themselves rather than the machines inside them. The knitters' self-discipline and restraint did not, of course, mitigate their criminal responsibility in the eyes of the law.

It has been estimated that the total number of stocking- and lace-frames wrecked in the three Midland counties during the Luddite troubles – 1811–16 inclusive – was around one thousand, or 4 per cent of all the frames in existence there. Darvall puts the number somewhat higher, at 1,300–1,400 frames, and if Revd Becher's figure of a thousand frames by February 1812 was correct (George Coldham had given the Home Office a figure of 800 frames early in December 1811), then Darvall's estimate would seem reasonable. Their total value as new was probably in the region of £30,000, with the total loss in both the Midlands and the north of England, due to machine-breaking, around £50,000.[36] The cost of damage to other property during the riots, especially in Lancashire, where the favourite tactic was to set mills on fire, was of course much greater. Colonel Fletcher reported to Henry Hobhouse on 26 July 1818 that a fire at Ormrod & Hardcastle's mill at Bolton had alone caused about £30,000 worth of damage.[37]

CHAPTER NINE

The Aftermath

Thomas Savage, one of the men hanged at Leicester, had attempted to save his skin by volunteering the information that he had knowledge of treasonable correspondence between Sir Francis Burdett, Major Cartwright, and the union leader Gravenor Henson. 'He says', a report to the Home Office said, 'he thinks Gravener Henson equal to the perpetration of anything that Robespierre committed.'[1]

Henson, ironically enough, had gone post-haste to London to appeal for the condemned men's lives, but he was arrested there under suspicion by the magistrates of having ordered the destruction of machinery. On 12 April the Nottingham police office had received a warrant from Lord Sidmouth to search Henson's house for 'treasonable and seditious papers'.[2] The *London Courier* was quoted as saying that 'this man Henson has long been an object of dread to the well-disposed inhabitants of Nottingham and its neighbourhood, both on account of the leading influence he was thought to have with the Luddites, and his supposed political principles.'[3] The Duke of Newcastle was informed by a Nottinghamshire county magistrate that Henson was 'supposed to have been a most active agent of the Luddites, one of the contrivers of mischief without personally engaging in it . . .'.[4]

Henson himself protested in a letter to Lord Sidmouth in June that his life had been threatened by the most extreme Luddites precisely because he was 'counteracting their designs, and for the freedom of language I have used at various times against their practices'.[5] And even the Tory *Nottingham Journal* editor pronounced himself ignorant of any connection between Henson and Luddite activities.[6] Nevertheless, Henson spent seven months in prison, during suspension of the Habeas Corpus Act. After his release, the *Nottingham Review* declared that 'we never before heard it even insinuated that the Luddites had any political objects in view – the direct reverse of this was always understood and believed in this neighbourhood.'[7]

The continuing plight of the stockingers and their families was almost universally acknowledged by this time. They were suffering the penalties of being trapped in a stagnant industry, which was not moving into centrally powered factories for mass-production, as in the northern textile industries. Lace-making was on the way to becoming a factory industry by 1816, but

Interior of a typical nineteenth-century stockinger's cottage, recreated at the museum of the
industry at Ruddington, Nottinghamshire.

hosiery remained a cottage occupation and its workers were still being exploited,
as before, by the masters and middlemen. A Leicester spokesman for the
knitters, William Jackson, wrote to Lord Sidmouth in February enclosing
resolutions of both knitters and hosiers at their recent meetings, and summarised
the situation in his covering letter, in which he said that the framework-knitters

> in consequence of the reduction of their wages are reduced to the lowest state
> of misery and wretchedness, and if the present system of giving low wages is
> persisted in, the whole of the common people must soon become paupers . . .
> The present system will eat up the vitals of the country, and your Lordship
> will find that a nation of paupers will ultimately produce an empty Exchequer
> and a national bankruptcy.[8]

It was widely believed that there was a conspiracy of master hosiers to maintain
wages at the lowest possible level. This would, of course, have been illegal under
the Combination Acts. (As long ago as the reign of James I a law had been
enacted forbidding clothiers to join forces in fixing rates for piece-work.) One
Leicestershire magistrate, Mr Mundy, went so far as to allege that the hosiers had

agreed between themselves that 'a yard of work shall consist of two-and-forty inches instead of six-and-thirty', although, when it was sold to the retailer, a yard was still thirty-six inches. Writing to Lord Sidmouth from Burton-on-the-Wolds, near Loughborough, Mr Mundy reported that the parish officers and himself were of the opinion that 'there exists a combination among the hosiers to keep down the prices of the workmen so low that the parishes are obliged to make up the earnings of the workmen so as to enable them to support their families, and thus carry on their trade in some measure out of the poor rates.'[9]

When the framework-knitters of Leicestershire met in the early months of 1817, and submitted resolutions to their employers, the latter forwarded the knitters' proposals to the Home Secretary, asking for them to be considered by the government, and incidentally praising the 'temperate and patient conduct' of the workers.[10] But the government had no intention of interfering in industrial relations, and an agreement made between the knitters and the more sympathetic hosiers soon broke down under economic pressures.

The Yorkshire croppers were also appealing for help, and 3,625 of them petitioned parliament in 1817. Only 860 of these men were in full employment, the rest being totally unemployed or having only part-time work. Despite their continued argument that gig-mills damaged the ground or texture of fine cloths, mechanisation was increasing rapidly in all branches of the woollen industry.[11]

Some framework-knitters became involved in the so-called 'Pentrich Rising' in June of that year, but this was not a Luddite affair, despite the suspicion that its leader, Jeremiah Brandreth, may have been a Luddite. He was an unemployed stockinger at the time of the rising, but had done various jobs in other areas, and seems to have been more of an itinerant fanatic than a skilled workman driven by economic desperation. No one knew where he came from originally, but as R.J. White put it: 'Everyone seems to have been intent on proving that he could not have come from the solid, sober stock of the English midlands.'[12]

On the night of Monday 9 June 1817 Brandreth, styling himself the 'Nottingham Captain', led a motley rabble of two or three hundred would-be revolutionaries from the village of Pentrich, in Derbyshire, towards Nottingham, where the plot was to 'storm the battlements' of the city, procuring arms from householders en route and making bullets from lead stripped from the roofs of churches along the way, a distance of scarcely fifteen miles! The ultimate object of this insurrectionary enterprise was, according to reports by more parliamentary Secret Committees, to consolidate a force of men sufficient to march on London, overthrow the government, and establish a republic. Brandreth, encouraged by William Oliver, representing himself as an emissary from the 'Hampden Club in London', deluded himself, and his followers, into believing that hundreds of thousands would rise in armed rebellion all over the country; that forces would 'come in the morning out of Yorkshire like a cloud';

that Nottingham would surrender before they even reached it, and the keys of
the Tower of London soon be handed over!

The revolutionary ardour of the insurgents, however, was dampened by
constant rain, and many, quickly disillusioned, dropped out of the column,
despite Brandreth's threat to shoot deserters. (The threat seems to betray a
certain lack of confidence on the Nottingham Captain's part.) When a troop of
cavalry led by Colonel Rolleston, a local magistrate, met the remnants of the
advancing army near Kimberley, just outside Nottingham, most of the
revolutionaries fled, throwing away their weapons.

Notwithstanding all the rumours and threats, the Derbyshire action was the *only*
armed rising during the Regency period in England. Both the government and
the local authorities were well informed about the rising before it occurred. Their
spies, chief among them being the notorious 'Oliver', Lord Sidmouth's own agent,
had infiltrated the movement and knew every detail. Oliver's real name was
Richards, and he was a book-keeper by profession. He went to the north and
Midlands as a spy and *agent provocateur*, and was instrumental in convincing
Brandreth that a revolutionary multitude in London was only waiting for men in
the north to raise the standard of revolution and march south to join them. He
corresponded with his dupes by cipher, according to the *Leeds Mercury*, and 'one
of the mottoes used by him for that purpose was – "*The Old Mother is sick, and
expects all her sons to arm*".'[13] After the collapse of the rising, 'Oliver the Spy' was
exposed by the *Leeds Mercury*. Lord Sidmouth had neglected to inform the local
magistrates that this shadowy figure was a Home Office agent, so the magistrates,
having been informed by their own spies that Mr Oliver was a dangerous
revolutionary, had arrested him, and were then obliged to release him, so that his
life was in great danger until he was able to make his escape back to London with
the help of Major-General Byng, the northern military commander.

Thirty-five men were eventually rounded up and charged with high treason.
The indictment stated that 'a great multitude of false traitors . . . arrayed and
armed in a war-like manner', had 'with great force and violence' maliciously and
traitorously attempted by force of arms to 'subvert and destroy the Government
and Constitution of this realm'. Thirteen of them were framework-knitters; the
rest miners, labourers and assorted craftsmen. Brandreth's fate was already sealed,
for he had shot dead a farmworker during an arms raid. He and three others were
sentenced to death – a stone-mason named William Turner, a quarry owner
named Isaac Ludlam, and a sawyer named George Weightman. The last-named
was granted a reprieve on account of his youth, and transported to Botany Bay
along with thirteen others. Brandreth, Turner and Ludlam were hanged at Derby
on 7 November 1817, and their heads severed from their bodies.[14]

Described in court as a 'sober, peaceable man' and 'a very civil and decent
character', Weightman was the man supposed to have gone to Yorkshire to

address Luddites five years earlier. One is inclined to attribute this tale to Frank Peel's dramatic inventiveness. A journalist by profession, writing more than sixty years after the events, Peel employed journalistic colouring in his account, inventing dialogue and using other fictional devices. For example: 'The intrepid Cartwright gazed silently at the man for an instant, his proud lip curling with contempt.'[15] (The surprising thing is surely that E.P. Thompson shows such faith in Peel's version of events.)

The only more-or-less coincident disturbance anywhere in the country had been during the previous night at Huddersfield, where a few dozen half-hearted local workers in the woollen industry – not all croppers – assembled and exchanged a few shots with the military, but fled when reinforcements appeared. This event was meant to have coincided with the Pentrich rising, but one of the leaders, Richard Lee, had declared that 'delay was dangerous' and that 'the business must be done tonight'. One of the rendezvous sites where these reluctant revolutionaries gathered to march on Huddersfield was appropriately called Folly Hall. No one was killed in this farcical incident, and no one was convicted of any crime, although Thomas Riley, charged with 'Procuring Riotous Assemblies to be held', tried to hang himself while being detained in Huddersfield gaol, and then cut his own throat in York Castle. Riley was the sixty-year-old Crosland Moor tailor who had threatened Radcliffe's life. There had been talk in Huddersfield of an earlier rising in concert with insurgents in the Manchester area, when 'a deal of arms that had been hid since the time of the Luddites' was to be brought into service, but nothing had come of it.[16] 'Oliver' had been active in this area, too.

Strikes for wage increases and riots against power-looms occurred in Stockport and the Lancashire cotton towns during the summer of 1818, when many windows were broken and two or three mills set on fire. An attack on Thomas Garside's factory at Stockport in July resulted in injuries to members of the local cavalry and others, among whom was John Lloyd's son, but twenty prisoners were taken, and the disturbances soon subsided. Indeed, Lloyd wrote to Henry Hobhouse on 25 July that 'Mr. Garside's turn-outs have all been with him to-day – have begged his pardon, asked to return, and he accepts their services! This is the triumph of firmness and perseverance.'[17] Elsewhere, several men were convicted of offences under the Combination Acts, and some spent two years in Lancaster Castle.

There were strikes for higher wages by the knitters of Leicestershire and Nottinghamshire in the summer of 1819, and workers marched through several towns. These demonstrations of solidarity were mostly peaceful and orderly, but Mr Enfield, George Coldham's successor as Nottingham town clerk, soon had to inform the Home Secretary that in an 'outrageous furtherance of their combination', some stockingers had dragged their frames through the streets and left them at the doors of their masters, refusing to operate them any longer at the current rates.[18]

When the Nottinghamshire stockingers petitioned the Lord Lieutenant in August to do something to relieve their piteous sufferings, and reminded him of 'that glorious precept of our Divine Master, "to love one another, to feed the hungry, clothe the naked",' etc, His Grace replied that 'your case shall be attentively examined by me, and . . . shall occupy my most serious consideration'. But six days later he advised them that the best he could do was to offer help and advice to any workmen who wished to help colonise the Cape of Good Hope![19] In September the Corporation of Nottingham agreed to a motion, by eleven votes to five, to subscribe a sum of £30 to a fund for the relief of distressed framework-knitters.[20]

Except for a revival of attacks on power-looms in the Lancashire cotton industry in 1826, Luddism's reign of terror was over. What had it achieved, if anything? In the north of England, nothing. Shearing machines and gig-mills

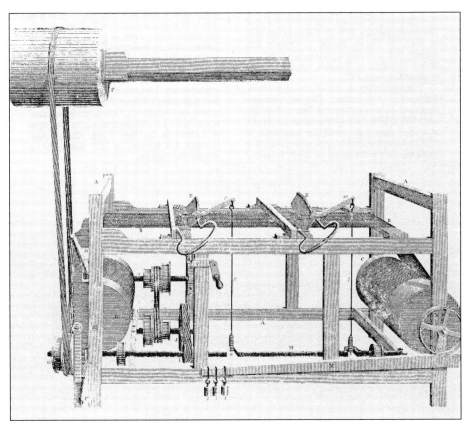

A shearing machine. This contraption was the chief object of the Yorkshire Luddites' fury. Its increasing use made the hand croppers redundant.

continued to increase in the Yorkshire woollen industry. Between 1806 and 1817, according to one historian of the industry, the number of shears operated by machinery increased 'from 100 to 1,462; and out of 3,378 shearmen no fewer than 170 were out of work while 1,445 were only partly employed'.[21] The number of power-looms grew apace in the Lancashire cotton industry. The Luddite belief in the north that new machinery would destroy their livelihoods was correct. In the short term, workers were made redundant and the skilled hand-finishing of woollen cloth was soon entirely destroyed.

Angus Bethune Reach, reporting on 'The Rural Cloth-Workers of Yorkshire' in 1849, described the poor housing of hand-loom weavers at Delph, near Saddleworth (then in the West Riding), and went on:

> The hand-jenny spinners, when in employment, earn, as a pretty general rule, about eight shillings a week. The weavers, as I have said, may, and often do, make fifteen and seventeen shillings per week; but, taking the year round, and the good webs with the bad ones, ten shillings in many parts of Yorkshire would be too high an average.[22]

The number of power-looms at work in the Lancashire mills almost trebled between 1835 and 1850, and the hand weaving of cotton disappeared. Looms were 'sold or broken up, and whole families have gone to the mills for employ'.[23]

The framework-knitters enjoyed a temporary illusion of success. Those manufacturers who had wide frames were forced to abandon the making of cut-ups, which were the chief objects of Luddite hostility in the Midlands. Skilled knitters achieved a price rise of two shillings a dozen pairs of stockings. Their standard of living recovered slightly. But any sense of satisfaction they may have felt was short-lived. Exploitation by truck payment (not abolished by law until 1831), by iniquitous stoppages in wages, and by the manufacture of cut-ups all returned after the violence had ended, and in the long run, the stockingers became even worse off than they were before.

In defiance of the Combination Acts, Revd Robert Hall founded a Friendly Relief Society, intended to afford some economic respite to the poorest of the knitters. Adult male members paid six pence a week, women and boys three pence. Mr Hall published an anonymous appeal to the public, which had been short-sightedly tardy in its support for the scheme, at first, in spite of the obvious fact, in Hall's view, that

> the framework-knitters and their families constitute the most numerous class of consumers in the county, and the quantity of their consumption must be

proportioned to the extent of their earnings. The circulation of money depends as much on the wages of labour, as on the profits of stock; and if thirty thousand persons rise from abject poverty to a capacity of commanding a larger share of the necessaries, and many of the comforts of life, the money which procures them will flow into every channel, so as to benefit alike the tradesman, the agriculturalist, and the landed proprietor. The infusion of a new *pabulum* of life into the extremities, will strengthen and invigorate the whole body.[24]

For some time the fund served its purpose, despite the scorn of Cobbett and others, who ridiculed what they saw as the propping up of low wages by artificial and unsustainable means. Hall published a reply to critics of the Friendly Relief Society, in which he denounced Cobbett as an 'arrogant and superficial declaimer', and called him 'the one-eyed monarch of the blind', who was 'intemperate, presumptuous, careless of the truth of his representations, and indifferent to their consequences, provided they make an impression . . .'.[25]

Dissecting Cobbett's reasoning, Hall detected an ulterior motive in his opposition to such relief schemes and to other remedies for the symptoms of poverty. Cobbett wanted the situation to deteriorate even further so that the obvious cure for the whole disease of society would then be forced upon them, i.e. parliamentary reform, the great object of Cobbett's rhetoric. But Mr Hall was not prepared to sit back and allow the Leicestershire knitters to sink into worse suffering, unaided, until this desirable object should come to pass. Another objection Hall had to answer was that 'the provision of a Fund for the support of such as are out of employ, affords a direct encouragement to idleness, the most baleful habit a poor man can contract'. But, he pointed out:

> The sum proposed to be paid from the Fund to such as are out of work, is at the most six shillings and sixpence a week, sufficient indeed to preserve them from lying utterly at the mercy of their masters, but certainly not such as to render their situation attractive, nor greater than the parishes would be under the necessity of paying shortly to a much greater number, were the Society abolished. While it provides a remedy for the existing evils, it leaves sufficient inducement to seek out other channels for their industry, whenever the state of society shall afford them.[26]

Nevertheless, by 1821 a quarter of its eight thousand members were unemployed, and the society failed because its resources were no longer equal to the task.

A framework-knitter at work. This old photograph shows one of the last survivors of the Midland cottage industry at work on a machine which had changed relatively little since the sixteenth century.

Several native Midlanders testified to the appalling conditions of the knitters during the 1830s and early 1840s, before hosiery manufacturing was transformed into a modern factory industry. General Booth, the Salvation Army founder, born in Nottingham in 1829, wrote:

When but a mere child, the degradation and helpless misery of the poor stockingers of my native town, wandering gaunt and hunger-stricken through the streets, droning out their melancholy ditties, crowding the Union or toiling like galley-slaves on relief works for a bare subsistence, kindled in my heart yearnings to help the poor which have continued to this day and which have had a powerful influence on my whole life.[27]

Thomas Cooper, the Chartist born in Leicester in 1805, recalled being sent as a journalist to report on a meeting in his native town in 1840, and was surprised, when he emerged at eleven o'clock at night, to see lights in the upper windows of working men's houses, and hear the creaking of stocking-frames:

'Do your stocking weavers often work so late as this?' I asked some of the men who were leaving the meeting.
    'No, not often: work's over scarce for that,' they answered; 'but we're glad to work any hour, when we can get work to do.'
    'Then your hosiery trade is not good in Leicester?' I observed.
    'Good! It's been good for nought this many a year,' said one of the men; 'We've a bit of a spurt now and then. But we soon go back again to starvation!'
    'And what may be the average earning of a stocking weaver?' I asked, – 'I mean when a man is fully employed.'
    'About four and sixpence,' was the reply.
    'Four and sixpence,' I said; 'well, six fours are twenty-four, and six sixpences are three shillings: that's seven-and-twenty shillings a week. The wages are not so bad when you are in work.'
    'What are you talking about?' said they. 'You mean four and sixpence a day; but we mean four and sixpence a week.'
    'Four and sixpence a week!' I exclaimed. 'You don't mean that men have to work in those stocking-frames that I hear going now, a whole week for four and sixpence. How can they maintain their wives and children?'
    'Ay, you may well ask that,' said one of them, sadly.[28]

A parliamentary Commission of Enquiry in 1844, set up in response to a petition signed by 25,000 framework-knitters, heard evidence from John Thurman, a knitter of Shepshed in Leicestershire, who had seven children, and worked for Messrs Cotton & Hammond. He told the commissioner, Richard Muggeridge, how he disposed of his weekly income of £1 2s 3d:

> The boy and me make four dozen [pairs of plain hose] in a week; then I have to pay 2s 3d frame-rent for the two frames; then I have to pay 2 shillings for seaming and I have to pay 7½d for needles for the two frames; then I have to pay for candles 4d per week. Then there is oil I have to pay 2d for; then I have the materials to buy towards the frame, wrenches, hammers, keys and everything of that sort. My little boy does the winding, that would be 6d if I was obliged to put anybody else to do it. Then I have coal 1s 3d per week, that is in the summer we do not use as much as that, but in the winter we use fire, that is, for the house and shop and all . . . The whole nine of us lie in two beds, and for these two beds we have one blanket for both; and it is out of my power, in any shape whatever, to buy any more without my earnings were more. I can positively say, and it is not my wish or principle to state one word of the least untruth, never a week goes by but I have to put my wife to bed for want of food; anybody that could come forward and knew me, would testify to that . . . when I have got my little on a Saturday, I pay every farthing I can, as far as it will go – and then when Monday morning comes I have not got 6d to buy a loaf with and there is nothing in the house. Then whatever few garments we have about us we take them and pledge them into the shop to get a bit of bread to go on with during the week, as long as it will last. . . .[29]

Joseph Ball, who worked for Mr Ratcliffe of Loughborough, told the commissioner:

> I have to grapple with all sorts of poverty, the same as the rest of my fellow-workmen, as respects not having the necessaries of life proper to the body nor the back, and sometimes there are sacrifices to be made for the necessaries of life in a way I am almost ashamed to name.

Mr Ball was asked if he had to pawn his clothes, and answered that there were 'very few housekeepers in the town working as stockingers that are not obliged to make those sacrifices many times, and in many cases every week, before they can have anything to eat.'[30] Little wonder that Thomas Cooper characterised the Leicestershire framework-knitter of the time as 'worn down, till you might have known him by his peculiar air of misery and dejection, if you had met him a hundred miles from Leicester'.[31]

Mr Muggeridge heard a great deal of evidence from framework-knitters all over the Midland counties that the former evils persisted. John Mayblin of Belper told him:

The frame-rent is considered a grievance by many; it is exacted whether you are in full, or only in part employment. I have known it taken when you have not had above 1s or 1s 6d to draw on Saturday night.[32]

William Bott, of Barwell, near Hinckley, thought that 'our frame-rents are a crying evil', and told the commissioner that there were 'somewhere near 300 frames' in the village, where the trade was conducted by bagmen.[33] Mr Muggeridge asked John Cheetham, of Hucknall, how many bagmen there were in that town:

> There are 10 or 12, I dare say.
> Do they all keep shops or deal in provisions?
> They all deal in provisions.
> Is there any manufacturer in Hucknall?
> No, they are all bagmen.
> . . .
> Is there much complaint of trucking going on at Hucknall?
> They do not complain much; they are afraid of being turned out of work.
> Is it notorious that it does exist to a considerable extent?
> Yes.[34]

Luddism, then, as a means of achieving improvements in the miserable living conditions of textile workers in the Midlands and the north, was an abject failure. It forced employers into temporary concessions because they feared for their property during a climate of conspiracy and violence against which the military and the local authorities were more or less impotent. But machine-breaking itself was a reaction to fear on the part of working men who were denied legal means of making representations to both masters and government. P. Mathias called it a negative response – 'a reaction characteristic of the pre-industrial world – the peasants' revolt . . .'.[35] But the state of industrial relations was also 'pre-industrial', and sophisticated and properly organised trade union negotiations were not possible, especially among isolated rural communities scattered over a large area of the Midlands, even if the law of the land had permitted them.

The long-term view prevailed, as always. 'Whenever the legislature attempts to regulate the differences between masters and their workmen,' Adam Smith had remarked, 'its counsellors are always the masters.' The desperate need of working men for bread had to give way to the interests of industrial evolution and profit. Even the alternative response of machine-breaking was defective in its organisation, in spite of the fact that the raiding gangs were regularly able to evade the military and carry out their intentions. The Midland men were most disciplined and efficient, and the Yorkshiremen most militant, but several historians have noted that machine-breaking in Lancashire and Cheshire was particularly chaotic.

From the shooting of John Westley at Bulwell in November 1811 to the executions at Leicester and Nottingham six years later, the Luddites and associated rioters suffered loss of life to the extent of forty-six people, thirty-five of whom were executed and the rest shot dead during raids on property. Although there were wounded soldiers and civilians on the other side, and no doubt a good deal of psychological stress in addition to Radcliffe's, there were only two deaths – those of Horsfall and the innocent bystander, Kilby. This tally surely tells us something about the lack of real passion or ferocity in any *political* designs the Luddites may have entertained, especially in Yorkshire, where most of the brave words were being uttered, and fanatics were chalking up notices of 'vengeance for the blood of the innocent'.

The known deaths by violence directly attributable to the Luddite campaign, 1811–17, are as follows:

Year	Luddites and associates	Others
1811	John Westley shot dead at Bulwell, Notts.	
1812	Samuel Hartley and John Booth shot dead at Rawfolds Mill, Yorks.	William Horsfall murdered near Huddersfield.
	Eight rioters fatally shot at Middleton, Lancs.	
	Seven men and one woman executed at Lancaster.	
	Two men executed at Chester.	
1813	Seventeen men executed at York.	
1814		Mr Kilby shot at Basford, Notts.
1816	James Towle executed at Leicester	
1817	Six men executed at Leicester.	
	Daniel Diggle executed at Nottingham.	

The so-called 'Swing' rioters, agricultural workers in the south of England, copied Luddite tactics in 1830, smashing up the new threshing machines which were threatening their jobs. They operated ostensibly under the orders of a mythical 'Captain Swing', in whose name they posted threatening letters, and many of them were subsequently executed or transported.

Some framework-knitters and other textile workers were involved in the Chartist riots of 1839 onward. Although not directly related to Luddism, this movement again revealed vital differences between Midland Chartists and those in the north, whose aims were fundamentally anti-industrialist. When Feargus O'Connor's Cooperative Land Company founded its first settlement at Chorleywood in Hertfordshire, however, its street names recalled the centres of the old industrial discontent – Nottingham Road, Halifax Road, Stockport Road, etc.

Despite all the protests, strikes, appeals and desperate acts of violence on behalf of the framework-knitters over a period of forty years, it was not until the mid-century conversion of hosiery manufacturing into a factory industry that any semblance of a fair system of employment for the workers began. The knitting industry had remained stagnant for so long partly because there were special technical problems involved in adapting knitting machinery to centrally powered operation. 'Stockings cannot be made by power,' a Derbyshire hosier told the commissioner on the condition of the framework-knitters in 1845. But the basis of the solution had already been made, ironically enough, during the Luddite period, in 1816, when Marc Brunel had patented a circular knitting machine called the 'tricoteur'. This and other ingenious new inventions were

Crag Mill, an early silk mill at Wildboarclough, Cheshire. Built around 1770, it was a pioneering textile factory. It now serves as the village post office.

long ignored by the manufacturers, who were quite happy to make their profits at the expense of starving hand-operatives.

In due course power-driven machinery brought long-term prosperity to the Midlands. The first power-operated factory to produce hosiery in Leicestershire was established at Loughborough around 1840, while in Leicester powered circular frames were being worked experimentally. In Nottinghamshire the first steam-driven hosiery factory was built at Nottingham in 1851. Within twenty years Leicester and Nottingham had nearly 120 hosiery factories between them, and by this time frame-rents had been abolished by law. Nottinghamshire also possessed most of the country's lace factories, while Derbyshire throve on cotton and silk.[36] By the end of the century the 25,000 knitting-frames in the three counties at the time of the Luddite riots had been reduced to a mere 5,000.

CHAPTER TEN

Hidden Agenda?

Gravenor Henson is reputed to have left at his death, in 1852, manuscripts revealing much of the inside story of Luddism, but they have never come to light, and even if they did, one presumes they would relate chiefly, and perhaps exclusively, to the Midland stocking- and lace-makers. In the absence of these or any other newly discovered contemporary documents, many – if not most – of the unanswered questions about the Luddite movement will remain as matters of some uncertainty. We can speculate, hypothesise and conjecture for as long as we like, but we cannot solve with complete confidence some of the historical problems the period presents, and can only propose possible answers based on the existing evidence.

The purpose of this chapter is to state my conclusions, and to consider the most vexed question of all: did the Luddite movement have a political as well as an economic objective in mind throughout – or at any point in – the campaign of violence? We have seen in the early chapters what is not in dispute: that the normally moderate Midland framework-knitters, driven by desperation resulting from high food prices, pitifully low wages and outrageous exploitation, adopted violence against machinery to try to force concessions from their employers. This was not because they were hostile to machinery as such, but because machinery was being used improperly by unscrupulous hosiers to make profit at the expense of their workers' living standards. There were many honourable manufacturers who, while not openly condoning sabotage, sympathised with the knitters' campaign, not only from humanitarian sentiments, but because unscrupulous opportunists were undermining *their* trade and profits, too. But the authorities had to act against what was, after all, criminal activity, and the government drafted in troops to assist the local militia in attempting to control the unrest.

There was not, at first, any suspicion of a political dimension to the rioting, but towards the end of 1811 some authorities began to think there might be some truth in rumours of foreign intervention. Napoleon might be secretly exploiting industrial unrest in order to undermine the British war effort. But the two Bow Street officers sent to Nottingham by the Home Secretary to investigate the causes and track down the perpetrators of violence found no evidence to support such fears, and the Home Secretary, Ryder, himself subscribed to the view that the riots were a purely local industrial relations affair.

The shearmen of Yorkshire and the hand-loom weavers of the north-west *were* opposed to new mechanical devices which threatened their livelihoods, not through their alleged misuse, as in the Midlands, but because of their very existence. For one reason or another, therefore, the use of machinery in the textile industries engendered a violent protest movement. But other fears were now growing among the local rulers and middle classes of England. The Duke of Newcastle, Lord Lieutenant of Nottinghamshire, who had formerly seemed almost complacently satisfied that local disturbances were only minor affairs which could be easily contained, wrote of a 'state of insurrection', and there began to be much talk of conspiracy and armed uprisings, and demands for increasing numbers of troops and martial law.

The government, mindful of recent events across the Channel, began to display exaggerated fears of revolution in Britain, and introduced a series of repressive measures to prevent what had never been seriously threatened, except in a few semi-literate inflammatory letters supposedly emanating from a mysterious 'General Ludd' hidden away in Sherwood Forest, and by a few rumour-mongers and rabble-rousers. The six years of the Luddite rebellion can be summed up quite easily, at the simplest level, in terms of a chain reaction:

1. Textile workers took to violence against property.
2. Local law officers were unequal to their responsibility of dealing with the crime wave.
3. The government adopted ferocious measures to compensate for the impotence or inefficiency of local authorities.

The more contentious arguments can perhaps best be summarised by reference to the enduring questions posed in the Preface:

1. Who *were* the Luddites?
It might be useful to satisfy ourselves first as to what is the correct definition of a 'Luddite'. If we mean simply one who took part in destroying machinery, then agricultural workers and many others were Luddites, too, and operative over a longer period than is normally considered. But the term has been used only in relation to textile workers in the Midlands and north of England, between 1811 and 1816, who themselves adopted the legendary 'Ludd' as their champion. If we were even more strict in our use of the term, however, only the framework-knitters of the three Midland counties, Nottinghamshire, Derbyshire and Leicestershire, would be regarded as genuine Luddites, conducting a long campaign of machine-breaking to force their employers into paying them wages which they could live on, and to urge the government into regulating the trade

so that it was free of corruption and exploitation. The Yorkshire, Lancashire and Cheshire men were impostors.

It was when the violence spread from the hosiery counties to other parts of the country that the situation assumed a wholly new dimension. Riots in the Midlands against wide frames had been going on for *almost a year* before similar machine-breaking activity began to appear in the textile industries of Yorkshire and the north-west. The northerners simply copied Luddite tactics to fight a different and perhaps less honourable battle, and soon gave up under pressure. But while it lasted, the Yorkshiremen's campaign was the most violent.

It is open to serious doubt whether there was any operational connection between those who planned and organised gang-raids on machinery and those who penned the various letters signed by or on behalf of 'King' or 'General' Ludd. The leaders of violent measures, men of action such as Towle in Nottinghamshire and Mellor in Yorkshire, are unlikely to have sat down to compose semi-literate manifestos and ultimata, although these men were possibly looked upon as the generals of their particular areas; the idea having been taken up in the north after its *succès de scandale* in the Midlands. The scribes were men of a more political turn of mind, with a taste for working-class rhetoric, who probably had little direct contact with the leaders of machine-breaking gangs. Their ideas were more radical, and they used Luddism as a highly convenient platform on which to erect their visions of revolution, associating the Luddites with a political ideology they did not have in the beginning, and perhaps never had at all.

Secrecy about the identities of those involved prevailed. Thousands of workers and their wives must have known who the machine-breakers were. These men were absent from their homes during the nights when attacks were made on local workshops. But only those few who became informers or turned King's Evidence to save their own necks ever betrayed anyone. Even sixty years after the events, Frank Peel claimed to have met old men who would not give anything away that might be considered incriminating.

2. Who were their leaders?
Who made the plans and issued the orders? Who, in fact, was 'King Ludd' or 'General Ludd'? Many of those in authority believed that it was Gravenor Henson, Janus-like, who was the chief architect of sabotage as a method of terrorising the master hosiers into compliance when more peaceful attempts at persuasion had failed. Francis Place, the reformer who promoted trade unions as a democratic right and managed to achieve repeal of the Combination Acts in 1824, believed that Henson was 'King Ludd', and, as we have seen, many others had deep suspicions about him. But Henson had no known connection with the Yorkshire croppers or the Lancashire and Cheshire hand-loom weavers, and the

invocation of 'General Ludd' seems to have been more frequent there than among the Midlanders. It is not without significance, surely, that there is no mention of Henson in, for example, the papers of Sir Joseph Radcliffe.

It is quite possible, of course, that Henson showed to the world one face and reserved another for meetings behind closed doors. There was – and is – nothing unusual about a figure in office who maintains a public image of correctness and respectability while secretly supporting unpopular measures and even criminal activities deemed expedient in the circumstances. (We need look no further than Sir Astley Cooper, President of the Royal College of Surgeons, for a contemporary analogy. Cooper, Henson's senior by seventeen years, was one of those who raised the science of surgery to a higher level. He lectured on the subject at St Thomas's Hospital, practised at Guy's, and numbered the Prime Minister and the Duke of Wellington among his patients. He was awarded a baronetcy for operating successfully on the king, George IV. But behind the scenes, Cooper was nicknamed 'King of the Resurrectionists'. He was paying professional body-snatchers, whom he described to a government Select Committee as 'the lowest dregs of degradation', to dig up corpses for his anatomical studies and lectures, because without them he could not have carried on.)[1]

Henson may have protested his innocence of any criminal act, for the public record, while giving encouragement to the machine-breakers when more legitimate appeals to government and manufacturers had failed, and a sharp reminder of the consequences of failure to negotiate a settlement seemed appropriate. The end would justify the means. There is a little circumstantial evidence to suggest that Henson *may* have given tacit approval to such tactical violence, but certainly none whatever to indicate that he was 'General Ludd', the moving spirit or chief organiser of the whole machine-breaking enterprise. There are hints in his character and his correspondence that he may have been capable of ordering violent attacks. By 1818 he had himself been reduced to poverty, and in April 1820 he and his wife Martha were ordered to be removed as paupers from St Mary's parish to the parish of St Nicholas, the place of their 'last legal settlement'.[2] Ten years later Henson was reported to the authorities in Nottingham for 'maliciously and contemptuously' disturbing a religious meeting.[3] Nevertheless, Henson's strong denials of any sympathy or involvement with the men of violence, and the absence of any hard evidence to the contrary, entitle him to the benefit of the doubt.

Although George Mellor has been widely regarded as the Luddite ringleader in Yorkshire, the magistrate Radcliffe thought that the 'Chief Lud' there was Thomas Brook, the 32-year-old cropper from Lockwood who was executed for his part in the attack on Rawfolds Mill. Brook was one of a large family, several members of which were among the defendants at York, although all of them except Thomas were discharged or acquitted.

In view of the legitimate doubts about strong links between framework-knitters and the croppers and weavers in the north, and the certain lack of organisational skill in obtaining a coordinated campaign throughout the textile industries (if such a thing *was* attempted), we must surely conclude that there was no single commander-in-chief of operations, disguised by the pseudonym 'General Ludd', with headquarters in Sherwood Forest or anywhere else.

One further interesting point arises here. E.P. Thompson has said that 'Men must be judged in their own context; and in this context we may see such men as George Mellor, Jem Towle, and Jeremiah Brandreth as men of heroic stature.'[4] The sentiment has been echoed, particularly with regard to Mellor, by one or two other writers, who have called him 'an heroic figure'. He was hardly that, I would suggest, and Towle and Brandreth even less so. It is true that a failure may still be a hero, but the objects of his actions and self-sacrifice must have been worthy ones in the eyes of his compatriots. There is little evidence to show that Mellor was anything more than a small-time gang-leader. He did not lack courage or boldness, certainly, but he failed to inspire reverence or admiration among the local working population. His story does not have the element of tragedy from which heroes are made, despite his betrayal. Reckless fanaticism, rather than nobility of purpose, was his inspiration, and led only to pointless deaths and disappointment in a lost cause.

3. How were they organised?
Having in mind the foregoing conclusions, it seems clear that machine-breaking raids were organised, in the Midlands at least, on a purely local basis by conspiracies among the more extreme young workers. There is no evidence of a systematic pattern or a carefully worked-out plan of campaign. Incidents appear to have occurred spontaneously, although word of intended attacks must have passed from one small town or village to another in the same district, and information was no doubt shared as to opportunities and objectives. Those hosiers who were targeted were the ones using wide frames to make cut-ups, and were obviously well known over a wide area, and deeply resented.

On the other hand, it is clear from the almost universal observance of discipline in the Midlands that local leaders were enjoined by some central individual or body of people to obey strict rules in pursuing their aims, so that the framework-knitters could not be branded as merely an unruly mob of hooligans and vandals. This in itself argues against ulterior political motives on their part, for it implies recognition of the social necessity of law and order even while they were engaged in lawless opposition to certain aspects of the system. And this self-control and unity of purpose, in turn, argues for a relatively small body of men who were carrying out the sabotage of knitting-frames at the height of the Luddite campaign. It is an almost impossible task, when letting

A framework-knitting workshop – a transitional stage between cottage and factory industry – with wide frames of the kind the Luddites regularly sabotaged; against the wall on the left is one of the obnoxious 'three-at-once' frames.

loose a large body of young men ready to commit riot and destruction, to prevent the eruption of base instincts. The restraint of the framework-knitters was quite remarkable in the circumstances, and the local organisers must have picked small groups of men who understood the objectives and whom they thought could be trusted. It was a different matter with the northerners, who assembled in chaotic and unruly hordes to raid the cotton and woollen mills.

As for the stories of missions from the Midlands to underground union meetings in the north, there is nothing to substantiate the rumours and statements made by unreliable witnesses, who had a vested interest in telling their inquisitors what they wanted to hear. The knitters as a body had nothing to gain by urging textile workers in the north to resort to sabotage, and as machine-breaking in the north was directed to different ends, organisational cooperation between the two parts of the country seems not only extremely unlikely, but positively counter-productive.

Robert Baker assured the Home Office in February 1812 that he and his colleague Conant had never neglected to try to discover if these people were abetted in an organised way by persons from a distance and particularly by other manufacturers at Manchester, Birmingham etc., but though such surmises have been constantly upon the minds of all descriptions of persons here, we have never been able to find any fact that gives countenance to it.[5]

Indeed, it is arguable that the framework-knitters had every good reason to *resent* northern appropriation of their methods. It stole their thunder and confused the signals received by the government and local authorities. The violence of the Yorkshire and Lancashire men was doing nothing to help the Midland knitters, and if a few politically motivated maverick or renegade extremists *did* travel to the north to stir workers there into action, they were certainly scoring own goals. That is perhaps the reason for a curious unexplained phenomenon of the Luddite riots. *Machine-breaking in the Midlands ceased promptly when the northern violence began, and only resumed when the northerners had given up sabotage, some months later.*

It has been argued that the Midlanders stopped wrecking stocking-frames because of the strong military presence, and because machine-breaking was about to be made a capital offence.[6] But if the Luddites were intimidated by troops and deterred by liability to the death penalty, why did they soon take up machine-breaking again? That does not make sense. The repetitive abandonment and resumption of machine-breaking by Luddite stockingers over a five-year period was invariably, without doubt, in reaction to their own economic interests and circumstances.

The truth is that the stockingers and lace-makers had no wish to be lumped together with another set of rioters with different objectives and thus become branded as subversives, their legitimate claims for economic aid only to be suppressed by troops clamping down wholesale on what was seen, wrongly in their case, as political rebellion. It appears that Henson and his colleagues were able to propagate this vital message even among the most violent extremists. The discipline and restraint of the Midland workers in targeting only the tools used for their exploitation, which is seen clearly in accounts of their attacks, and confirmed even by the authorities whose duty it was to arrest and punish them, are sufficient proof that the Midland knitters had one specific purpose only, from which they were not to be diverted.

4. Did the Luddites have a political agenda?
One of the aspects of the troubles which clearly caused considerable alarm to the authorities, and reinforced their fears of insurrection much more than acts of criminal damage, was the amount of secret and illegal oath-taking reported. Its frequency and significance were undoubtedly exaggerated by spies and informers reporting to the government and local magistrates, but there can be no doubt

that it was taking place on a significant scale, especially in the north-west, and that it alarmed the government. Combined with the incidents of arms thefts and reports of hidden caches of arms and ammunition, it is hardly surprising that there was genuine anxiety among the ruling classes about the security of the State. But was there any real danger of revolution from the Luddites? F.O. Darvall was categorical on the matter:

> Whatever danger of Revolution there might have been in Regency England . . . there was no such danger from the Luddites who, in so far as they had definite objects at all, wished only to prevent the introduction of new machinery, to coerce their employers into improving their wages and conditions of work, to prevent speculation in foodstuffs, and, by creating a state of public alarm, to secure local, immediate, economic advantages.[7]

This paragraph is a generalisation, misleading if taken to refer to the Luddites of all areas involved. It implies that they had hardly any discernible objects, whereas the majority of them undoubtedly did, though preventing the 'introduction of new machinery' was not one of them as far as the framework-knitters were concerned. Nor was 'creating a state of public alarm' any part of the Midland Luddites' intentions.

Nevertheless, most historians of Luddism have agreed with this general view. After all, there were none of the manifestations of revolutionary intent – no assassinations of political leaders, as Thomis and Holt point out; no armed attacks on town halls or military barracks. And it is difficult to argue with the calm judgement of the man on the spot best qualified to assess the situation, the military commander General Maitland, that the Luddites never had the capability of mounting an insurrection. They had neither the numbers, nor the arms, nor the organisational skill to pose a serious threat to the State. But that does not entirely dispose of E.P. Thompson's contention that the Luddites entertained a political as well as an economic agenda.

I trust it is by now perfectly clear that not only is there no shred of evidence for any political aims on the part of the Midland framework-knitters, who were the original, and in one sense the only true Luddites, but also that it would not have been in the nature of the working-class population of the Midland shires to entertain such notions. The educated leaders among them, such as Gravenor Henson and others, *may* have been politically motivated, but they would not have been regarded as leaders by *anyone* if they had ignored the distress of the workers they were supposed to represent, in order to further their own political interests. The priorities of the poor and largely rural workers were keeping their families fed and clothed. Anyone who preached the gospel of armed uprising to these people would have been wasting his breath.

It may well be a different matter when we consider the Yorkshire and Lancashire men. The Yorkshire croppers were skilled and well-paid craftsmen. They were not faced with imminent starvation, as the stockingers were. Their brief campaign of machine-breaking was directed solely at deterring their employers from installing machinery which they feared, correctly, would render them redundant. But they gave it up when they realised that the game was not worth the candle. The hangman's noose hung over them like the sword of Damocles, and they were a small and tightly-knit community, unlike the Midland knitters, and therefore more vulnerable to arrest and interrogation, and not immune from the laying of false information by fellow-workers with a grudge to settle or an eye on the main chance when a rich reward was in prospect.

Fears about the direction the croppers' protests might take had been expressed in Yorkshire since 1802, when secret meetings and links with the West Country wool finishers were known about. Lord Fitzwilliam had argued consistently then that any disturbances which might ensue would be limited to industrial relations. He wrote to the Home Secretary, Lord Pelham, in August of that year, for instance:

> There may be a combination of workmen: it is very probable that there is, from the state of the workmen of the West of England . . . not unlikely there is communication kept up between the two – but I am more and more inclined to hope that should unfortunately any flame burst out here, it will be found to originate, not in any principle of a public nature, but in the partial cause of jarring interests of masters and workmen.[8]

But the more extreme among the Yorkshiremen, not content to sit back and do nothing when the wrecking of machinery had been given up, and having absorbed revolutionary ideas in the meantime, were persuaded that they could form part of a nationwide armed revolt, beside which the smashing of a few shearing frames seemed a trivial sideline. They soon found, however, that they could not get widespread support.

It seems fairly clear that some of the younger and more militant among the Yorkshire croppers were infected with the spirit of revolution and republicanism emanating from underground movements and secret societies in the industrial heartland of the West Riding, and openly espoused by men such as John Baines of Halifax, the disciple of Tom Paine. Baines and his friends no doubt saw the potential of an outbreak of industrial rioting as the cradle of a mass movement of disaffection from the government, and wasted no time in infiltrating the local Luddites and spreading the republican gospel among them. But that is not to say that the whole Luddite campaign was, or became, a political cause. The majority of machine-breakers remained indifferent to philosophical ideas, even if they were capable of understanding them, and were concerned only with their immediate dilemma of how to feed and clothe their wives and families in the face of spreading unemployment.

Cheshire and Lancashire were already rife with civil unrest when machine-breaking was adopted by the poor hand-loom weavers of Manchester and its satellite towns. Machinery had crept almost surreptitiously into the Lancashire cotton industry over a long period, and resentment against it was more in the nature of a revival of old opposition, inspired by news of the Luddite rioting elsewhere, than a fresh campaign against a new enemy. The Luddites did not instigate political action in that area, but many of them evidently embraced it, and it culminated in the infamous 'Peterloo Massacre' in Manchester in 1819. As E.P. Thompson has put it, it is

> difficult to know how far the unrest in Lancashire may be described as authentic Luddism. It was made up in part of spontaneous rioting, in part of illegal but 'constitutional' agitation for political reform, in part of incidents fabricated by *provocateurs*, and in part of genuine insurrectionary preparations.[9]

After Peterloo, there was much renewed talk in the north of armed risings, and links between Manchester and Huddersfield, arms from Birmingham, and so on. The Midlands had nothing to do with all this. The lace and hosiery workers still had their own occupational hazards to worry about.

If it were possible to redefine Luddism as a movement of Midland stockingers only, with some northern textile workers copying a tried and, to a limited extent, effective method of coercion, and *then* ask if the Luddites had a political agenda, the clear answer would be emphatically, No! If Luddism had remained confined to the three Midland counties where it originated, little would have been heard of oath-taking, arms raids or political agendas. Given, however, that the term Luddism is universally understood to include the machine-breaking riots of the Yorkshire croppers and the Lancashire and Cheshire hand-loom weavers, I find it impossible to agree entirely with those historians – the majority, in fact – who totally reject any suggestion of political aims on the part of the Luddites. The northerners' priorities may have been to improve their immediate economic situations, but many of them were undoubtedly carried along on a wave of insurrectionary clamour. The weight of evidence for this seems to me to be much too strong to dismiss it *all* as the false information of spies and the mischievous actions of *agents provocateurs*. Even so, taken as a whole, the political overtones of Luddism were, as George Rudé concluded, 'intrusive rather than intrinsic' to the movement.[10]

The northern Luddites were hopelessly misguided, easily duped by rabble-rousing extremists and impulsively aggressive towards those in authority. But many of them, particularly in the north-west, were insurrectionary in temper. Political agitation in the north-west was reinforced, if not actually led, by Irish immigrants, but was unfocused and disorganised, with no hope of a successful outcome. In Yorkshire it may have had a more philosophical basis, but its leaders did not succeed in firing the plebeians with sufficient revolutionary ardour to produce any significant impact. Many may have talked excitedly about revolution in secret union meetings over their ale in the local public houses, but few had the stomach for it when it came to bearing arms and marching in defiance of a large military presence.

The truth of the matter is that we do not know, and never can know, what was going through the minds of hundreds, possibly thousands, of men who went out to break machines, demand arms, or collect money. History deals with waves washing over the shore, not with each individual drop of water that makes up the incoming tide. No doubt some of those who were called, or called themselves, Luddites, were intelligent men, and some were not. Some knew exactly why they were carrying out acts of violence and destruction of property, and others had only the vaguest idea. Some felt the thrill of defiance and the excitement of risk as they smashed machines; others hung back nervously and feared discovery. Some may have had visions of the different world they were trying to establish, while others had only a blind resentment of authority as their incentive.

Use of what are called 'loaded' or 'value-oriented' terms like 'mob' or 'rabble' has been exercising the minds of some historians in recent years. They are seen as words used exclusively by the upper classes to describe their mindless inferiors. I do not entirely go along with this argument. Dostoevsky said: 'The more I love humanity, the more I hate individuals.' My own position is rather the reverse. The more I love individuals, the more I hate humanity. I do not mean it literally, any more than Dostoevsky did. But a crowd is always less attractive than each of the separate individuals who make it up. When a number of people join together, something of the individuality of each one is sacrificed to the collective interest. 'Mob' seems to me an apt word, whoever uses it, for a crowd of people whose character is formed by some external and malicious force more than by the personalities of the people in it. 'The mob', as Fuller said, 'has many heads but no brains.' A mob may sometimes deserve sympathy or compassion, rather than condemnation, but it is still a mob for all that.

What is perfectly plain is that the herd instinct operated among the strong and active young men in both the Midlands and the north of England as the chief impetus behind machine-breaking. After all, it was not the old men of wisdom and experience who went out at dead of night with blackened faces to break into workshops with axes and heavy hammers. Nearly 60 per cent of the prisoners held in York Castle after the Rawfolds Mill affair were under thirty years of age, and nearly 90 per cent were under forty. Most of them had been toddlers or babes in arms when the French Revolution took place. George Mellor had not been born when the Bastille was stormed.

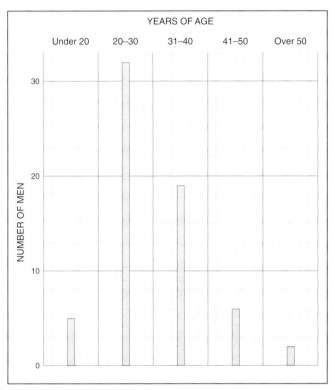

Ages of the 64 men held in York Castle in January 1813 for trial before the Special Commission.

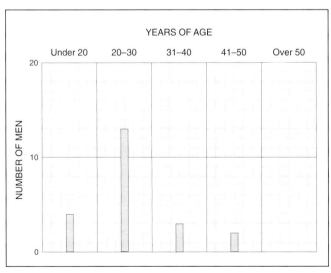

Ages of the 22 men charged with arms stealing and/or tumultuously assembling after the Pentrich rising in June 1817.

The significance of these facts has not been sufficiently emphasised, in my view. Impulsive young men and boys, impatient for action, want to force the pace rather than wait upon events like their more world-weary elders. It is important to keep in mind that there were tens of thousands of middle-aged and elderly framework-knitters who, though they were as hard-pressed economically as the younger men, and perhaps more so, had *nothing whatever* to do with machine-breaking. Most of the men executed or transported for crimes during the Luddite rebellion were described by various commentators as young men in the prime of life. The six convicted at Nottingham of machine-breaking in March 1812, whose sentences of transportation were considered lenient by Radcliffe and others, were all under twenty-three years old – three of them were teenagers. Those who attacked the armoury at Sheffield in April 1812 were described as 'young men'. The six hanged at Leicester for the Loughborough attack were described as 'young men, in the prime of life, health and vigour'.

The herd instinct is a feature of tribal preservation and ensures that each individual's behaviour is consistent with that of the community as a whole. When an individual does anything that deviates from what is, by common consent, society's self-interest, it is called 'crime' or 'rebellion' or 'treason', and is punished accordingly. Thus each individual will tend not only to accept, quite unquestioningly, the beliefs of his tribe or community, but will also carry out orders with equally uncritical obedience. Any national war effort depends on this instinct. But it also works in smaller tribal units than the national one. A perceived threat to the tribe acts as a stimulus to herd action, and this is exploited by political or religious leaders. Rabble-rousing tribal leaders are able to harness and mobilise this herd instinct in a kind of mindless hysteria, conditioning men into believing, often without the slightest rational basis, that their acts are a necessity of tribal self-protection. It is the fit young men of the tribe who respond to any need for collective physical force. They do not always understand fully the reasons for their actions. A sudden alert to communal danger passes from one to another member of the tribe like an electric current, and fortifies their collective courage. We must not overlook the family, either, as a smaller tribal unit. Among the sixty-four accused at the York Special Commission in 1813 were six members of the Brook family, three each of the Baines, Haigh and Walker families, and two each of Hill, Hey, Schofield, Smith and Thornton families.

It only needed a committed revolutionary like John Baines to gain one or two young and aggressive disciples such as George Mellor, and they could inflame the mob with a hot-headed revolutionary zeal which sometimes obscured the purely economic purpose of their collective action. Then one or two would go out at night with guns instead of sticks, and another would write a threatening letter, and so the process would escalate, and the more soldiers sent in to quell the riots, the more tribal resistance was generated. It is no use Mr Thompson calling this view the 'condescension of posterity'. This is the way human beings are. Social psychologists know that the objective judgements of individuals are influenced by being part of a group. The 'group mind' reveals what has become common to the individuals in it by virtue of being in the group rather than being in isolation. But complicated thought arrives at less precise conclusions in the collective mind. This has all been shown by experiment. 'Autonomy of judgement is abandoned in favour of the central tendency exhibited by the group. Thus the individual's perceptive reactions are often adaptations to cultural norms.'[11] We do not all sit down and spend time making calm judgements and act according to our reason or our consciences. We follow the leader, or 'jump on the bandwagon', almost instinctively. We act impulsively, fearing isolation, and trusting to safety in numbers. Young men do not want to be seen standing on the sidelines being jeered at by the majority. They have learned during childhood that being an outsider is not a pleasant experience. So they join the consensus, and this is how unruly mobs are formed. As Freud's biographer Ernest Jones expressed it, the group or crowd's 'irrationality, intolerance, illogical type of thinking, and its deterioration in moral standards and behaviour, strongly suggest a reversion to some more primitive level'.[12]

It is perfectly true, as Mr Thompson says, that 'the poor stockinger, the Luddite cropper' and others whom he wishes to rescue from the 'enormous condescension' he writes of, 'lived through these times of acute social disturbance, and we did not'.[13] So, of course, did the harassed authorities who, whatever the moral rights and wrongs of the matter in hindsight, were faced with a worrying and spreading crime wave and fears – real or imagined – of an armed insurrection of workers, within a few years of the cataclysmic revolt by the *sans-culottes* of France.

That does not mean, however, that the Luddites are to be dismissed as a mob of ignorant and misguided barbarians. The Luddite campaign may have failed, in the long run, to achieve a better standard of living for textile workers, but the attempt was not dishonourable, especially in the Midlands, where the movement started and finished as a last resort of working men reduced to mere shadows of human beings of dignity and self-respect, in the midst of a wealthy and so-called civilised country. We are entitled to make judgements about individual behaviour, and censure those we know acted wrongly or irresponsibly. But the advantage of hindsight and a clear view of the great sweep of industrial progress does not give us the right to condemn those who, driven by fear, did what they believed they had to do, at that time and in those circumstances. The fear they felt was of the consequences for them and their families if they sat back and did

A Radical Reformer. George Cruikshank's cartoon of 1819 shows the Prince Regent and Lords Liverpool, Castlereagh and Eldon panicking at the English radical movement, seeing it as a French guillotine breathing fire and dripping blood.

nothing to help themselves. The instinct of self-preservation is more powerful than submission to rational thought. Misguided the Luddites may have been; stupid they were not.

In any great survey of the whole sweep of history, the Luddite Rebellion merits no more than a sentence or two. It was a mere blip in the irresistible march of industrial progress. But was the machine-breakers' campaign wholly negative and useless? Did the Luddites have any *positive* effect at all? Undoubtedly: they added an unacknowledged drop to that meandering stream of common experience which flowed inexorably, though with desperately frustrating slowness, to a more equitable social landscape.

Appendix I

LETTER FROM REVD JOHN T. BECHER
TO THE HOME OFFICE

Southwell, 11th February 1812

Sir,

As the attention of parliament will soon be directed to the outrages, prevailing in the county of Nottingham, I shall not, I hope, be censured for intrusion, if I venture to transmit such observations as have been suggested to me by the subject.

In bringing the state of our manufacturing concerns under your consideration, I must beg leave to request your particular attention to the principle, upon which the machinery, employed in the fabrication of lace & stockings is supplied. The conditions are, I believe, almost peculiar to this branch of business; and to this origin, as I humbly conceive, the present grievances may, in a great measure, be imputed.

The Frames, upon which Lace & Stockings are woven, are hired by the workmen at stipulated weekly rents, seldom amounting to less than 12 per cent, & occasionally to 20 per cent, upon the original cost. – The prices of these frames vary from £16 to £50, without including additional machinery; and the interest arising from capital so vested has induced Farmers, Servants, Laborers, & others, totally unacquainted with the interests & management of the trade, to become frame owners & to embark their money in this speculation, which was artfully recommended by those hosiers who were desirous of engaging in the lace or hosiery business or of extending their concerns without possessing sufficient pecuniary resources. The frames thus introduced are denominated 'Independents'.

Until the commencement of the present war the demand for the Nottinghamshire manufactures exceeded the produce of the machinery & labour in the market. The frames were regarded by every workman as the tutelary guardians of his house. To these the family was indebted for food and raiment, so that they became the objects of their attentive care & most vigilant protection. – Females and children attained the art of using them; and those who declined this exertion, were occupied in seaming stockings, ornamenting clocks, or embroidering lace. Abundance thus rapidly acquired by those who were ignorant of its proper application hastened the progress of luxury &

licentiousness, and the lower orders were almost universally corrupted by profusion & depravity, scarcely to be credited by those who are strangers to our district. – Among the men, the discussion of politics, the destruction of game or the dissipation of the alehouses was substituted for the duties of their occupation during the former part of the week; and in the remaining three or four days a sufficiency was earned for defraying the current expenses. These emoluments contrasted with the wages of common laborers presented inducements too powerful to be resisted, and the children of the poor were consequently withdrawn from agriculture to trade. – The difficulty of procuring servants created general complaints; and this inconvenience was aggravated by want of diligence in the males & of virtue in the females. – Such was the condition of the inferior classes – and, if we examine the conduct & character of the Hosiers or Masters, much will appear deserving reprehension. – Some were distinguished by liberality towards their workmen & by their firm attachment to the established government, but these were not the features of the majority. – The bulk of the Hosiers had commenced their pursuits without fortune or education, and were far more inclined to censure the conduct of administration, than to correct their own ignorance & inhumanity: Hence an incessant struggle arose between the high & the low party. – This in the elections of members of parliament was signalized by flagrant outrages, which at length subverted entirely the freedom of election, and produced the act 43 Geo 3. ch5 by which the justices for the county were empowered to exercise a coordinate jurisdiction with the Mayor & Corporation of Nottingham within their precincts. – Keeping pace with these changes in the habits & characters of the lower ranks, an increasing population exhibited to every considerate mind a prospect, at no great distance, of complicated distress whenever the manufactured articles should glut the markets. – The policy of our enemies, by prohibiting the introduction of British commodities upon the continent, may have accelerated the crisis; but altho it might possibly have been postponed, it could not have been prevented. – For nothing but the fall of the structure could have demonstrated to the artificers the impossibility of sustaining it at the height to which it had been raised; and, when the crash convinced them of their error, the subsistence of numbers was inevitably overwhelmed by the event.

The check imposed upon the trade of Nottinghamshire was, at first, but partially felt, because the stock on hand was comparatively of little value; but, as the practice of multiplying Frames & Artificers was continued with unabated zeal, long after the demand for them had ceased, the period arrived, when the warehouses were crowded with goods for which no vent could be found: and the Hosiers, sensible of their difficulties, began to devise arrangements for preventing their increase.

In this emergency, if the Hosiers had acquainted the Workmen with the true situation of the trade; if they had retained those who by long services or large families possessed the best title to protection, the young men would have engaged in other employments, or would have entered into the army or navy; – and none of our present disturbances would have occurred. But the workmen had, in the season of prosperity, dictated with insolence to their Masters; and an opportunity for retaliation now appeared, of which the latter indiscreetly & unfeelingly availed themselves.

The first attempt to abate the prices of labor originated, as I have been informed, with Mr. Nun the lace manufacturer above seven years ago. – As the proposal was novel to the workmen they could not reconcile their minds to a reduction upon the compensation allowed for work; but, after many conferences, they tendered an increased rent for their frames to which the agent of Mr. Nunn acceded & all parties were perfectly satisfied. – This agreement however was erroneous in its principle & injurious in its operation, since it assisted in concealing the redundancy of labor in the market, while it encouraged the introduction of independent frames with which the trade was then overstocked, and facilitated the projects of needy adventurers who carried on their business by means of the 'Independents'. About two years since, the consequences were severely felt; and an endeavour was made by many eminent lace manufacturers to reduce the rents of the lace frames to such sums as might entirely preclude all profit upon the machinery & thus annihilate the system of trafficking by the aid of 'Independents'. – This measure gave rise to much contentious discussion; but has now, I am told been carried completely into effect, with advantage, as I conceive, to the trade; but with considerable loss to those, who had ventured to furnish the independent machinery. – This ferment in which both Masters & workmen were involved was followed by a diminution of the prices for work; & by the fabrication of very imperfect article called single pressed lace, which was highly disapproved & publickly reprobated by respectable tradesmen, as disgraceful to the general character of the business.

Meanwhile the Hosiers were pursuing the same object by a different path. – Knowing that the Framework-knitters would be little disposed to endure an abatement of prices which had been sanctioned by uninterrupted usage, about two years ago the Masters determined to change the fashion & figure of the work & to effect their purpose by deducting from the workmans prices more than a proportionate consideration. As soon as one change in the fashion & prices was established another was proposed. – The quality of the manufactured goods was progressively deteriorated; and the Workmen found their utmost industry incapable of securing a livelihood. – Some Masters in addition to these arrangements delivered out only half the usual weekly work to the Artificers, while they claimed the full rent of their frames while the means of employing them was denied.

Under these circumstances representations were urged by the workmen, and the example of many respectable tradesmen, who discharged their supernumary men & continued the remainder in full work, at equitable prices, was urged as a model for imitation. – A meeting of the Hosiers was convened and standard prices were fixed & published in the Newspapers. – But the result was only a fresh source of irritation & disappointment to the Petitioners. When they looked for the operation of the advertisement they were mortified by the galling refusal of their application; while their claims were countenanced by those Masters, who had from the commencement behaved with honor & humanity; and who now saw others enabled to undersell them in the market by petty profits, oppressively extorted from the starving necessities of the poor. – It is not be supposed, that liberal men could behold this surreptitious traffic without indignation & comment. – Neither could their sentiments remain long concealed from the objects of their commiseration. – Pressed with hunger & exasperated by faithless promises of redress, the Framework-knitters denounced vengeance, & their threat has been amply fulfilled. – They began their destructive work last spring by demolishing a few of the frames belonging to those who were most obnoxious - but as this warning did not produce any advances in their favor - they recommenced their outrages in November last, directing their fury against the machinery of every person by whom they conceived themselves to be aggrieved or oppressed. – In one or two instances they have destroyed the property of their best employers, but this has been unintentional. – The general tendency of their system is a proscription against persons & work of a specific description; and their designs have been generally accomplished by an understanding, if not a conspiracy, between the frame breakers & the frame renters, who mutually rejoiced in the event. – The number of frames broken is supposed to exceed 1000; and the value of them may be estimated at £10,000. – By individuals the loss will be severely felt but as far as the general interests of the trade are concerned, it is universally allowed, that the machinery remaining is still abundantly more than sufficient for the market. –

In the commencement of the disturbances three haystacks, belonging to those who had assisted the civil power, were burned; and some threatening letters were sent, but no such crimes have been recently committed: – so that, altho I listened with attention to those, who at first taught me to believe, that the outrages were connected with political views; & that money might have been supplied, thro' secret channels, I now am firmly persuaded from diligent enquiry & vigilant observation that these opinions are not supported by facts. – I ascribe the origin & progress of our present offences solely to internal animosities between the manufacturers themselves, and between the manufacturers & their workmen, acting upon the passions of a necessitous & dissolute class, who had been trained for insubordination by those who are now the objects of their vengeance; and who had been repeatedly told by many of their employers, & by the licentious paper brooded under their patronage, that the sovereignty resided in the people; and that it was their province as well as their duty to avenge their wrongs & to retaliate upon their oppressors.

Even at this juncture the Manufacturers who have endangered the safety of the county by their misconduct, continue spectators of the mischief without having, to my knowledge, done any act as a collective body to subdue the evils or to bring the offenders to punishment. Indeed they seem to be more occupied in murmuring against the executive government & in abusing the magistracy than in vindicating their own proceedings or in recommending any plan for effecting reciprocal conciliation.

Possibly it may be asked how are the Frame-breakers or 'Luddites' supported. – To this I reply, that they are not numerous, that they receive contributions from the people in work; and that there is scarcely a Stockinger who will not give half his victuals or his money to these 'friends of the poor man', as they are styled, who beg in the evening from house to house, exposing to sale the Framework-knitters act, as a protection against the vagrant laws.

Upon a review of the circumstances which have been stated, the means of restoring the public peace and of preventing similar occurrences in future, appear to demand attention.

The Bill now preparing for parliament, if the duties are executed by principals & not by substitutes, with the cooperation of the military force, will, in all probability, enforce good order especially as the distresses & opportunities peculiar to the winter season will soon have ceased.

But if tranquillity is to be permanently established it will be necessary to adopt some plan for preventing the frequent renewal of such alarming conflicts. I am aware of the delicacy attaching to any interference with regulations of trade, yet I beg leave most respectfully to submit for your consideration the expediency of passing an act to prescribe by a regulated table, what could be easily drawn, the rent to be paid for every species of frame used in the lace or stocking trade, which might be so estimated, as not to exceed 7½ per cent upon the prime cost, – and to prohibit any person not supplying a frame with full work from demanding more than half the rent. – The advantages which, I humbly conceive, likely to result from such a measure are these. – It would remove all temptation to overstock the market with machinery by means of the independent frames – It would prevent the speculations of needy adventurers - It would create a closer connection between the manufacturers & the machinery, and render them more circumspect in their conduct from a consciousness that they must by oppression endanger their own property, which, under the present system, in many instances is not the case – It would materially conduce to settle the minds of the workmen if they learned that Parliament was not unmindful of their distress; and, as far as I can judge from the opinion of those to whom I have mentioned the plan it would prove acceptable to the substantial manufacturers. Since the late depreciation of wages is the first that has occurred within the memory of man in the lace & stocking manufactures of this county the poor have been less prepared than those in other districts for the indigent situation to which they are unexpectedly reduced; and may therefore have been incited to the perpetration of more flagrant excesses than would otherwise have prevailed.

   I have now, Sir, to apologize for having so extensively trespassed upon your attention for which the importance of the subject will I trust supply some excuse.

> I have the honour to be, Sir
> your most obedient and very humble servant
> John T. Becher.

Appendix II

LORD BYRON'S MAIDEN SPEECH IN THE
HOUSE OF LORDS, 27 FEBRUARY 1812

My Lords,

The subject now submitted to your Lordships for the first time, though new to the House, is by no means new to the country. I believe it had occupied the serious thoughts of all descriptions of persons, long before its introduction to the notice of that legislature, whose interference alone could be of real service. As a person in some degree connected with the suffering county, though a stranger not only to this House in general, but to almost every individual whose attention I presume to solicit, I must claim some portion of your Lordships' indulgence, whilst I offer a few observations on a question in which I confess myself deeply interested.

To enter into detail of the riots would be superfluous: the House is already aware that every outrage short of actual bloodshed has been perpetrated, and that the proprietors of the frames obnoxious to the rioters, and all persons supposed to be connected with them, have been liable to insult and violence. During the short time I recently passed into Nottinghamshire, not twelve hours elapsed without some fresh act of violence; and on the day I left the county I was informed that forty frames had been broken the preceding evening, as usual, without resistance and without detection.

Such was then the state of that county, and such I have reason to believe it to be at this moment. But whilst these outrages must be admitted to exist to an alarming extent, it cannot be denied that they have arisen from circumstances of the most unparalleled distress: the perseverance of these miserable men in their proceedings tends to prove that nothing but absolute want could have driven a large, and once honest and industrious, body of the people, into the commission of excesses so hazardous to themselves, their families, and the community. At the time to which I allude, the town and county were burdened with large detachments of the military; the police was in motion, the magistrates assembled; yet all the movements, civil and military, had led to nothing. Not a single instance had occurred of the apprehension of any real delinquent actually taken in the fact, against whom there existed legal evidence sufficient for conviction. But the police, however useless, were by no means idle: several notorious delinquents had been detected, – men, liable to conviction, on the clearest evidence, of the capital crime of poverty; men, who had been nefariously guilty of lawfully begetting several children, whom, thanks to the times! they were unable to maintain. Considerable injury has been done to the proprietors of the improved frames. These machines were to them an advantage, inasmuch as they superseded the necessity of employing a number of workmen, who were left in consequence to starve. By the adoption of one species of frame in particular, one man performed the work of many, and the superfluous labourers were thrown out of employment. Yet it is to be observed, that the work thus executed was inferior in quality; not marketable at home, and merely hurried over with a view to exportation. It was called, in the cant of the trade, by the name of 'Spider-work'. The rejected workmen, in the blindness of their ignorance, instead of rejoicing at these improvements in arts so beneficial to mankind, conceived themselves to be sacrificed to improvements in mechanism. In the foolishness of their hearts they imagined that the maintenance and well-doing of the industrious poor were objects of greater consequence than the enrichment of a few individuals by any improvement, in the implements of trade, which threw the workmen out of employment, and rendered the labourer unworthy of his hire. And it must be confessed that although the adoption of the enlarged machinery in that state of our commerce which the country once boasted might have been beneficial to the master without being detrimental to the servant; yet, in the present situation of our manufactures, rotting in warehouses, without a prospect of exportation, with the demand for work and workmen equally diminished, frames of this description tend materially to aggravate the distress and discontent of the disappointed sufferers. But the real cause of these distresses and consequent disturbances lies deeper. When we are told that these men are leagued together not only for the destruction of their own comfort, but of their very means of subsistence, can we forget that it is the bitter policy, the destructive warfare of the last eighteen years, which has destroyed their comfort, your comfort, all men's comfort? that policy, which, originating with 'great statesmen now no more', has survived the dead to become a curse on the living, unto the third and fourth generation! These men never destroyed their looms till they were become useless, till they were become actual impediments to their exertions in obtaining their daily bread. Can you, then, wonder that in times like these, when bankruptcy, convicted fraud, and imputed felony are found in a station not far beneath that of your Lordships, the lowest, though once most useful portion of the people, should forget their duty in their distress, and become only less guilty than one of their representatives? But while the exalted offender can find means to baffle the law, new capital punishments must be devised, new snares of death must be spread for the wretched mechanic, who is famished into guilt. These men were willing to dig, but the spade was in other hands: they were not ashamed to beg, but there was none to relieve them; their own means of subsistence were cut off, all other employments pre-occupied; and their excesses, however to be deplored and condemned, can hardly be subject of surprise.

It has been stated that the persons in the temporary possession of frames connive at their destruction; if this be proved upon inquiry, it were necessary that such material accessories to the crime should be principals in the punishment. But I did hope, that any measure proposed by his Majesty's government for your Lordships' decision, would have had conciliation for its basis; or, if that were hopeless, that some previous inquiry, some deliberation, would have been deemed requisite; not that we should have been called at once, without examination and without cause to pass sentences by wholesale, and sign death-warrants blindfold. But, admitting that these men had no cause of complaint; that the grievances of them and their employers were alike groundless; that they deserved the worst; – what inefficiency, what imbecility has been evinced in the method chosen to reduce them! Why were the military called out to be made a mockery of, if they were to be called out at all? As far as the difference of seasons would permit, they have merely parodied the summer campaign of Major Sturgeon; and, indeed, the whole proceedings, civil and military, seemed on the model of those of the mayor and corporation of Garratt. – Such marchings and counter-marchings! – from Nottingham to Bullwell, from Bullwell to Banford, from Banford to Mansfield! And when at length the detachments arrived at their destinations, in all 'the pride, pomp, and circumstance of glorious war', they came just in time to witness the mischief which had been done, and ascertain the escape of the perpetrators, to collect the 'spolia opima' in the fragments of broken frames, and return to their quarters amidst the derision of old women, and the hootings of children. Now, though, in a free country, it were to be wished that our military should never be too formidable, at least to ourselves, I cannot see the policy of placing them in situations where they can only be made ridiculous. As the sword is the worst argument that can be used, so should it be the last. In this instance it has been the first; but providentially as yet only in the scabbard. The present measure will, indeed, pluck it from the sheath; yet had proper meetings been held in the earlier stages of these riots, had the grievances of these men and their masters (for they also had their grievances) been fairly weighed and justly examined, I do think that means might have been devised to restore these workmen to their avocations, and tranquillity to the county . . . At present the county suffers from the double infliction of an idle military and a starving population. In what state of apathy have we been plunged so long, that now for the first time the House has been officially apprised of these disturbances? All this has been transacting within a hundred and thirty miles of London; and yet we, 'good easy men', have 'deemed full sure our greatness was a-ripening', and have sat down to enjoy our foreign triumphs in the midst of domestic calamity. But all the cities you have taken, all the armies which have retreated before your leaders, are but paltry subjects of self-congratulation, if your land divides against itself, and your dragoons and your executioners must be let loose against your fellow-citizens. – You call these men a mob, desperate, dangerous and ignorant; and seem to think that the only way to quiet the 'Bellua multorem capitum' is to lop off a few of its superfluous heads. But even a mob may be better reduced to reason by a mixture of conciliation and firmness, than by additional irritation and redoubled penalties. Are we aware of our obligations to a mob? It is the mob that labour in your fields and serve in your houses, – that man your navy, and recruit your army, – that have enabled you to defy all the world, and can also defy you when neglect and calamity have driven them to despair! You may call the people a mob; but do not forget that a mob too often speaks the sentiments of the people. And here I must remark, with what alacrity you are accustomed to fly to the succour of your distressed allies, leaving the distressed of your own country to the care of Providence or – the parish. When the Portuguese suffered under the retreat of the French, every arm was stretched out, every hand was opened, from the rich man's largesse to the widow's mite, all was bestowed, to enable them to rebuild their villages and replenish their granaries. And at this moment, when thousands of misguided but most unfortunate fellow-countrymen are struggling with the extremes of hardships and hunger, as your charity began abroad it should end at home. A much less sum, a tithe of the bounty bestowed on Portugal, even if those men (which I cannot admit without inquiry) could not have been restored to their employments, would have rendered unnecessary the tender mercies of the bayonet and the gibbet. But doubtless our friends have too many foreign claims to admit a prospect of domestic relief; though never did such objects demand it. I have traversed the seat of war in the Peninsula, I have been in some of the most oppressed provinces of Turkey; but never under the most despotic of infidel governments did I behold such squalid wretchedness as I have seen since my return in the very heart of a Christian country. And what are your remedies? After months of inaction, and months of action worse than inactivity, at length comes forth the grand specific, the never-failing nostrum of all state physicians, from the days of Draco to the present time. After feeling the pulse and shaking the head over the patients, prescribing the usual course of warm water and bleeding, - the warm water of your mawkish police, and the lancets of your military, – these convulsions must terminate in death, the sure consummation of the prescriptions of all political Sangrados. Setting aside the palpable injustice and the certain inefficiency of the Bill, are there not capital punishments sufficient in your statutes? Is there not blood enough upon your penal code, that more must be poured forth to ascend to Heaven and testify against you? How will you carry the Bill into effect? Can you commit a whole country to their own prisons? Will you erect a gibbet in every field, and hang up men like scarecrows? or will you proceed (as you must to bring this measure into effect) by decimation? Place the country under martial law? depopulate and lay waste all around you? and restore Sherwood Forest as an acceptable gift to the crown, in its former condition of a royal chase and an asylum for outlaws? Are these the remedies for a starving and desperate populace? Will the famished wretch who has braved your bayonets be appalled by your gibbets? When death is a relief, and the only relief it appears that you will afford him, will he be dragooned into tranquillity? Will that which could not be effected by your grenadiers be accomplished by your executioners? If you proceed by the forms of law, where is your evidence? Those who have refused to impeach their accomplices when transportation only was the punishment, will hardly be tempted to witness against them when death is the penalty. With all due deference to the noble lords opposite, I think a little investigation, some previous inquiry, would induce even them to change their purpose. That most favourable state measure, so marvellously efficacious in many and recent instances, temporising, would not be without its advantages in this. When a proposal is made to emancipate or relieve, you hesitate, you deliberate for years, you temporise and tamper with the minds of men; but a death-bill must be passed off-hand, without a thought of the consequences. Sure I am, from what I have heard, and from what I have seen, that to pass the Bill under all the existing circumstances, without inquiry, without deliberation, would only be to add injustice to irritation, and barbarity to neglect. The framers of such a bill must be content to inherit the honours of that Athenian law-giver whose edicts were said to be written not in ink but in blood. But suppose it passed; suppose one of these men, as I have seen them, – meagre with famine, sullen with despair, careless of a life which your Lordships are perhaps about to value at something less than the price of a stocking-frame; – suppose this man surrounded by the children for whom he is unable to procure bread at the hazard of his existence, about to be torn forever from a family which he lately supported in peaceful industry, and which it is not his fault that he can no longer so support; – suppose this man – and there are ten thousand such from whom you may select your victims – dragged into court, to be tried for this new offence, by this new law; still, there are two things wanting to convict and condemn him; and these are, in my opinion, twelve butchers for a jury, and a Jeffreys for a judge!

Appendix III

PROCLAMATION BY HIS ROYAL HIGHNESS THE PRINCE OF WALES, REGENT OF THE UNITED KINGDOM OF GREAT BRITAIN AND IRELAND, IN THE NAME AND ON BEHALF OF HIS MAJESTY

WHEREAS it hath been represented unto us, that divers unfortunate and misguided persons, who have been induced by the artifices of wicked and designing men to take some oath or engagement, contrary to the Acts of Parliament in that behalf made in the 37th and 52nd years of His Majesty's reign, or one of those acts, or to steal ammunition, fire arms, and other offensive weapons, for the purpose of committing acts of violence and outrage against the persons and property of His Majesty's peaceable and faithful subjects, and who are not yet charged with such their offences, may be willing and desirous to make a disclosure or confession of such their offences, and to take the oath of allegiance to His Majesty, upon receiving an assurance of His Majesty's most gracious pardon for such their offences;

We, therefore, acting in the name and on the behalf of His Majesty, being willing to give such assurance upon such conditions as are hereinafter mentioned, and earnestly hoping that the example of the just and necessary punishments which have been inflicted in the counties of Lancaster, Chester, and York, upon certain offenders lately tried and convicted in those counties, may have the salutary effect of deterring all persons from following the example of their crimes by a renewal of the like atrocities, have thought fit, by and with the advice of His Majesty's privy council, to issue this proclamation; and as an encouragement and inducement to His Majesty's misguided subjects to relinquish all disorderly practices, and return to their due and faithful allegiance to His Majesty, we do hereby, acting in the name and on the behalf of His Majesty, promise and declare, that every person, not having been charged with any of the offences hereinbefore mentioned, who shall, previous to the first day of March next ensuing, appear before some justice of the peace or magistrate, and declare his offence, and the oath or engagement by him taken, and when and where the same was taken, and in what manner, or the ammunition, fire arms, or other offensive weapons by him stolen, and when, where and from whom the same were stolen, and the place where the same were deposited; and also, according to the best of his knowledge and belief, the place where the same may be found; and who shall, at the same time, take before such justice of the peace or magistrate, the oath of allegiance to His Majesty, shall receive His Majesty's most gracious pardon for the said offence; and that no confession so made by any such person shall be given in evidence against the person making the same in any court, or in any case whatever.

Given at the Court at Carlton House the 18th of January, 1813, in the 53rd year of His Majesty's reign.

GOD SAVE THE KING

Notes

Preface

1. *Nottingham Review*, 20 December 1811.
2. Geoffrey of Monmouth: *Histories of the Kings of Britain*, tr. Sebastian Evans (Dent, Everyman's Library edn, 1928), p. 54.
3. *The Anglo-Saxon Chronicle*, ed. & tr. G.N. Garmonsway (Dent, Everyman's Library edn, 1975), pp. 60, 61.

Introduction

1. Quoted in A. Aspinall: *The Early English Trade Unions. Documents from the Home Office Papers in the Public Record Office* (Batchworth Press, 1949), p. xiii.
2. F.O. Darvall: *Popular Disturbances and Public Order in Regency England* (Oxford University Press, 1969), p. 19.
3. Ida Macalpine & Richard Hunter: *George III and the Mad Business* (Allen Lane, 1969), p. 165.
4. Brian Bailey: *The Resurrection Men* (Macdonald, 1991), p. 58 *et seq.*
5. Quoted in H.C. Darby (ed.): *A New Historical Geography of England after 1600* (Cambridge University Press, 1976), p. 140.
6. Malcolm I. Thomis: *The Luddites: Machine-Breaking in Regency England* (David & Charles, 1970), p. 45.

1. The Midland Framework-knitters

1. Daniel Defoe: *A Tour through the Whole Island of Great Britain* (Penguin edn, 1971), p. 408.
2. G.H. Dury: *The East Midlands and the Peak* (Nelson, 1963), p. 255.
3. Thomas Pennant: *A Tour in Wales* (Hughes, 1778–83), vol. II, pp. 76–7.
4. Arthur Raistrick: *The Pennine Dales* (Eyre Methuen, 1968), p. 119.

5. Joseph Budworth: *A Fortnight's Ramble to the Lakes* (3rd edn, London, 1810), p. 39.
6. Defoe: *Tour*, p. 513.
7. *Ibid.*, p. 214.
8. F.A. Wells: *The British Hosiery and Knitwear Industry: Its History and Organisation* (David & Charles, 1972), p. 16.
9. William Felkin: *History of the Machine-Wrought Hosiery and Lace Manufacture* (David & Charles edn, 1967), p. 17.
10. Lee's authorship of the knitting frame has not been proven beyond all reasonable doubt, but is now generally accepted by historians of the industry. Felkin's *History* discusses the question at length (Chapter III).
11. *Ibid.*, p. 51.
12. Wells: *British Hosiery and Knitwear Industry*, p. 220.
13. William Gardiner: *Music and Friends* (Longman, Orme, Brown, & Longman, 1838), vol. I, pp. 43–4.
14. Colin Ellis: *History in Leicester* (City of Leicester Publicity Dept, 2nd edn, 1969), p. 92.
15. Felkin: *History*, chapter XIV.
16. Dury: *East Midlands*, p. 255.
17. Felkin: *History*, pp. 437–8.
18. Wells: *British Hosiery and Knitwear Industry*, p. 68.
19. *Leicester and Nottingham Journal*, 7 March 1778.
20. J.L. & Barbara Hammond: *The Skilled Labourer* (Longman, 1979 edn), p. 182.
21. Felkin: *History*, p. 435.
22. *Ibid.*, p. 436.
23. J. Stevenson: *Popular Disturbances in England, 1700–1870* (Longman, 1979), pp. 92–4.
24. *Leicester Journal*, 12 September 1800.

25. M. Dorothy George: *London Life in the Eighteenth Century* (Penguin edn, 1966), p. 188.
26. Stevenson: *Popular Disturbances*, p. 119.
27. Felkin: *History*, pp. 116–7, 228–9.
28. Quoted in Ellis: *History in Leicester*, p. 98.
29. *London Gazette*, 1799, p. 507.
30. Quoted in E.P. Thompson: *The Making of the English Working Class* (Penguin edn, 1991) p. 574.
31. Hammond: *Skilled Labourer*, pp. 137–9.
32. Beckett to Fitzwilliam, 28 January 1803, quoted in Adrian Randall: *Before the Luddites: custom, community and machinery in the English woollen industry, 1776–1809* (Cambridge University Press, 1991), p. 144.
33. Hammond: *Skilled Labourer*, p. 143.
34. Select Committee on the State of the Woollen Manufacture (House of Commons, 1806), pp. 308 and 355; Randall: *Before the Luddites*, pp. 131–8 and 173.

2. The Advent and Escalation of Luddism

1. *Nottingham Journal*, 20 and 23 March and 20 April 1811.
2. E.J. Hobsbawm: *Labouring Men: Studies in the History of Labour* (Weidenfeld & Nicolson, 1964), p. 13.
3. Darvall: *Popular Disturbances*, p. 67.
4. A. Temple Patterson: *Radical Leicester* (University College, Leicester, 1954), pp. 52 and 58–9.
5. Darvall: *Popular Disturbances*, p. 75.
6. Quoted in Thompson: *English Working Class*, p. 607.
7. *Nottingham Review*, 9 November 1811.
8. *Nottingham Journal*, 16 November 1811; HO 42/119.
9. Felkin: *History*, p. 232.
10. HO 42/117.
11. HO 42/119. 'This letter cannot be answered' a Home Office official wrote on the document.
12. HO 42/117.
13. *Ibid.*
14. *Nottingham Journal*, 30 November 1811.
15. HO 42/117.
16. HO 42/118.
17. *Ibid.* (Lord Middleton to Home Office, 12 December 1811).
18. HO 42/118.
19. *Leeds Intelligencer*, 20 January 1812.
20. HO 40.1/4.
21. *Leeds Mercury*, 28 December 1811.
22. Parliamentary Debates, XXI, 808 *et seq.*, 14 February 1812.
23. Richard Holmes: *Shelley: The Pursuit* (Penguin edn, 1987), p. 98.
24. C. Southey (ed): *Life and Correspondence of Robert Southey* (London, 1848–50), vol. III, pp. 326–7.
25. HO 42/118 (William Milnes to Sir Joseph Banks, 22 December 1811), quoted in Aspinall: *Early English Trade Unions*, p. 118.
26. HO 42/118.
27. HO 42/117.
28. *Leeds Mercury*, 25 January 1812.
29. *Manchester Exchange Herald*, 21 April 1812.
30. George Walker: *The Costume of Yorkshire in 1814* (Richard Jackson, 1885 edn), pp. 19–20.
31. HO 42/66 (Earl Fitzwilliam to Lord Pelham, 27 September 1802), quoted in Aspinall: *Early English Trade Unions*, p. 63.
32. Elizabeth Gaskell: *The Life of Charlotte Brontë* (Dent, Everyman's Library edn, 1946), pp. 6–7.
33. HO 42/66, quoted in Aspinall: *Early English Trade Unions*, p. 64.
34. Thomis: *The Luddites*, pp. 177–86.
35. *Nottingham Review*, 7 February 1812; *Leeds Mercury*, 15 February 1812.
36. HO 42/119.
37. *Leeds Mercury*, 15 February 1812.
38. HO 42/120.
39. Parliamentary Debates, XXI, 808 *et seq.*, 14 February 1812.
40. *Leeds Mercury*, 15 February 1812.
41. *Leeds Mercury*, 28 January 1811.
42. *The Times*, 1 February 1812.
43. Frank Peel: *Risings of the Luddites, Chartists and Plug-drawers* (Cass edn, 1968), p. 9.
44. Thompson: *English Working Class*, p. 12.
45. *Ibid.*, p. 604.
46. Darvall: *Popular Disturbance*, p. 174.
47. HO 42/119.

3. Local Responses and Government Reactions

1. HO 42/119.
2. Darvall, *Popular Disturbances*, p. 75.
3. E. Lipson: *History of the Woollen and Worsted Industries* (A. & C. Black, 1921), p. 181.
4. HO 42/117.
5. HO 42/121.
6. HO 42/120, letter dated 11 February 1812 to unknown correspondent, quoted in Aspinall: *Early English Trade Unions*, p. 120.
7. Darvall: *Popular Disturbances*, p. 75.
8. Thompson: *English Working Class*, p. 605.
9. *Ibid.*, p. 630.
10. See, for instance, Aspinall: *Early English Trade Unions*, pp. 95n, 98, 99, 121.
11. HO 42/118. Letters from Duke of Newcastle and Revd R. Hardy, JP, dated 9 and 19 December respectively.
12. HO 42/127.
13. Radcliffe MSS, 126/50.
14. HO 42/126; Radcliffe MSS; A. Brooke & L. Kipling: *Liberty or Death: Radicals, Republicans and Luddites* (Huddersfield, 1993), pp. 30–1.
15. HO 42/120.
16. Quoted in Thomis: *The Luddites*, p. 143.
17. HO 42/120.
18. F.K. Donnelly & J.L. Baxter, 'Sheffield and the English revolutionary tradition, 1790–1820', in S. Pollard & C. Holmes (eds): *Essays in the Economic and Social History of South Yorkshire* (South Yorkshire County Council, 1976), pp. 102–4.
19. HO 42/120.
20. HO 42/118 (William Nunn to Home Office, 6 December 1811).
21. HO 42/121.
22. Robert Reid: *Land of Lost Content* (Heinemann, 1986), p. 92.
23. Darvall: *Popular Disturbances*, p. 63.
24. *Nottingham Journal*, 10 December 1811.
25. *Leeds Mercury*, 16 May 1812.
26. HO 42/119.
27. Parliamentary Debates, XXI, 808 *et seq.*, 14, 17, 18 and 20 February 1812.
28. Peter Gunn (ed.): Byron: *Selected Prose* (Penguin, 1972), pp. 104–6.
29. *Ibid.*, pp. 113-4; Annual Register, 1812, pp 35-8.
30. HO 42/123.
31. *Nottingham Review*, 21 February 1812.
32. *Leeds Mercury*, 29 February 1812; Brooke & Kipling: *Liberty or Death*, p. 17.
33. *Leeds Mercury*, 29 February 1812.
34. Darvall: *Popular Disturbances*, p. 62.
35. Henry Heginbotham: *Stockport: Ancient and Modern* (Sampson Low, Marston, Searle & Rivington, 1882), pp. 74–5.
36. Radcliffe MSS, 126/26.
37. *Ibid.*, 126/19.
38. *Ibid.*, 126/24.
39. Felkin says (*op cit.*, p. 235) that four men were sentenced to fourteen years and three to seven years. Darvall (*op cit.*, p. 86) says that five men were sentenced to fourteen years and two to five years. R.J. White: *Waterloo to Peterloo* (Penguin edn, 1968) says (p. 124) that seven were sentenced to transportation for life. None of these accounts tallies with Mr Justice Bayley's own report to the Home Office, dated 18 March, in HO 42/121.
40. Radcliffe MSS, 126/96.
41. HO 42/122.
42. HO 42/123; Hammond: *Skilled Labourer*, p. 219.
43. HO 40/11. Quoted in full in R. Offor, 'The Papers of Benjamin Gott in the Library of the University of Leeds' in W.B. Crump (ed.): *The Leeds Woollen Industry, 1780–1820* (Thoresby Society, 1931), pp. 229–30.
44. *Ibid.*, p. 229.
45. Radcliffe MSS, 126/27.
46. *Leeds Mercury*, 28 March 1812.
47. *Ibid.*, 11 April 1812.

4. Yorkshire Climax

1. Peel: *Risings*, p. 56.
2. Gaskell: *Life of Charlotte Brontë*, p. 70.
3. My account of the attack on Rawfolds Mill is based on reports in the *Leeds Mercury*, 18 April 1812; the *Leeds Intelligencer*, 20 April 1812; and evidence given at the trial in January 1813 of eight men accused of participation in

the raid. See E. Baines: *Proceedings under the Special Commission at York* (Leeds, 1813).

4. *Leeds Mercury*, 18 April 1812.

5. *Ibid.*

6. HO 40.1/4.

7. HO 42/130.

8. HO 40/18, Houldsworth to Robert Peel, 19 April 1823, quoted in Aspinall: *Early English Trade Unions*, p. 365.

9. Radcliffe MSS, 126/32.

10. Baines: *Proceedings*, p. 12.

11. Radcliffe MSS, 126/26.

12. *Leeds Mercury*, 2 May 1812.

13. HO 42/123.

14. HO 40.1/1 and HO 40.1/7.

15. Thompson: *English Working Class*, pp. 588–9.

16. *Nottingham Journal*, 2 May 1812; *The Times*, 3 May 1812; HO 42/123.

17. HO 42/123.

18. Radcliffe MSS, 126/41.

19. *Leeds Mercury*, 20 June 1812.

20. Radcliffe MSS, 126/46.

21. *Leeds Mercury*, 16 May 1812.

22. *The Times*, 9 July 1812.

23. Ezekiel, 21:26.

24. HO 42/125, 129; Hammond: *Skilled Labourer*, p. 257.

25. Quoted in E.P. Greenleaf & J.A. Hargreaves: *The Luddites of West Yorkshire* (Kirklees Leisure Services, 1986) p. 27.

26. HO 42/129; Peel: *Risings*, pp. 112–13.

5. Rumour and Repression

1. *Leeds Mercury*, 25 April 1812.

2. HO 40/1.

3. *Leeds Mercury*, 25 April 1812.

4. HO 42/122.

5. Hammond: *Skilled Labourer*, p. 229.

6. *Leeds Mercury*, 2 May 1812.

7. State Trials, XXXI, 1070.

8. HO 42/123.

9. *Ibid.*, and HO 40.1/2.

10. Quoted in Peel: *Risings*, p. 159.

11. HO 42/120.

12. Radcliffe MSS, 126/75.

13. Quoted in Offor, 'Papers of Benjamin Gott', in Crump: *Leeds Woollen Industry*, pp. 230–1.

14. Hammond: *Skilled Labourer*, pp. 224–5.

15. Thomis: *The Luddites*, p. 83; HO 40.1/1.

16. HO 42/123.

17. *The Times*, 1 July 1812.

18. *Manchester Mercury*, 26 May, 9 and 16 June 1812; Hammond: *Skilled Labourer*, pp. 238–40.

19. Thomis: *The Luddites*, p. 110.

20. *The Times*, 11 July 1812.

21. HO 42/121 and 123; Hammond: *Skilled Labourer*, pp. 247 and 254.

22. Parliamentary Debates, XXIII, 986 *et seq.*, 10 July 1812.

23. HO 42/123.

24. HO 42/124.

25. *Ibid.*

26. HO 42/122.

27. Francis Raynes: *An Appeal to the Public* (A. Stark, 1817), pp. 29–31.

28. *Ibid.*, pp. 40–1.

29. Parliamentary Debates, XXI, 1167.

30. Annual Register, 1812, pp. 385–93.

31. *Ibid.*

32. Raynes: *Appeal to the Public*, pp. 53–6.

33. Hammond: *Skilled Labourer*, pp. 241–3.

34. HO 42/126.

35. *Ibid.* and 130.

36. Thompson: *English Working Class*, p. 529.

37. HO 40/1.

38. Raynes: *Appeal to the Public*, pp. 91-2.

39. Fitzwilliam MSS, quoted in Randall: *Before the Luddites*, p. 269. (Letter from Mayor of Leeds to Earl Fitzwilliam, 16 August 1802.)

40. Broadside in Manchester Central Library, Local Studies Unit, f1812/26.

6. Gravenor Henson and the Framework-knitters' Union

1. See Roy A. Church & S.D. Chapman: 'Gravener Henson and the Making of the English Working Class' in E.L. Jones & G.E. Mingay (eds): *Land, Labour and Population in the Industrial Revolution* (Edward Arnold, 1967); also Stanley D. Chapman, Introduction to G. Henson: *The Civil, Political and Mechanical History of the Framework-Knitters* (David & Charles edn, 1970).

2. *Nottingham Review*, 1 June 1834.

3. *Records of the Borough of Nottingham*, vol. VIII, 1800–1835, eds. Duncan Gray and Violet W. Walker (Thos. Forman, 1952), pp. 75–6.

4. *Ibid.*, p. 141.

5. *Ibid.*, pp. 141–2. The reference to beans is an allusion to the old nickname, 'bean-belly Leicestershire'. Beans used to form part of the staple diet in the county in times of poverty. 'Shake a Leicestershire yeoman by the collar,' it was said, 'and you will hear the beans rattle in his belly.'

6. *Ibid.*, p. 143.

7. *Ibid.*, pp. 146–7.

8. *Ibid.*

9. *Report and Minutes of Evidence from the Select Committee on Petitions from the Framework-Knitters* (House of Commons, 1812), pp 3 and 9.

10. *Records of the Borough of Nottingham*, p. 151.

11. *Ibid.*, pp. 151–2.

12. *Ibid.*, p. 154.

13. *Ibid.*, p. 153.

14. *Ibid.*, p. 155.

15. *Ibid.*

16. *Ibid.*, pp. 156–7.

17. *Ibid.*

18. *Ibid.*, p. 159.

19. *Ibid.*, p. 162.

20. *Ibid.*

21. Felkin: *History*, p. 451.

12. *An Historical Account of the Luddites of 1811, 1812, and 1813, with Report of Their Trials at York Castle* (Cowgill, 1862 edn), p. 20.

13. Leman Thomas Rede: *York Castle in the Nineteenth Century* (J. Saunders, 1831), p. 477.

14. Kipling & Hall: *On the trail of the Luddites*, p.50; Brooke & Kipling: *Liberty or Death*, p. 28.

15. Raynes: *Appeal to the Public*, pp. 124–6.

16. Rede: *York Castle in the Nineteenth Century*, p. 463.

17. HO 42/128; *Leeds Mercury*, 2 May 1812.

18. Peel: *Risings*, pp. 277–8.

19. D.F.E. Sykes, a Huddersfield solicitor, who wrote a novel about Walker entitled *Ben O'Bills, the Luddite*, said that Walker died a pauper and that his body was exhumed by resurrection men and sold for dissection.

20. Holmes: *Shelley*, p. 185.

21. Radcliffe MSS, 126/18.

22. HO 42/132.

23. Thompson: *English Working Class*, p. 604.

24. Brooke & Kipling: *Liberty or Death*, p. 29.

25. Radcliffe MSS, 126/105, 106, 109.

26. *Ibid.*, 126/136.

27. See Raynes: *Appeal to the Public*, especially pp. 138–84.

28. See John D. Gay: *The Geography of Religion in England* (Duckworth, 1971), pp. 144–67.

29. Peel: *Risings*, p. 267.

30. Printed leaflet in Manchester Central Library, Local Studies Unit, F1812/23B.

7. Trials and Tribulations

1. HO 40.2/3.

2. Radcliffe MSS, 126/92.

3. *Leeds Mercury*, 5 December 1812.

4. *The Times*, 3 December 1812.

5. Brooke & Kipling: *Liberty or Death*, p. 39.

6. HO 42/123.

7. HO 40.2/4 and 2/8.

8. Brooke & Kipling: *Liberty or Death*, p. 99.

9. HO 42/132; L. Kipling & N. Hall: *On the trail of the Luddites* (Pennine Heritage Network, 1982) p. 49.

10. See Brooke & Kipling: *Liberty or Death*, pp. 49 and 96.

11. *Ibid.*, p. 39.

8. Midland Dénouement

1. HO 42/137.

2. HO 42/138.

3. *Ibid.*

4. *Ibid.*

5. *Ibid.*

6. HO 42/139.

7. *Ibid.*

8. HO 42/138.

9. *Ibid.*

10. HO 42/139.

11. Patterson: *Radical Leicester*, p. 62.

12. Felkin: *History*, p. 237.

13. Darvall: *Popular Disturbances*, p. 155.

14. Brooke & Kipling: *Liberty or Death*, p. 51.

15. Hammond: *Skilled Labourer*, p. 194.

16. Wells: *The British Hosiery and Knitwear Industry*, pp. 125–6 and 129.

17. Robert Hall: *An Appeal to the Public on the subject of the Framework-Knitters' Fund* (Thomas Combe, 4th edn, 1821), pp. 15–16.

18. Quoted in J.B.Firth: *Highways and Byways of Leicestershire* (S.R. Publishers edn, 1969), p. 90.

19. Heginbotham: *Stockport: Ancient and Modern*, vol. I, p. 76.

20. Felkin: *History*, p. 202.

21. My account of the raid on Heathcoat's factory is based on the confession of John Blackburn, HO 40/3, and Felkin: *History*, pp. 238–41.

22. Felkin: *History*, p. 242.

23. HO 42/152.

24. HO 42/155.

25. Thompson: *English Working Class*, p. 627.

26. HO 40/3.

27. *Ibid.*

28. Gardiner: *Music and Friends*, vol. II, p. 575(n).

29. *Leicester Journal*, 4 April 1817; Patterson: *Radical Leicester*, p. 114.

30. Hobsbawm: *Labouring Men*, p. 7.

31. Felkin: *History*, p. 238.

32. HO 40/3.

33. Rede: *York Castle in the Nineteenth Century*, pp. 550–1.

34. HO 42/120.

35. HO 42/119.

36. See Thomis: *The Luddites*, pp. 177–86; Darvall: *Popular Disturbances*, pp 209–10.

37. HO 42/178.

9. The Aftermath

1. HO 42/163.

2. *Records of the Borough of Nottingham*, p. 223.

3. *Nottingham Journal*, 19 April 1817.

4. Quoted by Church and Chapman, 'Gravener Henson', in Jones & Mingay: *Land, Labour and Population*, p. 139.

5. HO 42/166.

6. *Nottingham Journal*, 19 April 1817.

7. *Nottingham Review*, 23 January 1818.

8. HO 42/160.

9. HO 42.168/9. (C.G. Mundy to Home Office, 22 July and 13 August 1817.)

10. Hammond: *Skilled Labourer*, p. 201.

11. Parliamentary Debates, XXXV, 1817, p. 322; Randall: *Before the Luddites*, p. 230.

12. White: *Waterloo to Peterloo*, p. 175.

13. *Leeds Mercury*, 19 July 1817.

14. State Trials, XXXII.

15. Peel: *Risings*, p. 91.

16. Brooke & Kipling: *Liberty or Death*, pp. 55–66.

17. HO 42/178.

18. HO 42/194, H. Enfield to Viscount Sidmouth, 1 & 2 September 1819, quoted in Aspinall: *Early English Trade Unions*, pp. 327–8. George Coldham, who had been Nottingham's town clerk for twenty years, was killed in an accident at Brighton on 18 September 1815. (*Records of the Borough of Nottingham*, p. 195.)

19. HO 42/193.

20. *Records of the Borough of Nottingham*, p. 252.

21. Lipson: *History of the Woollen and Worsted Industries*, p. 181.

22. *Morning Chronicle*, 26 November 1849.

23. Darby: *A New Historical Geography*, pp. 192–3.

24. Hall: *Appeal to the Public*, p. 13.

25. Robert Hall: *A Reply to the Principal Objections advanced by Cobbett and others against the Framework-Knitters' Friendly Relief Society* (T. Combe, 1821), pp. 25–6.

26. *Ibid.*, pp. 27–8.

27. William Booth: *In Darkest England and the Way Out* (London, Salvation Army, n.d.), Preface.

28. Thomas Cooper: *The Life of Thomas Cooper. Written by Himself*, 1872 (Leicester University Press edn, 1971), pp. 137–9.

29. *Report of the Commissioner appointed to inquire into the Condition of the Framework-Knitters* (HMSO, 1845), Minutes of Evidence, Pt I, 5548–60.

30. *Ibid.*, 5628–47.

31. Cooper: *Life*, p. 140.

32. *Report into the Condition of the Framework-Knitters*, Pt II, 4779–86.

33. *Ibid.*, Pt I, 4783–4813.

34. *Ibid.*, Pt II, 3440–61.
35. P. Mathias: *The First Industrial Nation: An Economic History of Britain* (Methuen, 1969), p. 364.
36. Dury: *The East Midlands and the Peak*, pp. 159–63.

10. Hidden Agenda?

1. Bailey: *Resurrection Men*, pp. 62–3.
2. *Records of the Borough of Nottingham*, pp. 242 and 273.
3. *Ibid.*, p. 389.
4. Thompson: *English Working Class*, p. 648.
5. HO 42/120.

6. See, for instance, Thompson: *English Working Class*, p. 608.
7. Darvall: *Popular Disturbances*, p. 175.
8. HO 42/66, quoted in Aspinall: *Early English Trade Unions*, p. 49.
9. Thompson: *English Working Class*, p. 618.
10. George Rudé: *The Crowd in History* (Lawrence & Wishart edn, 1981), p. 90.
11. Robert Thompson: *The Pelican History of Psychology* (Penguin, 1968), p. 376.
12. Ernest Jones: *Sigmund Freud, Life and Work* (Hogarth Press, 1953–7), vol. III, p. 362.
13. Thompson: *English Working Class*, p. 12.

Bibliography

Official and Government Documents
Annual Register for 1812
Home Office papers in the Public Record Office
Parliamentary Debates (Hansard)
Report of the Committee on the State of the Woollen Manufacture in England (House of Commons, 1806).
Report of the Select Committee appointed to consider Petitions from the Framework-Knitters (House of Commons, 1812).
Report of the Commissioner appointed to inquire into the Condition of the Framework-Knitters (HMSO, 1845).
State Trials

Manuscripts
The Radcliffe Papers, Leeds City Archives

Newspapers and Journals
Cobbett's Weekly Register
Leeds Mercury
Leeds Intelligencer
Leicester Journal
Leicester and Nottingham Journal
London Gazette
Manchester Exchange Herald
Manchester Mercury
Morning Chronicle
Nottingham Journal
Nottingham Review
The Times

Other Primary Sources
Records of the Borough of Nottingham, vol. VIII, 1800–1835 eds. Gray, D. & Walker, V.W. (Nottingham, Thos. Forman & Sons, 1952)
An Historical Account of the Luddites of 1811, 1812, and 1813, with Report of Their Trials at York Castle (Huddersfield, Cowgill, 1862 edn)

Aspinall, A. (ed.). *The Early English Trade Unions. Documents from the Home Office Papers in the Public Record Office* (London, Batchworth Press, 1949)

Baines, E. *Proceedings under the Special Commission at York* (Leeds, Baines, 1813)

Hall, Robert. *An Appeal to the Public on the subject of the Framework-Knitters' Fund* (Leicester, Thos Combe, 4th edn, 1821)

—. *A Reply to the Principal Objections of Cobbett and others against the Framework-Knitters' Friendly Relief Society* (Leicester, Thos Combe, 1821)

Raynes, Francis. *An Appeal to the Public* (Gainsborough, A. Stark, 1817)

Secondary Sources
Place of publication is London unless stated otherwise.

Bailey, Brian. *The Resurrection Men* (Macdonald, 1991)

Booth, William. *In Darkest England and the Way Out* (Salvation Army, n.d.)

Brooke, Alan & Kipling, Lesley. *Liberty or Death: Radicals, Republicans and Luddites* (Huddersfield, Workers History Publications, 1993)

Budworth, Joseph. *A Fortnight's Ramble to the Lakes* (London, 3rd edn, 1810)

Byron, Lord. *Selected Prose*, ed. Peter Gunn (Penguin Books, 1972)

Cooper, Thomas. *The Life of Thomas Cooper. Written by Himself* (Leicester, Leicester University Press edn, 1971)

Crump, W.B. (ed.) *The Leeds Woollen Industry, 1780–1820* (Leeds, Thoresby Society, 1931)

Darby, H.C. (ed.) *A New Historical Geography of England after 1600* (Cambridge, Cambridge University Press, 1976)

Darvall, F.O. *Popular Disturbances and Public Order in Regency England* (Oxford, Oxford University Press, 1969)

Defoe, Daniel. *A Tour through the Whole Island of Great Britain* (Penguin edn, 1971)

Dury, G.H. *The East Midlands and the Peak* (Nelson, 1963)

Ellis, Colin. *History in Leicester* (Leicester, City of Leicester Publicity Dept, 2nd edn, 1969)

Felkin, William. *History of the Machine-Wrought Hosiery and Lace Manufactures* (Newton Abbot, David & Charles edn, 1967)

Firth, J.B. *Highways and Byways of Leicestershire* (Wakefield, S.R. Publishers edn, 1969)

Gardiner, William. *Music and Friends*, 3 vols (Longman, Orme, Brown and Longman, 1838)

Garmonsway, G.N. (ed. and tr.) *The Anglo-Saxon Chronicle* (Dent, Everyman's Library edn, 1975)

Gaskell, Elizabeth. *The Life of Charlotte Brontë* (Dent, Everyman's Library edn, 1946)

Gay, John D. *The Geography of Religion in England* (Duckworth, 1971)

Geoffrey of Monmouth. *Histories of the Kings of Britain*, tr. Sebastian Evans (Dent, Everyman's Library edn, 1928)

George, M. Dorothy. *London Life in the Eighteenth Century* (Penguin edn, 1966)

Greenleaf, E.P. & Hargreaves, J.A. *The Luddites of West Yorkshire* (Huddersfield, Kirklees Leisure Services, 1986)

Hammond, J.L. and B. *The Skilled Labourer* (Longman, 1979)

Hay, Douglas, *et al*. *Albion's Fatal Tree* (Penguin edn, 1988)

Heginbotham, Henry. *Stockport: Ancient and Modern*, 2 vols (Sampson Low, Marston, Searle & Rivington, 1882)

Henson, Gravenor. *The Civil, Political and Mechanical History of the Framework-Knitters* (Newton Abbot, David & Charles edn, 1970)

Hobsbawm, E.J. *Labouring Men: Studies in the History of Labour* (Weidenfeld & Nicolson, 1964)

Holmes, Richard. *Shelley: The Pursuit* (Penguin edn, 1987)

Jones, E.L. & Mingay, G.E. (eds) *Land, Labour and Population in the Industrial Revolution* (Edward Arnold, 1967)

Jones, Ernest. *Sigmund Freud, Life and Work*, 3 vols (Hogarth Press, 1953–57)

Kipling, L. & Hall, N. *On the trail of the Luddites* (Huddersfield, Pennine Heritage Network, 1982)

Lipson, E. *History of the Woollen and Worsted Industries* (A. & C. Black, 1921)

Macalpine, Ida & Hunter, Richard *George III and the Mad Business* (Allen Lane, 1969)

Mathias, P. *The First Industrial Nation: An Economic History of Britain* (Methuen, 1969)

Nichols, John. *The History and Antiquities of the County of Leicester*, 4 vols (Nichols, Son & Bentley, 1795–1811)

Patterson, A. Temple. *Radical Leicester* (Leicester, University College, 1954)

Peel, Frank. *Risings of the Luddites, Chartists and Plug-drawers* (Cass edn, 1968)

Pennant, Thomas. *A Tour in Wales*, 2 vols (Hughes, 1778–83)

Pollard, S. & Holmes, C. (eds) *Essays in the Economic and Social History of South Yorkshire* (Sheffield, South Yorkshire County Council, 1976)

Porter, Roy. *English Society in the Eighteenth Century* (Penguin Books, 1982)

Raistrick, Arthur. *The Pennine Dales* (Eyre Methuen, 1968)

Randall, Adrian. *Before the Luddites: custom, community and machinery in the English woollen industry, 1776–1809* (Cambridge, Cambridge University Press, 1991)

Rede, Leman Thomas. *York Castle in the Nineteenth Century* (Leeds, J. Saunders, 1831)

Reid, Robert. *Land of Lost Content* (Heinemann, 1986)

Rudé, George. *The Crowd in History* (Lawrence & Wishart, 1981)

Rule, John. *The Experience of Labour in Eighteenth-Century Industry* (Croom Helm, 1981)

Southey, C. (ed.) *Life and Correspondence of Robert Southey*, 6 vols (London, 1848–50)

Stevenson, John. *Popular Disturbances in England, 1700–1870* (Longman, 1979)

Thomis, Malcolm I. *The Luddites: Machine-Breaking in Regency England* (Newton Abbot, David & Charles, 1970)

— & Holt, Peter. *Threats of Revolution in Britain 1789–1848* (Macmillan, 1977)

Thomson, Robert. *The Pelican History of Psychology* (Penguin Books, 1968)

Thompson, E.P. *The Making of the English Working Class* (Penguin edn, 1991)

Trotter, W. *Instincts of the Herd in Peace and War* (T. Fisher Unwin, 1916)

Walker, George. *The Costume of Yorkshire in 1814* (Leeds, Richard Johnson, 1885 edn)

Wells, F.A. *The British Hosiery and Knitwear Industry: Its History and Organisation* (Newton Abbot, David & Charles edn, 1972)

White, R.J. *Waterloo to Peterloo* (Penguin edn, 1968)

Williams, Neville. *Elizabeth I, Queen of England* (Weidenfeld & Nicolson, 1967)

Index